Writing Public Policy

*A Practical Guide to Communicating
in the Policy Making Process*

FOURTH EDITION

Catherine F. Smith

New York   Oxford
OXFORD UNIVERSITY PRESS

Oxford University Press is a department of the University of Oxford.
It furthers the University's objective of excellence in research,
scholarship, and education by publishing worldwide.

Oxford   New York
Auckland   Cape Town   Dar es Salaam   Hong Kong   Karachi
Kuala Lumpur   Madrid   Melbourne   Mexico City   Nairobi
New Delhi   Shanghai   Taipei   Toronto

With offices in
Argentina   Austria   Brazil   Chile   Czech Republic   France   Greece
Guatemala   Hungary   Italy   Japan   Poland   Portugal   Singapore
South Korea   Switzerland   Thailand   Turkey   Ukraine   Vietnam

For titles covered by Section 112 of the US Higher Education
Opportunity Act, please visit www.oup.com/us/he for the
latest information about pricing and alternate formats.

Published by Oxford University Press
198 Madison Avenue, New York, New York 10016
http://www.oup.com

Oxford is a registered trademark of Oxford University Press.

Library of Congress Cataloging-in-Publication Data
Smith, Catherine F. (Catherine Findley), 1942-
  Writing public policy : a practical guide to communicating in the
policy making process / Catherine F. Smith. -- Fourth edition.
      pages cm
  Includes bibliographical references and index.
  ISBN 978-0-19-938857-8
 1. Communication in public administration. 2. Written communication.
 3. Public policy. 4. Public administration. I. Title.
  JF1525.C59S64 2015
  320.6--dc23
                                                          2015028697

Printing number: 9 8 7 6 5 4 3 2

Printed in Canada
on acid-free paper

Brief Contents

To my family

Ian and Lauren, exemplars
John, still best friend and best critic

Contents

Preface

Following a summer internship in a Washington, DC, public policy think tank, a student said this about the lesson she learned: "In public policy work, if you can't write it or say it, you can't do it."

Public policy professionals will recognize the truth of her observation. I recognize it, too, as a writing teacher and communications consultant to government and nongovernmental organizations. I wrote this book to prepare students, policy professionals, and active citizens to do public policy work by writing, speaking, and interacting effectively in democratic public processes.

What Is the Purpose of This Book?

This practical guide aims to develop communication know-how and skill. Know-how means understanding what to do. Know-how includes awareness of the policy process, as well as situational and contextual awareness. Skill means knowing how to do or having ready competencies. Skill is capability, competence, and craft.

This guide:

- describes public policy making and communication processes;
- identifies communication's functions and limitations;
- describes contexts, situations, and experiences of policy communication;
- explains standards and expectations for communicating in the public sector; and
- offers guidance on method and practice of selected public policy communication genres.

It does not:

- engage theory of public policy, writing, or communication; or
- teach policy analysis, public administration, written composition, or public speaking.

Although it is not about theory, this guide is conceptually influenced by disciplines of professional communication, written composition, rhetoric, cognitive linguistics, discourse studies, and policy studies. Influential sources are cited as references or suggested further reading.

What Is This Book About?

Instruction here focuses on actual practices of communicating for policy purposes. For this guide's purposes, public policy making in democracy is an institutional process of addressing collectively experienced problems and acting on collectively held ideals (Wagenaar, 2001, p. 278).

Policy making involves these interdependent activities:

- defining the problem;
- developing knowledge of problematic circumstances and causal conditions; of prior action or inaction on the problem; of reasons for acting or not acting;
- choosing a purpose and a direction for intervention;
- developing a political strategy, a plan for implementation, and a communication strategy;
- legislating and administering intervention; and
- reviewing, renewing, or redirecting intervention.

These are expected phases of an institutional policy cycle. The real progression of policy is not as linear as this list might suggest. Activities do not always occur in order, in a single pass, or in a simple way. Each activity might develop slowly or quickly, stop and restart, or stop abruptly and end inconclusively.

Largely invisible in the list are the writing, speaking, and interacting on which each activity depends. For example, problem definition might require any or all of the following documents or interactions: notes by participants on personal experiences with problematic conditions, an expert briefing for an elected official on the problematic conditions, a position paper framing the problem presented by the conditions as seen from an advocacy group's perspective, a briefing memo to a legislator by an aide summarizing policy options, or a statement by a legislative aide addressed to the readers of the opinion section of a major newspaper to raise public awareness. This guide makes such communications visible and holds the spotlight on them.

Who Is the Intended Audience?

Primarily, this book addresses undergraduate and graduate students of public policy, environmental policy, political science, public administration, public health, public communication, professional communication, education, and writing, along with their teachers.

Entry-level professionals in government, management, nonprofit organizations, politics, public policy, public relations, public affairs, public administration, social work, public safety, or public health will find the guide useful.

Active citizens who are engaged in community issues, politics, or government will find the guide useful, too.

Special Features of This Book

- Illustrations and scenarios to show policy making in political and cultural contexts.
- Writing samples by professionals, students, and citizens participating in government and nonprofit organizations.
- Commentary to show how the writing samples apply communication principles, perform thinking or communication tasks, and meet expected standards.
- A general method for communicating in policy work, with checklists for planning, producing, and assessing documents.
- Specific instruction for selected document types.

Every illustration, scenario, and sample is taken from actual policy work in governmental, organizational, or academic settings. Most represent the work of professionals in government or nonprofit organizations; some represent the work of students in classroom simulations of policy activity. A few represent both. Students who, at the time of writing, were also government professionals or organization interns produced communications that crossed over into actual use in a policy process. The samples are examples, not models. They are actual work products, presented as written. When requested, names have been removed. Most samples are condensed because of space limitations. When possible, information on accessing the full sample is provided.

How Is This Book Organized?

The illustrations, scenarios, and samples provide a realistic and multifaceted view of policy communication without oversimplifying. This guide's immersion approach to developing know-how assumes that broad exposure develops a feel for the territory and a sense of its predictability as well as variability. Consequently, you will not find here a singular case of policy making to which all the scenarios and samples relate. Instead, you will find exemplification drawn from multiple legislative and administrative processes.

Coherence is signaled in several ways to invite readers to integrate their knowledge with what they read here (Williams & Colomb, 2012, p. 108). Sustained topics such as health, safety, fairness, and environmental protection turn up here like themes in a novel. Exemplars appear in several chapters to show a policy actor writing his or her way through phases of a policy process. These exemplars' documents are presented in several chapters to show a policy actor reusing information for different purposes or audiences across contexts or, more generally, to illustrate varied calls for communication. In the present edition, structural cues are added to make using the text easier. Major section headings—Processes, Practices, Principles—mark the clustering of chapters and appendices.

Why Is This Book Needed?

Public policy making is demanding work. Communication can be difficult, frustrating work. This guide aims to make it doable. It assumes that policy communicators need both general know-how and specific skills. So, a general method of rhetorical and strategic communication planning is provided here, along with detailed task-by-task instructions for commonly used genres or document types. Also offered are a general approach to interpreting research results for policy purposes and specific instruction on writing clear and concise sentences. Together, the methods and instructions provide a disciplined approach to communicating under the typical working conditions of public policy activity.

Limits of this guide should be noted. First, the emphasis is on communicating in, or with, government. The emphasis is justified because government makes most public policy and because people know too little about what government does and does not do. Other actors are certainly involved. Nonprofit organizations, advocacy groups, individual policy analysts, and active citizens are included here as influential participants.

Second, writing samples and commentary refer only to U.S. domestic policy communication. Global and international policy communications are outside the scope of this short guide.

Third, this guide does not cover everything. Less familiar types of governmental communication such as witness testimony and formal written public comment are included, whereas familiar types of public communication such as letters to the editor or press releases are excluded because they are widely taught elsewhere. Finally, some types of policy documentation cannot be adequately addressed in a compact guide. However, this guide's principles of communication apply broadly in policy workplaces.

What Is New in the Fourth Edition?

- Improved organization.
- Updated illustrations, scenarios, and samples in Chapters 7, 8, 9, and 10.
- New appendix on interpreting research results and writing research papers.
- New appendix on writing clearly.
- More consideration of language use, symbolic representation, and political discourse.

The fourth edition reflects its times. Increased political polarization, sharp debate about government's role, institutional change, and uncivil policy discourse bear out a need for this edition's emphasis on language use. In particular, new examples and commentaries show

how symbolic devices such as story and metaphor operate to influence perception. Not new, but more emphatic in this edition is appreciation for the political and discursive nature of policy communication (Stone, 2012; Wagenaar, 2012).

Acknowledgments

This book results from my interaction with professionals and executives in federal and state government, elected and appointed officeholders in local government, and undergraduate and graduate policy-writing students at four universities. There are too many to be given full credit here, although I am very aware of contributions by each from the beginning to now.

In summary, I thank continuing contributors JoAnn Crandall, formerly of the Center for Applied Linguistics and the Government Accountability Office (GAO) Training Institute, as well as numerous GAO executives and professionals; Orange County (North Carolina) former Commissioner Margaret W. Brown; Gregg Township (Pennsylvania) supervisor Douglas P. Bierly; Penns Valley (Pennsylvania) Conservation Association board members; Pennsylvania Association for Sustainable Agriculture executive director Brian Snyder; National Sustainable Agriculture Coalition policy director Ferd Hoefner; and (former) policy director of the U.S. Department of Transportation's National Highway and Traffic Safety Administration Carl E. Nash. I thank new contributors Marion K. Hook, City of Tucson; Tom Driscoll and Michael Slattery, National Farmers Union, and David Bullock, Research Triangle Institute.

For content and critique, I thank academic colleagues William D. Coplin, Carol Dwyer, Frank Lazarski, Natasha Cooper, Lesley Pease, Stephen Thorley, Frederick Gale, Molly Voorheis, and Peter Wilcoxen at Syracuse University; Krista Perreira, Daniel Gitterman, Lucy S. Gorham, and Jessica L. Dorrance of the University of North Carolina at Chapel Hill; David Helfert of George Mason University and the LBJ School of Public Affairs, University of Texas at Austin. I thank Susan Warner-Mills, Jinx Crouch, and Suzanne D. LaLonde for critique from the active citizen's viewpoint.

I thank student contributors Elizabeth Graves, Felicia Feinerman (Syracuse University), Ashley O'Neill, Lynda Deaton, Michael Cavanagh (East Carolina University), and Gary Redding (University of the District of Columbia David A. Clarke School of Law). Along with many other students not included here, they are the reasons for the book.

These contributors' accomplishments and generosity are responsible for the book's richness. They ground its abstraction, deepen its reality, and widen its reach. Any distortions or errors introduced by my purposeful descriptions of their work are mine. Although contributors might not agree with instructional lessons I draw from their examples, I hope and believe that they endorse the aims of the guidance.

For each edition, Carl E. Nash has enthusiastically responded when I needed more know-how or new samples of his exemplary policy communications. Cliff Nelson has been on call for editing of drafts. John B. Smith has engaged the project with unique perspective, patient draft review, on-point critique, and fresh ideas. They are true friends of this book.

I appreciate Oxford University Press reviewers for their practical, pedagogical insights. Reviewers who use this guide in the classroom are silent partners for each new edition, even when I can only partially use the advice or fill the requests. Reviewers for the fourth edition were:

Severa Austin, *University of Wisconsin–Madison*
Victoria Gordon, *Western Kentucky University*
Marcus D. Mauldin, *The University of Tennessee at Chattanooga*
Kimberly Ratcliff, *The Ohio State University*
Jonathan Rogers, *New York University–Abu Dhabi*
John Scott, *University of North Carolina at Chapel Hill*
Steven D. Stehr, *Washington State University*

Editors Jennifer Carpenter, Matthew Rohal, and Michael Kopf brought forth the current edition. Former acquisitions editor Tony English first liked the idea and signed the project for the Press.

References

Stone, D. (2012). *Policy paradox: The art of political decision making* (3rd ed.). New York, NY: Norton.

Wagenaar, H. (2001). *Meaning in action: Interpretation and dialogue in policy analysis.* Armonk, NY: Sharpe.

Williams, J. M., & Colomb, G. (2012). *Style: The basics of clarity and grace* (4th ed.). New York, NY: Pearson Longman.

Introduction:
How to Use This Book

To benefit from this book, you do not need prior experience as a student of public policy, as an intern in government, as a student in community-based learning, as an activist in campus or community affairs, or as a volunteer in a nonprofit organization. Any such experience will be helpful, and you can draw on it often as you use this book. But it is not required. Experience or training in professional or business or administrative communication will be helpful, too, but it also is not required.

You will find this book useful if:

- you are majoring in the social sciences or humanities to prepare for a career in politics, government, public relations, law, public policy, journalism, social work, or public health.

- you are (or might in the future be) an intern in government, in a think tank, or in a nongovernmental organization concerned with public affairs.

- you are preparing to enter (or you are already practicing in) a publicly regulated industry or business.

- you have (or seek) a job as a communications aide in government or a political action organization.

- you have (or seek) a job as a public policy/public relations director in a nonprofit organization or as a public affairs liaison in a corporation, trade organization, professional association, or community service agency.

- you are a writer and you write about public affairs.

- you are concerned about a local, national, or world problem and you want to do something about it.

- you want or are asked to comment publicly on a controversy and you do not feel you have the authority or knowledge or skill to do so.

How Should You Use This Book?

It is a manual of practice or guide, not a textbook. You can use it whenever you have a wish or face a demand to enter a public forum or to participate in a public policymaking process. Here's the intended model of use, whether you are a student, professional, or active citizen. You bring experience, knowledge, willingness to learn, persistence, and a motivating topic of concern. In the book, first read the foundational chapters, Chapters 1 and 2. Before you write or speak on the topic of concern, answer general questions about the policy process (General Method, Chapter 2) to make yourself aware of the cultural context and the rhetorical situation of your intended communication and to plan the product. Then follow the specific instructions (Chapters 3 through 10) to compose the product with awareness of the context and your plan. If you are using research results to write a policy paper, consult Appendix B for help in communicating your findings. After you compose any communication, use the checklists of expected qualities in policy communications (Chapter 2) to assess the product. If its sentences are long and unclear, consult Appendix A for help in revising for clarity. If you want to assess your product's readability, refer to the plain writing guides listed at the end of Appendix A.

Do you need all of the book or only parts? That depends on your intentions and circumstances. The chapters build on one another, but they can be used separately. If you are a student in a policy writing course, you might use the entire guide. Start with a topic of concern; then compose the necessary communications to work the topic through a typical policy process. The benefits of using the entire book are that you gain an overview of policy making and your subject knowledge increases as your communication competencies develop. Even if you skip a chapter, skim its examples and commentary for tips.

If you are writing in a team, divide the communication responsibilities and designate individuals to produce particular documents or presentations using relevant chapters. That way, team members gain practical experience with one or more of the types of communication while the group collectively gains an overview of the process.

If you are learning independently, use the chapters that fit the demand. For broader learning, skim each chapter's examples and commentary. Tips to communicators are distributed throughout.

If you feel intimidated because you don't know enough about a subject or about policy making or about policy writing, do not worry. Your confidence and your knowledge will grow as you practice the communications this book teaches. (This tip comes to you directly from evaluations by students who used this book.)

Tip: Several chapters (Chapters 3, 5, 9, and 10) anticipate research and communication tasks that may be given without much warning to interns, volunteers, and professionals new on the job, ready or not. If that happens to you, first review Chapter 2 on communicating in context. Then, depending on the task, you might find Chapter 3 on problem definition, Chapter 5 on legislative records research, Chapter 9 on witness testimony, or Chapter 10 on written public comment particularly helpful.

Finally, pay special attention to the book's instructional features. Chapter 2 contains a general method for communicating and includes checklists for planning, producing, and assessing documents. Appendix B includes a general method for interpreting research results to make a policy argument. Appendix A presents a technique for achieving sentence-level clarity and concision. In each chapter, you will find instructions for a specific genre or type of communication. Illustrations supplement the instruction. Writing samples by professionals, students, and citizens in government or nonprofit organizations are presented throughout the book. Scenarios show the samples in context. Accompanying commentary shows how the samples apply communication principles, meet expected standards, and do policy work.

List of Writing Samples

✦◦

CHAPTER 1

Public Policy Making

Key Concepts

- Politics
- Values
- Pluralism
- Information

This guide to communication is informed by the idea of public policy making as a democratic process of acting on values to address problems affecting society. This chapter frames the process from the perspective of communication. Other ways to think about public policy making are found in suggested readings at the end of this chapter.

Policy is an effort to order reality for a purpose (Stewart, 2009, p. 32). In public policy making, the effort involves defining public problems, deciding to act, and constructing and administering interventions. All of this happens in a political context of pluralism. The framework for decision is governmental. Decision often demands compromise and reflects institutional constraints. Effective action is practical and adaptive. Communication is integral.

Two illustrations show the process, first in administration and then in budget legislation.

Illustration 1: Milk Labeling

On October 24, 2007, Pennsylvania announced a new standard of food safety aimed to prevent "mislabeling" of food products, especially "misleading" labels. That's *public policy*, a standing decision by government. An administrative agency, the state's department of agriculture, targeted dairy food as the problem. Specifically, milk produced or sold in Pennsylvania could not be labeled "hormone-free." Labels could not say that milk came from cows not treated with "artificial growth hormone" or with "rBGH" or "rBST," common acronyms for recombinant bovine somatotropin growth hormone.

Politics influenced the decision. Arguably, the agency's decision to target milk labeling favored one set of stakeholders, the maker of rBST and dairy farmers who use it. Those interests had long argued that milk labels stating "no artificial growth hormone" or using similar language harmed sales of their products by implying that milk from cows treated with rBST is unsafe. They cited Federal Drug Administration (FDA) approval for rBST use and scientific evidence of its safety. The state agriculture secretary agreed.

The agency's decision was immediately controversial in Pennsylvania and elsewhere. News and reaction spread through newspapers, telephone, e-mail, blogs, and chat outlets. Dairy farmers who did not use rBST and who wanted to say so on milk labels rapidly organized to oppose the ban. Advocates for sustainable agriculture joined these farmers in support. They countered that the science on rBST's safety is inconclusive, that farmers have a right to inform consumers about their product, and that consumers have the right to make informed choices. Plans for litigation against the state were announced. In parallel opposition, farmers who did use rBST organized to react with other advocacy groups in support of the ban. Conflicting *values* or ideas of public good drove the discourse.

In mid-November, Pennsylvania's governor postponed the ban and then canceled it. On January 17, 2008, the governor, along with the secretary of agriculture, announced two policy changes: a revised standard for dairy product labeling and new procedures for oversight of labeling claims. Under rule revisions, labels are permitted to claim that milk came from cows not treated with rBST, along with a disclaimer regarding its potential for health risk. Dairy food processors are required to verify label claims by having dairy farmers sign affidavits regarding production methods. That's *pluralistic, practical policy making* in institutional democracy.

This snapshot captures the basics. For a more comprehensive view, read the participants' own communications. They reveal dimensions of debate, and they illustrate a typical mix of policy writing styles. Extracts selected from key participants' statements are presented here. To read the full text of these and related communications, go to the source cited. The following extracts start with the state's initial announcement and follow the story as it developed.

Government Chooses a Problem

Memorandum
To: Agriculture and Food Labeling Stakeholders
From: Secretary Dennis C. Wolff
Subject: Product Label Review Update
Date: October 23, 2007

The Pennsylvania Department of Agriculture (PDA) is increasingly being made aware of concerns from consumers, farmers, and public policy makers regarding mislabeled food products. These include concerns as to whether label claims are accurate and verifiable, and whether label claims are misleading.

For example, concerns have been raised that some labels are misleading consumers by promoting what is *not* in the product. . . . I recently called upon help from a group of dietitians, consumer advocates, and food industry representatives on current issues relating to food labeling by establishing the Food Labeling Advisory Committee. . . . While widespread food labeling concerns existed, the Committee recommendation is to begin by addressing dairy labeling improprieties. This is a logical starting point, in that PDA has current legal responsibility to review certain milk and dairy product labels before they are used in commerce.

Local and National Media Disseminate the News and Opinion

"Milk-Labeling and Marketing Integrity"
By Hon. Dennis C. Wolff, Pennsylvania Secretary of Agriculture, *Lancaster Farming*, November 3, 2007

Consumers rely upon the labeling of a product when deciding what to buy for their families. Recently, concern has risen over the way milk products are labeled and the Department of Agriculture has taken action to help consumers make informed decisions about what to buy and to feed their families.

Some labels mislead by promoting what is not in the product, a practice called absence labeling. This marketing strategy is confusing and implies a safe versus not safe product.

. . .

I take issue with the fact that companies use false food labeling tactics to gain a market advantage. . . . Ultimately, we are seeking a solution to the labeling issue that will benefit those who produce Pennsylvania's food and those who consume it.

"Consumers Won't Know What They're Missing"

By Andrew Martin, *The Feed*, NYTimes.com, November 11, 2007, http://www.nytimes.com/2007/11/11/business/11feed.html?_r=2& oref=slogin&oref =slogin/.

The Pennsylvania Department of Agriculture has decided that consumers are too dim to make their own shopping decisions. Agriculture officials in Ohio are contemplating a similar decision. . . .

Dairy Farmers React to Oppose the Ban

Opinion by Todd Rutter, dairy farmer, president of Rutter's Dairy in York, Pennsylvania. *Harrisburg Patriot News*, November 9, 2007. Quoted in Sherry Bunting, "Milk Label Issue Comes to a Boil in Pennsylvania," *Farmshine*, November 16, 2007; reprinted in Consumer Attitudes about Biotechnology, Science & Education, rbST Public Discussion, Penn State Dairy and Animal Science Blogs, Terry Etherton Blog on Biotechnology. http://blogs.das.psu.edu/tetherton/2007/11/17/milk-label-issue-comes-to-a-boil-in-pennsylvania/

. . . The state's untenable position has only emboldened Rutter's in this regard, prompting us to plan a series of very public activities designed to educate the community and our customers about artificial growth hormones and our strong stance against their use in our milk production, not to mention our right to say so on our labels.

In the next couple of weeks, we will be running full-page newspaper ads, handing out more than 100,000 information cards through Rutter's Farm Stores, posting content at http://www.rutters.com, and, on Nov. 13, hand-delivering letters to every member of the Pennsylvania General Assembly. Of course, we're also pursuing all legal avenues available to us to protect our right to provide consumer information.

Dairy Farmers React to Support the Ban

Opinion by Daniel Brandt, dairy farmer, Annville, Pennsylvania; PA Holstein Association State Director; Lebanon County Farm Bureau Director, November 17, 2007 at 12:16 pm. Filed under Consumer Attitudes about Biotechnology, Science & Education, rbST Public Discussion, Penn State Dairy and Animal Science Blogs, Terry Etherton Blog on Biotechnology.http://blogs.das.psu.edu/tetherton/2007/11/17/rutter-hormone-stutter/

In Todd Rutter's little rant in the November 9th *Harrisburg Patriot News*, it is shameful that he had no scientific documents to back up his claims. . . . He does nothing to promote milk for what it is and the unprecedented benefits of drinking milk. . . .

Advocates Opposing the Ban Reframe the Debate

"Time to Do the Right Thing with Food Labeling"

E-mail action alert, November 11, 2007, by Brian Snyder, Executive Director, Pennsylvania Association for Sustainable Agriculture, http://pasafarming.org; Leslie Zuck, Executive Director, Pennsylvania Certified Organic, http://www.paorganic.org; Timothy LaSalle, CEO, The Rodale Institute, http://www.rodaleinstitute.org

On its face, the recent decision by the Pennsylvania Department of Agriculture to conduct a crackdown on what it considers to be false or misleading claims on dairy product labels may seem to be in everyone's best interest. . . . The essential question to ask is "What's really in everyone's best interest over the long term?" . . . The whole labeling controversy itself is only a sideshow to the real issues involved here, which have more to do with ethics and the industry-perceived need for the use of performance enhancing drugs in livestock production. . . . The use of artificial growth hormones (rBST or rBGH) is certainly not the only example of such drugs being used on farms today. In fact, the majority of antibiotics sold in America are actually used in livestock production as growth promoting agents, not as treatment for disease in humans or animals as many uninformed, potentially confused consumers might assume.

. . . By all means, it makes perfect sense to employ the "precautionary principle" when research on any aspect of food production is not conclusive—in doing so, the countries of Canada, Australia, New Zealand, Japan and all 25 members of the European Union have already banned the use of rBST/rBHG in the production of milk.

So what's so wrong if an individual farmer or group of them working together wishes to advertise, even on a label, the choice made not to use such drugs at all, or at least not unless clinically indicated? While we are so busy debating when and how it is proper to put an absence claim on food labels, when do we get to consider the value of being completely forthcoming with consumers and letting them make informed choices?

Expert Comments

"rBST Certified Milk: A Story of Smoke and Mirrors"

By Terry Etherton, Distinguished Professor of Animal Nutrition and Head of the Department of Dairy and Animal Science, The Pennsylvania State University, October 3, 2006 at 4:23 pm. Filed under Agricultural Biotechnology, The Food System, rbST Public Discussion Penn State Dairy and Animal Science Blogs, Terry Etherton Blog on Biotechnology. http://blogs.das.psu.edu/tetherton/2006/10/03/rbst-certified-free-milk-a-story-of-smoke-and-mirrors/

The *Boston Globe* ran a story on Sept. 25th on the decision by H. P. Hood and Dean Foods to switch New England milk processing plants to "rbST-free" milk. In this story, a spokesperson for Dean Foods said, "Even though conventional milk is completely safe and . . . recombinant bovine somatotropin (rbST) is completely safe, some people don't feel comfortable with it" . . . There's little doubt that consumers who have no understanding are easily gulled by such labels. . . . "If the future of our industry is based on marketing tactics that try to sway consumers with 'good milk' versus 'bad milk' messages, we are all in trouble," Kevin Holloway, President of Monsanto Dairy, told a group of dairy producers at a September 13th meeting in Washington D.C. . . .

The reality I have observed is that it is easy to scare the public in a 30-second media message. It is impossible to give them a sound scientific

understanding about the benefits of biotechnology in the barnyard in 30 seconds. . . . One can ask, who wins? Junk science by a knockout.
. . .

Government Revises the Policy

"Governor Rendell says Consumers Can Have Greater Confidence in Milk Labels"

Office of the Governor, Commonwealth of Pennsylvania, Press Release, November 17, 2007

Governor Edward G. Rendell today announced that labels informing customers the milk they intend to buy is produced without rBST . . . can continue to be used . . . under new guidelines for accountability. "The public has a right to complete information about how the milk they buy is produced," said Governor Rendell.

Government Promulgates a New Ruling

William Chirdon, Bureau Director, Commonwealth of Pennsylvania, Department of Agriculture, Bureau of Food Safety and Laboratory Services.

Dear Fluid Milk Permit Holder . . . PDA has received a great deal of input on the standards set forth [in October 2007]. . . . Enclosed please find a new document titled 'Revised Standards and Procedure for the Approval of Proposed Labeling of Fluid Milk' dated January 17, 2008. . . . Please review this document carefully and govern yourself accordingly. . . .

From the revised standard:

"7. Label Representations.

(A) No labeling may be false or misleading. . . .

    i. In no instance shall any label state or imply that milk from cows not treated with recombinant bovine somatotropin (rBST, rbST, RBST, or rbst) differs in composition from milk products made with milk from treated cows. . . .

    ii. No labeling may contain references such as 'No Hormones, Hormone Free, . . .'

    iii. References such as 'No rBST,' 'rBST Free,' 'Free of rBST,' 'No added rBST' may be considered misleading labeling based upon the entirety of the particular label under review. By way of guidance, a label containing such references may be approved if such references are part of language defined in paragraph 7(B) as a 'Claim,' and is accompanied as set forth in paragraph 7(B) by a 'Disclaimer.' An example of such a Claim and Disclaimer would be 'No rBST was used on cows producing this milk. No significant difference has been shown between milk derived from rBST-treated and non-rBST-treated cows.' In such cases, the reference 'No rBST,' or the other references listed above, may be accentuated by different type style or size but not more than twice the size of the other Milk Labeling Standards 2.0.1.17.08 language in the Claim and Disclaimer. . . .

(B) Permitted Claims. The following claims are permitted:
   (i) RBST (referenced to FDA February 10, 1994 Guidance on the Voluntary Labeling of Milk. . . .)
      1. 'From cows not treated with rBST. No significant difference has been found between milk derived from rBST-treated and non-rBST treated cows' or a substantial equivalent. Hereinafter, the first sentence shall be referred to as the 'Claim' and the second sentence shall be referred to as the 'Disclaimer. . . .'"

. . .

(Standards 2.0.1.17.08. http://www.portal.state.pa.us/portal/server.pt/gateway/PTARGS_0_2_24476_10297_0_43/AgWebsite/Files/Publications/milk_labeling_standards_new.pdf/.)

Advocates Opposing the Ban Reflect on the Outcome

"A Day for Celebration and Humility"
By Brian Snyder, Pennsylvania Association for Sustainable Agriculture. E-mail, January 1, 2008

This is truly a cause for celebration for all of us, especially those who responded to our alerts by sending letters and emails or making phone calls to Governor Rendell's office and the Pennsylvania Department of Agriculture. . . . This is also a day for reflection and humility. There were many farmers on both sides of this issue right from the start, and the damage done to the agricultural community in Pennsylvania will take some time to heal. . . . Yesterday's announcement preserved the right of farmers to communicate with eaters about the way food is being produced in a straightforward way. If you think about it, this is just about as fundamental as it gets.

News Media Reports Ongoing Advocacy Supporting the Ban

"Fighting on a Battlefield the Size of a Postage Stamp"

By Andrew Martin, *The Feed*, NYTimes.com, March 9, 2009. http://www .nytimes.com/2008/03/09/business/09feed.html

A new advocacy group closely tied to Monsanto has started a counter-offensive to stop the proliferation of milk that comes from cows that aren't treated with synthetic bovine growth hormone. The group, called American Farmers for the Advancement and Conservation of Technology, or Afact, says it is a grass-roots organization that came together to defend members' right to use recombinant bovine somatotropin, also known as rBST or rBGH. . . .

National News Media Reports Continuing Debate

"'Hormone-free' milk spurs labeling debate"

Christian Science Monitor, April 21, 2008. http://www.csmonitor.com/ Environment/2008/0421/p13s01-sten.html

Ohio, Missouri, Kansas, Indiana, and Michigan all have pending legislation or rule changes that would limit labeling claims about hormones. . . . Some say Monsanto is behind attempts to remove mentions of hormones. "Clearly what's going on is Monsanto is trying to get states to thwart the market from working," says Michael Hansen, senior scientist for Consumers Union. . . . But Monsanto contends that milk from cows treated with [its rBST product called] Posilac is safe. . . . Monsanto has unsuccessfully petitioned the Federal Trade Commission for a rule change about what it says is deceptive labeling. Other legal action taken by the company and lobbying by farm bureaus to block such labeling has largely failed. Legal precedent appears to uphold the free-speech interest of dairies and the consumer's right to know. . . . As other new agricultural technology reaches the market, labeling debates appear likely to increase, industry analysts say. For example, milk made from cloned animals and their offspring, approved January 15, 2008 by the FDA, has already prompted one labeling bill in California . . . "This [milk labeling] issue will not go away," says the Consumer Union's Mr. Hansen.

────────────

●─• **What This Illustration Shows.** Common features of policy making are shown here. For example, typical complexity is shown in defining the problem. At least five policy problems with associated issues are conceivable: (1) agricultural biotechnology with issues of impacts on people, animals, and ecosystems; (2) food safety with issues of consumer protection; (3) labeling with issues of free speech; (4) trade with issues of marketing and advertising; and (5) ethics with issues of conflicting values. These conceptions of the problem are not mutually exclusive. That's typical, too. Problems usually are blends.

Pluralism of several kinds—constituencies, values, interests, positions, roles—is shown. Dairy farmers are geographically distributed, operationally diverse, and politically mixed. Consumers here are an undifferentiated mass. Agencies serve many masters. The product manufacturer is ambiguously good or bad. Advocates articulate opposed interests and values. News media disseminate multiple versions of the problem. Again, that's typical.

Solutions are selective. In this example, several alternatives were considered. The state could accept the status quo without further action or it could intervene, perhaps with limitations. To accept the status quo, Pennsylvania could follow federal FDA guidelines that allow rBST use in milk production and do not call for labeling. Instead, the state chose to regulate labeling, first to ban a specific practice and then later to allow it with limitations.

In the governmental framework all three branches—legislative, executive, and judicial—make public policy. This illustration shows administrative policy making that involves federal and state government. The federal agency acted to the limit of its authority to monitor food safety, whereas the state agency went on to act within its authority to monitor product labeling.

Debate about the use of scientific evidence in policy making emerged in the process. On the subject of rBST use, U.S., Canadian, and European Union policies differ. The United States permits its use and the other governments do not. The variation is attributable partly to different interpretations of evidence and partly to national differences in regulatory agencies' power.

Communication technology's impact on public process is evident here. Far exceeding print media's impact on opinion in rural communities, the Internet's capacity to rapidly distribute information by e-mail, online news, blogs, chat, and other media altered and accelerated Pennsylvania's process. Elsewhere, in other states, the network of information helped to organize interest groups across boundaries as more state governments took up the problem. Continuing access to online news archives kept the unofficial public record open and the issues alive as the problem moved beyond Pennsylvania.

Policy making is not always as topical or as visible as in the milk-labeling illustration. Important policy work goes quietly on every day in government. Budgeting is a good example. Communications move a budget cycle along. To illustrate, state budget development is described next, shown from the viewpoint of the communications director for the state senate's budget committee chairman.

Illustration 2: Budgeting

The annual state budgeting process occurs over six months with preset deadlines or milestones. In January, the governor proposes a budget for the coming year that represents the administration's priorities and politics. The legislative committees respond in March (for the house) and in May (for the senate) with recommendations based on their priorities and politics. Effectively, three budget proposals—the governor's, the house's, and the senate's—must culminate in a single adopted budget by July 1, the mandated start of the state's new fiscal year.

In early January, the state governor holds a press conference to announce the release of his proposed budget for the coming year. Immediately after the governor's press conference, the chairs of the state's house of representatives and senate budget committees comment publicly on the governor's proposed budget in other press conferences, newspaper interviews, and radio and television talk show appearances. The communications director for the senate budget chair tracks public response to the governor's budget and to the senate chair's comments on it.

At the same time, work begins on the senate and house budget recommendations. In the senate, the current chair of the ways and means committee brings his staff (an administrative assistant and the communications director) to a meeting with staff for the permanent committee. Present are the ways and means chief of staff, chief legal counsel, and chief budget analyst. The chair has authority, as a member of the majority political party, to set the senate's current budget policy. The permanent committee staff has responsibility for developing, with the help of the chair's staff, the senate's recommendations for budgeting according to current priorities.

In the first meeting in January, the chair and the combined staffs review budget history (what's carried over from last year and what's new this year), the state of the economy (current and projected conditions), and the politics of individual budget items (item is nice to have but can be sacrificed if necessary, item is nonnegotiable, we expect a fight on the item, or we go to the mat with the item). They compile a rough list of potential priorities for the coming year's budget. Because he will draft text for the senate recommendations, the communications director starts taking notes.

After the first meeting, the committee staff fans out in January and February to consult with federal and state fiscal experts, as well as with experts on specific issues in state agencies, government watchdog groups, and advocacy groups. They get more projections for the economy, and they seek external corroboration for their rough list of budget priorities. The communications director goes along to all these consultations.

Next, the committee staff solicits budget requests internally from senate members, state departments, and state agencies. Staffers meet with the members, departments, and agencies about their requests. They begin an initial breakdown of line items to include in the senate recommendations. The communications director stays in touch with the staff. In parallel, he maintains daily or weekly contact with editors and reporters of major news media. He develops relationships and educates the press. They, in turn, keep him up to date on budget-relevant news. He maintains good contact both internally and externally because he has dual responsibilities to anticipate debate about the senate's recommendations and to present them in a way that will promote their acceptance by government officials and the public.

A second working meeting is held. The chair and combined staffs intensely debate priorities and preliminarily decide on key priorities. Later in March, when the house budget proposal is released, the combined staffs analyze it, compare it with the governor's proposal, and compare it with their own developing proposal. The communications director participates in the meetings and continues to track press and public responses to the governor's proposal and to the house recommendations. Most important, he translates the key priorities (decided at the second working meeting) into key messages, simple statements that identify a key issue, and the senate's proposed way of using tax dollars to address the issue. He gets the chair's and committee senior staff's commitment to emphasize the key messages at every communication opportunity. Whenever they speak or write, they agree that the key messages will be appropriately included.

Throughout March and April, the senate budget committee staff finalizes its recommendations and interacts with the governor's and house committee's staffs. The communications director's attention increasingly turns to his primary responsibility of drafting the document that will both present senate recommendations and publicize them; he must also prepare for debate in the legislature and for negotiation with the governor's office during the budget approval process.

In March, he writes preliminary drafts of the chairman's introduction and the executive summary for the document. (He knows that when the lengthy and detailed document is released, many people, including the press, will read only the chair's introduction and the executive summary.) He emphasizes the key messages in both. He writes (or edits senior staff's) descriptions of major budget categories (health care, education, housing, and so forth). From his notes taken in budget working meetings, he develops arguments to support proposed dollar figures for existing line items and new initiatives in each category.

Also in March, he plans a comprehensive internal and external presentation strategy to be carried out in June. Along with internal distribution to the governor, the legislature, and government departments and agencies, the senate's recommendations will be publicized through an external news media and public events campaign conducted before, during, and after formal release of the recommendations document.

In April and early May, he revises the document based on committee staffers' review of his preliminary drafts and edits of their drafts. He coordinates with news media and advocacy groups regarding a public relations campaign to accompany release of the senate recommendations. By mid-May, the finished 600-page document presenting the recommendations is delivered to the printer. He fields inquiries by the press and the public about the soon-to-be-released recommendations, and he focuses on writing, editing, and revising press releases, other public announcements, and the chairman's comments for the senate budget release press conference.

In late May, the senate recommendations are released, distributed, and announced. Simultaneously, the planned public relations campaign is conducted. Throughout June, while the senate and house debate the budget and the governor responds to their debates, events all around the state (preplanned jointly by the communications director and advocacy groups) direct public attention to senate priorities and funding proposals during "health-care week" or "education week" or "citizenship assistance week." Meanwhile, back in the senate, the communications director puts out daily press releases, follows up phone contacts by the press or the public, and prepares comments for the chair's use in responding to unexpected developments, politically significant news, or budget controversies.

WHAT THIS ILLUSTRATION SHOWS. The problem here is the need to finance state government operations and public services in the coming year. The process is the annual budgeting cycle. The major actors are three elected officials (the governor and the chairs of the state senate and house of representatives budget committees). Five appointed professional staffs (those of the governor, the two chairs, and the two committees) advise and assist the elected officials. Other players are experts inside and outside state government with knowledge on specific topics, policy analysts who will advise authorities on ways to approach the problem, and advocates representing special civic, commercial, or political interests in the solution. The resulting policy is a set of priorities and related recommendations for spending.

In this example, you can see policy making in a flow of actions on a timeline to conduct a process. In budgeting, basic institutional actions are to define priorities in relation to current conditions and goals; to review previous goals; to take reasoned positions on needs, argue for them, and negotiate with others who reason differently; to propose specific objectives and spending levels; to deliberate alternative proposals and decide; and to inform and invite public participation. The flow of activity in this particular process is typical of institutional policy making.

Typical integration of communication and action is shown here, too. Communication products formalize conceptions and enable further action. For example, what most people call "the budget" is not the policy itself; rather, it is an intentionally persuasive document (composed by the communications director, in this instance) that argues for objectives based on the priorities and that proposes funding allocations to accomplish them. It is the last of many documents that move the process along. At earlier stages, working discussions are materialized in draft documents. Circulation of the drafts for comment, editing, and revision facilitates negotiation about priorities. The final budget document serves both general public discourse (persuasive expression of priorities and objectives) and institutional discourse (dollar amounts) about governmental spending in the coming year.

Practical communications in this illustration deserve comment, too. From a communicator's viewpoint, budgeting, although orderly as a policy cycle, is quite messy as a real process. The illustration shows the typical density of information, number of writing demands, need to balance competing interests, need to coordinate actors, and even the juggling of schedules that characterize a policy process and create the working conditions for communicators.

Summary and Preview

Public policy making is shown here as lived experience. Two illustrations exemplify what policy actors do and how they do it. Basic components of their working world, a problem, a definition of the problem, a process, and a policy, are shown to be contingent, not predetermined or arbitrary.

Most important for this guide's purpose, the examples show that the origin as well as the outcome of policy making is information. Communication is the means of creating, presenting, and receiving information. Need description and problem definition are information, as are label claims or disclaimers and budget item justifications. Actors in the process use language to create and deliver information needed to achieve policy purposes, not always successfully, but necessarily.

Next, Chapter 2 explains how communication functions in policy making and offers a disciplined approach to practices of writing and speaking in the process.

Reference

Stewart, J. (2009). *Public policy values.* New York, NY: Palgrave Macmillan/ St. Martin's Press.

Further Reading

Baumgartner, F. R., & Jones, B. D. (2009). *Agendas and instability in American politics* (2nd ed.). Chicago, IL: University of Chicago Press.

Baumgartner, F. R., & Jones, B. D. (2002). *Policy dynamics.* Chicago, IL: University of Chicago Press.

Kingdon, J. W. (2011). *Agendas, alternatives, and public policies* (2nd ed.). New York, NY: Pearson.

Sabatier, P. (Ed.). (2007). *Theories of the policy process* (2nd ed.). Boulder, CO: Westview Press.

↝

CHAPTER 2

Communicating

Key Concepts

- Context
- Process
- Strategy
- Standards

Policy communication requires both know-how and skills. To develop know-how or conceptual and contextual awareness, this chapter describes communication to do policy work from four viewpoints. Each brings out a different dimension or emphasizes a different variable in the activity. A cultural view characterizes the policy work context. An experience view shows what happens when readers read and writers write. A process view traces the transformation of thought into written product. A methodology constructs a framework for producing needed documents (or talks). Subsequent chapters invite you to apply these viewpoints strategically to specific practical communications.

Viewpoint 1: Cultural Context

Who generates public policy information? Actors in the policymaking process do. Actors are participants. Actors create and use information in accordance with their roles in the process. As the term is used here, a role is a function or job with specific responsibility in the process.

Interests motivate actors and influence their role performance. Interests are stakes or concerns, which might be organized (collectively held, ready for action) or unorganized (individually held, latent). For example, a trade association or an advocacy group has organized interest, whereas a dispersed, affected population has unorganized interest. Typically, organized interests acting as groups are most influential. However, individuals acting alone can be influential, too.

For all actors, roles and interests might relate in complex ways, and lines between them can be unclear. Some ambiguity is normal, as when an elected officeholder represents constituency interests in seeking a particular committee assignment or in proposing legislation. But other ambiguity might be unethical, as when an officeholder communicates false or misleading information. Ethics guidelines and enforcement procedures, internal and external to government, protect the policymaking process. Even better protection comes from consciously ethical actors who aim to do no harm (Svara, 2007).

Typical actors in public policy processes include:

- providers of goods, services, or activities related to the problem;
- consumers of goods or services (if organized);
- experts with specialized knowledge;
- advocates and lobbyists representing specific interests;
- advocates representing the public interest; and
- officials with power to decide and authority to intervene.

For example, in making policy for highway safety, the following actors would be involved:

- Automotive and insurance industries as providers of goods, services, or activities;
- Organizations of automobile drivers as consumers;
- Specialists in automobile design or analysts of the economics of transportation as experts;
- Lobbyists for law-enforcement associations as representatives of specific interests;
- Advocates for accident victims as representatives of the public interest; and
- Members of Congress, cabinet secretaries, or state governors as authorities with power.

Whether they write or speak themselves or authorize others to do it for them, policy actors generate information in relation to their role. Credibility, or the perceived reliability of information, is judged partly on the information source's role in the process. In the auto safety example, automotive industries credibly generate technical information on safety features of vehicles. Similarly, insurance industries credibly generate information on the economic consequences of accidents. Consumer groups credibly provide accounts of experience in using automotive products and credibly identify problematic conditions. Specialists in automobile design or materials credibly report results of research on ways to make cars safer. Expert policy analysts might credibly offer advice on policy options, such as regulation of manufacturers versus education of consumers. Advocates and lobbyists might credibly provide germane information about interested or affected groups, propose policy, and argue for or against policy based on group interests. Elected and appointed officials credibly generate the policy instruments, for instance, to reallocate funds, create a new program, or provide more oversight for existing programs.

To suggest the range of practical policy communications, a listing that sorts actors by role and associated communication practices is provided next.

Professionals Inside Government
Within government, career or consulting professionals generate most of the working information of a policy process. They communicate in roles as, for example, legislative aides to members of a legislature, experts on the staffs of legislative committees, legal counsels to legislative committees and agencies, executive agency administrators, policy analysts, and technical specialists attached to many offices. To carry out their responsibilities, they might use any of the following document types:

- one-page fact sheets (summaries limited to one page);
- memos (more developed summaries of varying length);
- position papers or white papers (extensive reportage or analysis including evidence);
- legislative concept proposals (outlines of model or idea or strategy for policy, without details);

- legislative histories (reports of government action or inaction, based on government records);
- committee reports (synthesis of committee decision and history of action on a topic);
- speeches (to be delivered by elected or appointed officials); and
- testimonies (to be delivered by executives or professionals).

For some inside professionals, communication is the entire job. The communications director in the state budgeting illustration (Chapter 1) is an example. A communications director is a generalist who:

- writes and produces internal documents of many kinds;
- writes external public announcements of many kinds; and
- produces kits of information for news media to use.

Other professional communicators in government are specialists. They include:

- speechwriters who draft talks for officials to deliver;
- legislation writers who draft bills for deliberation and formulate laws for codification;
- debate reporters who produce stenographic transcripts and the published records of deliberation and debate; and
- webmasters who maintain government websites.

Professionals Outside Government

Significant amounts of information used in policy making come from outside government. Experts of many kinds in universities, industries, policy institutes or think tanks, nonprofit organizations, and businesses contribute to white papers and reports of many kinds and also testify as witnesses in governmental hearings. Because they are not constrained as government employees are from engaging in public debate, they may write opinion in print or online publications. The expert's blog in the milk-labeling illustration in Chapter 1 exemplifies this practice. In addition, professionals and managers in publicly regulated industries and businesses might provide needed information.

For some outside professionals, communication for public policy purposes is the main focus of their job. Lobbyists are an example.

They are experts in a subject and are employed by organizations to ensure that policy makers have information about the subject that is germane to the interests of the employing organizations and to ensure that policy makers are exposed to the full range of arguments on a given issue. Lobbyists might brief legislators and their staffs or they might draft legislation for consideration. Policy analysts are a different example. They may be either inside or outside government. They are experts in using quantitative and qualitative methods to examine problems and options for solving problems. Analysts might advise policy makers on the choice of policy instruments or interpret research results to aid the formulation of policy (Appendix B).

Active Citizens

Ordinary people in daily life inform and influence public policy making when they:

- write or e-mail officials;
- provide formal written remarks on their experience relevant to a problem or a policy in response to a call for comment;
- testify about effects of a problem or a policy on their life or their livelihood;
- conduct letter-writing campaigns, create e-mail lists, and use phone trees;
- form a coalition to cooperate in solving a problem;
- create a mechanism, such as a lawsuit or a boycott, to force response by institutional authorities; or
- lobby as a representative of civic organizations, trade associations, professional associations, communities of interest, or constituencies.

The milk-labeling illustration in Chapter 1 exhibits citizen participation in several of these ways.

In the culture of public policy work, communication is not sufficient, but it is necessary. What does communication do? The following are its key functions.

1. Communication produces useful information. Useful information in a public policy process has four major characteristics: it

is relevant, it serves action, it has consequences, and it is publicly accessible.

(i) Is relevant: Every phase of a policy process—to frame a problem, to analyze issues, to argue approaches, to decide on intervention—demands information. Only relevant information helps, however. In deciding whether to provide information, always ask (re-ask, if necessary) and answer these questions: To what does this relate? To whom does it matter?

(ii) Serves action: In policy work, information makes things happen. In deciding whether and how to inform in a policy process, always ask and answer these questions: How does this help? What or whom does it help? What or whom do I want to help?

(iii) Has consequences: A problem, intervention, and implementation affect other concerns in many contexts. Information's effects can be wide ranging. Although you cannot foresee all consequences, you should try. In deciding whether and how to inform in a policy process, always ask and answer these questions: What is likely to happen as a result of this information? What impacts might this information have?

(iv) Is publicly accessible: Policy makers are answerable to the people who give them authority. Therefore, information used in public processes must be publicly available. Officially, it is recorded and preserved by government as an authoritative public record. Unofficially, news media of all kinds and people in everyday social interactions distribute information as well. In deciding whether and how to inform a policy process, always ask and answer this question: How will this information be made public?

2. Communication makes information intelligible. Intelligible here means understandable and applicable in context. Defined narrowly, context means a particular policy cycle, or, broadly, government and its political environment. Intelligibility occurs when expectations are activated and met. For meaningful communication to occur, information presenters and recipients must have similar expectations.

What expectations? The most basic is interaction, or give and take between people. Presenters expect to give information. Recipients expect to get information. That reciprocity is fundamental to human communication for any purpose.

Other expectations influence communication's effectiveness. Genre or communication type is powerfully influential. Some say that effective communication begins with making the right genre choice. That is the selection of an appropriate communication type (or skillful use of a prescribed type) fitted to the presenter's purpose, the recipient's purpose, and the relevant policy process.

Other powerful influences on effectiveness are utility and credibility. In public policy work, communication must be useful. What matters most is not how much you know. Rather, what matters most is how much your readers or listeners know after taking in what you say and whether they trust your information.

Finally, policy communication is expected to be efficient. Information products must be coherent, concise, and to the point. Efficient communication is universally appreciated in policy making because working conditions demand it. Public policy work is information overloaded. Especially in government and nonprofit organizations, time is scarce, schedules are nearly impossible, and attention is always fragmented. Rarely does anybody have patience for disorganized, wordy documents or talks without obvious and relevant purpose and authority.

In summary, the cultural view shows us that information functions best in a policy context when it meets expectations. That is, it succeeds when it can be comprehended quickly, recognized as relevant, trusted as accurate, traced to authoritative sources, and used with confidence by its intended readers.

Viewpoint 2: Experience

How do expectations function in readers' and writers' minds? A second viewpoint looks at communication as intellectual experience. Here's a quick sketch of what recipients experience. The sketch represents a recipient reading a policy document. It could also represent listening to an oral summation.

Recipients hunt and gather. As they attend to a communication, their attention is dynamic. They make numerous quick, tacit decisions about the information and its presenter—its subject (explicit or implicit), for whom it's intended, who is presenting it, what motivates it, what its point is, and, most importantly, whether it matters. In other words, recipients don't just consume a communication; rather, they form a perception of it as they attend to it. This perception is the basis of the recipient's understanding of the communication's meaning, what they think and feel it is saying. (The familiar remark "What you are telling me is . . ." refers to this perception.) Moreover, recipients evaluate the perceived information and its source. For instance, as they hunt for structural cues in the text's layout, they judge the presenter to be competent in the subject and caring about the recipient's time and interest or not. If they have a choice, they choose whether it's worth their time to continue reading (or listening). If they continue, they choose how they will proceed. Typical strategies are to skim all, to dip in and out, or to read selectively, perhaps only the summary. Recipients' criteria for selection are functional, based on relevance.

Now, here is a sketch of the other side of the experience. This sketch shows you, the presenter.

There is a demand for information. You are responding to the demand alone or in a team of people. You (or you and the team) will present the information in a communication. These are your possible working conditions: You might choose the way you will communicate, or you might use a prescribed way. You might have ready access to relevant information or not. The recipients might be known to you or not entirely. The recipients' uses for the information might be known to you or not entirely. Your intentions or purpose for providing information or what you want your contribution to achieve might be clear to you or not entirely. You are aware of (or your team agrees on) the perspective you will take or not entirely. Similarly, you are sure of your position on the topic (and your team agrees with you) or not entirely. You have limited time. You (or you and the team) must decide how to plan and produce the information product in the time available. You know that your product might be the only means by which recipients will get needed information and know what you think. You know that the product must be designed to fit recipients' needs and circumstances, although you can't be sure what that will be for all recipients.

These sketches depict experience as it might occur in any setting of policy work. Whether the presenter is a policy student writing to an instructor or a policy professional writing to a legislator, similar uncertainties might be present. The same intellectual activity is required. What goes into that activity?

A third viewpoint on policy communication brings out the relationship between a writer's thinking process and its manifestation in a written product.

Viewpoint 3: Process and Product

Process means change. Change transforms a state of existence into a different state. When understanding occurs, a presenter's information changes to become the recipient's information. Functionally, thinking in one mind must also occur in other minds. An information product such as a written document is the instrument of transformation. How? A document functions when its form or genre and its intentionally constructed features and content prompt a comprehending response. In Table 2.1, elements of thinking are associated with product features. Recipients hunt for these elements in the features of a document.

Table 2.1 Elements of a presenter's thinking manifest in product features

Element	Product Feature
Knowledge	Content specific to the domain and selected for relevance
Perspective	Characterization of content from a viewpoint
Position	Statement of message with disclosure of reasoning
Adaptation	Content made relevant to the context
Documentation	Genre, form, style appropriate to the demand

To round out this process-and-product view of communication, consider the policy communicator's need for control under hectic working conditions. A system for conceiving and producing communications is advisable. Most important is a goal. Communicators who know what they want to achieve can better assess and resolve any constraints on achieving it. They can make wiser choices of strategy and tactics. Looking forward in this guide, in the "how to" section of each chapter you will find a suggested goal, objective, strategy, and tactics (sequenced tasks) for a particular communication type.

Here, next, you will find a general approach to managing any policy communication.

In earlier times, public policy thinkers employed self-questioning to discover relevant information and valid arguments. It is still a good methodology. So, this overview's fourth viewpoint on policy communication reduces the required intellectual activity to a comprehensive set of questions. The questions are distilled from the experience of many practitioners who generously contributed to this outline. (If you are experienced, you should add your own tried-and-true questions to the outline.) These questions constitute a methodical approach to writing or speaking that is fitted to the policymaking process and to the culture of policy communication. They translate the culture into questions you should routinely ask when you initiate a communication. At the end of the questions are two checklists of expected qualities that public policy documents or talks should exhibit. The checklists are intended for your use in assessing the functionality and quality of a policy communication you have produced.

Now, you should only read the outline and checklists for perspective and for familiarity. Later, when you have an actual need to communicate, you should use the method to plan before you write. Use the checklists after you write. Make a habit of using both.

If you have had mainly classroom writing experience, you may be surprised by the method's questions. They represent policy workplace writing conditions. For orientation to workplace writing, see any professional communication textbook.

Ask and answer the method's questions to plan and produce a communication. They prompt you to consider all the usual aspects of a writing situation and to take note of significant particulars that might affect your work. Your answers to the questions are your guide to writing or planning the needed product.

Practice this questioning methodically (even if tediously at first) until it becomes routine. At first, jotting down your answers and keeping your notes nearby as you write will be helpful. Later, when you habitually use this method, you will comfortably adapt it to particular or unusual demands. A word of caution: even if you skip some questions, do not omit whole steps in the method. All the steps are needed to cover the basics. Omitting a step in the preparation wastes time when you are writing or causes other trouble later.

If you are writing for someone else or if you are producing a document with many contributors, as state budgeting illustrates in Chapter 1, remember to consult with others as needed to answer the questions.

Viewpoint 4: General Method of Communicating in a Policy Process

Step 1: Prepare

First, ask questions about the policy process.

Policy

- To what policy action (underway or anticipated) does this communication relate?
- Does a policy already exist?

Problem

- What conditions are problematic?
- What problem do these conditions present?
- How do I define the problem?
- How do others define the problem?
- What narrative does my definition suggest?
- How do I frame or characterize the problem? What is it like, metaphorically?
- What stories, frames, or metaphors are apparent in other definitions of the problem?

Actors

- Who are the actors?
- What are their roles?
- What are their interests?
- Who else has a significant role or interest in the process?

Politics

- What are the major disagreements or conflicts?
- What are the major agreements or common interests?
- Which actors are most likely to influence the process or the outcome?

Step 2: Plan

Second, ask questions about the communication.

Purpose

- Why is this communication needed?
- What do I want to accomplish?

Message

- What story do I want to tell?
- What is my message?
- How does my message differ from that of others on the topic?
- What argument will I make to support my message?
- How does my argument relate to that of others on the topic?

Role

- What is my role in this process?
- What is my interest in the outcome?

Authority

- Whose name will be on the document(s): Mine? Another's? An organization's?
- For whom does the communication speak?

Reception

- Who is (are) the named recipient(s)?
- Who will use the information?
- How do I want the information to be used?
- Will the document(s) be forwarded? Circulated? To whom? Summarized? By whom?

Response

- What will recipients know after reading the document(s)? What will users of its information do?
- What is likely to happen as a consequence of this communication?

Setting and Situation

- What is the occasion? What is the time frame for communicating?
- Where, when, and how will this communication be presented?
- Where, when, and how will it be received? Used?

Form and Medium

- Is there a prescribed form or do I choose?
- What is the appropriate medium for presentation and delivery? A written document? A telephone call? E-mail?

Contents

- What information will support the message?
- Where will a succinct statement of the message be placed?
- How should the contents be arranged to support the message?
- How will the document's design make information easy to find?

Tone and Appearance

- How do I want this communication to sound? What attitude do I want to convey?
- How do I want the document(s) to look? Is a style or layout prescribed, or do I choose how to present the contents?

Document Management

- Who will draft the document? Will there be collaborators?
- Who will review the draft? Who will revise it?

Step 3: Produce

Based on your preparation and planning, write the document. Do it in three separate passes: draft first, review second, and revise third. Do not mix the tasks. Separating those tasks allows you to manage your time and handle distractions while you write and to communicate better in the end.

The tasks are outlined here. Use this outline to stay on track if you're working alone or under pressure or if you're producing a short document. If you're collaborating or team-writing, or if you're creating a multidocument product (such as the budget described in Chapter 1), adapt the task outline to your circumstances.

Draft

- Produce a complete working draft in accordance with your preparation and plan (your answers to the questions listed earlier).

Review

- Compare the draft to the plan and highlight any differences.
- Get additional review of the draft by others, if advisable.
- Refer to the checklists (shown next here) to assess the draft's effectiveness and quality and to highlight needs for revision.

Revise

- Make the changes called for by review.

Two Checklists

───────

➤ **FEATURES OF EFFECTIVENESS.** A public policy communication is most likely to be useful if it addresses a specific audience about a specific problem, has a purpose related to a specific policy action, represents authority accurately, uses the appropriate form, and is designed for use.

- ☐ Addresses a specific audience about a specific problem: In policy work, time is scarce. Specifying a communication's audience or intended recipient(s) and the subject or problem saves thinking time for both writer and reader (or speaker and listener). The information's relevance for the recipient should be made clear.
- ☐ Has a purpose related to a specific policy action: Policy cycles have several phases. Multiple actions and cycles are underway simultaneously. Timing matters. Agendas change. Stuff happens. Therefore, explicitly stating a communication's purpose and relevance to the recipient makes it more likely to get timely attention.
- ☐ Represents authority accurately: Policy communications do more than present information; they also represent a type of

participation and power. For a policy communication to be taken seriously, to have influence, and to influence rightly, the communicator's role and status—a citizen with an opinion, an expert with an opinion, a spokesperson for a nongovernmental organization, a government official—must be accurately represented.

☐ Uses appropriate form: Settings of policy work have their own conventions for communicating. Use the document type, style, and tone of presentation that are expected for the purpose and that accommodate working conditions in the setting of its reception.

☐ Is designed for use: People's attention is easily distracted in settings of policy work. Dense, disorganized text will not be read or heard. For people to comprehend under conditions of time pressure and information overload, contents must be easy to find and to use. Written documents should chunk information, use subheadings, and organize details in bulleted lists or paragraphs or graphics. Spoken texts should cue listeners' attention with similar devices.

―――――

►― MEASURES OF EXCELLENCE. No two communications are exactly alike, but every public policy communication should try to meet criteria for clarity, correctness, conciseness, and credibility.

☐ Clarity: The communication has a single message that intended recipients can find quickly, understand easily, recognize as relevant, and use.

☐ Correctness: The communication's information is accurate.

☐ Conciseness: The communication presents only necessary information in the fewest words possible, with aids for comprehension.

☐ Credibility: A communication's information can be trusted, traced, and used with confidence.

Example

For practice, apply this overview to an actual policy communication. Keep the four viewpoints in mind as you read a professional writing sample, a report by the Congressional Research Service. Because of space limitations, the full report is not shown. The complete summary is shown. At the summary's end, you will find access information for the full report.

The Federal Food Safety System: A Primer

Renee Johnson
Specialist in Agriculture Policy
January 11, 2011
Congressional Research Service
7-5700
www.crs.gov
RS22600
CRS Report for Congress
Prepared for Members and Committees of Congress

Summary

Numerous federal, state, and local agencies share responsibilities for regulating the safety of the U.S. food supply. Federal responsibility for food safety rests primarily with the Food and Drug Administration (FDA) and the U.S. Department of Agriculture (USDA). FDA, an agency of the Department of Health and Human Services, is responsible for ensuring the safety of all domestic and imported food products (except for most meats and poultry). FDA also has oversight of all seafood, fish, and shellfish products. USDA's Food Safety and Inspection Service (FSIS) regulates most meat and poultry and some egg products. State and local food safety authorities collaborate with federal agencies for inspection and other food safety functions, and they regulate retail food establishments.

The combined efforts of the food industry and government regulatory agencies often are credited with making the U.S. food supply among the safest in the world. However, critics view this system as lacking the organization, regulatory tools, and resources to adequately combat foodborne illness—as evidenced by a series of widely publicized food safety problems, including concerns about adulterated food and food ingredient imports, and illnesses linked to various types of fresh product, to peanut products, and to some meat and poultry products. Some critics also note that the organizational complexity of the U.S. food safety system as well as trends in U.S. food markets—for example, increasing imports as a share of U.S. food consumptions, increasing consumption of fresh often unprocessed foods—pose ongoing challenges to ensuring food safety.

The 111th Congress passed comprehensive food safety legislation in December 2010 (FDA Food Safety Modernization Act, P.L. 111–353). Although numerous agencies share responsibility for regulating food safety, this newly enacted legislation focused on foods regulated by FDA and amended FDA's existing structure and authorities, in particular the Federal Food, Drug, and Cosmetic Act (FFDCA, 21 U.S.C. §§ 301 *et seq.*). This newly enacted law is the largest expansion of FDA's food safety authorities since the 1930s; it does not directly address meat and poultry products under the jurisdiction of USDA. The 112th Congress will likely provide oversight and scrutiny over how the law is implemented, including FDA's coordination with other federal agencies such as USDA and the Department of Homeland Security (DHS).

In addition, some in Congress have long claimed that once FDA's food safety laws were amended and updated, it would be expected that Congress would next turn to amending laws and regulations governing USDA's meat and poultry products. Food safety incidents and concerns regarding USDA-regulated meat and poultry products are similarly well documented. A series of bills were introduced and debated in the previous few Congresses. These bills may be re-introduced and debated in the 112th Congress.

(The full report can be found at opencrs.com/document/RS22600/.)

•➤ **WHAT THIS EXAMPLE SHOWS.** This report summary manifests the transformation of process into product. Knowledge, perspective, position, adaptation, and documentation are effectively represented.

The first paragraph identifies the subject, food supply safety policy. The policy actors, federal agencies and their state counterparts, are recognized. In broad strokes, the writer demonstrates knowledge of the domain.

The second paragraph recognizes another actor, the private-sector food industry, before summarizing the consensus viewpoint that federal government and the industry have together achieved a safe U.S. food supply. Complication of this consensus view immediately follows. Cueing the reader with a "however," the writer introduces a disagreement that challenges the consensus. Critics point to a problem, food-borne illness, that has exposed gaps in protection of the food supply. The consensus and the critical viewpoints differ. The author's own perspective is neutral, as that of an informed observer rather than a partisan.

The third paragraph opens with a sentence introducing the primary actor, who is also the report's intended recipient, the U.S. Congress. This legislative actor makes policy that agency actors will administer and industry actors will implement. With the primary actor ("who cares?") in focus, attention shifts to that actor's concerns ("so what?"). Again, in broad strokes, the author describes the previous 111th Congress's legislative solution to the problem of foodborne illness. Possible next steps by the 112th Congress are previewed. The preview is tailored to the policy cycle and timely for the legislators' purposes, agenda setting and problem recognition, at the start of a new session. This fitting of the report to recipients' particular purposes at a particular time shows adaptation.

Other features of the documentation adapt to recipients' fragmented attention and to their need for confidence in the report's accuracy:

- An advance summary tells readers what the report offers.
- In that summary, four short sections (each a paragraph long) begin with a sentence telling the reader that paragraph's main point, followed by subsequent sentences that consistently fill in the point.
- After first use, domain-specific vocabulary is immediately explained.
- At the summary's end, citations enable readers to trace the writer's sources.

Another way to recognize adaptation in this summary is to look at the story it tells. Policy communications tell a story. Look for the storyline in the CRS report sample.

The sample tells a story of agenda setting and problem recognition. As the story opens, government characters are poised to act further on a new law. The characters are legislators, bureaucrats, producers of goods, providers of services, consumers, and subject-matter experts. There are no heroes or villains, only ordinary characters performing their relative roles in a system of governance. A problem has emerged to reveal flaws in the system. Characters have previously devised a solution to the problem. Will that solution work as intended? Is it sufficient to solve the problem? To learn the answers, stay tuned.

This story helps to move the reader's attention along. It is compactly told in four sequenced paragraphs. The first paragraph, or prologue, sets the scene and introduces the lead actor. The second paragraph introduces supporting actors and the complication, a problem the readers care about and for which the solution is not obvious. The third paragraph examines the current situation. The fourth paragraph sets the stage for continued action.

Summary and Preview

Multiple actors in varied roles communicate to do policy work. Distilled into a general method for practical writing and speaking, their working knowledge of the process and communication's role can instruct you. This method keeps you on track, enables you to produce under pressure, to behave ethically, and to be accountable.

It is hard to get communication right. The know-how summarized in this chapter gives you a broad foundation. Refer to it often as you take up specific communication tasks. Problem definition, perhaps the most consequential task of policy communication, is described in Chapter 3.

Reference

Svara, J. (2007). *The ethics primer for public administrators in government and nonprofit organizations.* Sudbury, MA: Jones & Bartlett.

Further Reading

Allison, L., & Williams, M. F. (2007). *Writing for the government.* New York, NY: Pearson Longman.

Coplin, W. D., with Sandefer, E. (2007). *The Maxwell manual for good citizenship: Public policy skills in action.* Lanham, MD: Rowman & Littlefield.

CHAPTER 3

Definition: Frame the Problem

Key Concepts

- Frame the problem as an advocate
- Rhetorical awareness

This chapter focuses on defining a problem for the purpose of getting it onto the public policy agenda. Advocacy is emphasized as a means of achieving that purpose. In the next chapter, analysis is emphasized.

How does public policy making begin? From the perspective of advocacy, it might start with values. Or it might start with perception of a wrong. Somebody perceives a condition in society or its environment to be wrong. Perceptions differ, so conflict might be involved in defining the wrong as a policy problem. Or cooperation might be involved.

Problems come to public attention and a public policy agenda in various ways. Sometimes the problem chooses you. Something happens, you are affected by it, and you seek public action to address the problem. The triggering event might be large scale, as when the destructive hurricanes Katrina and Rita damaged American coastal cities and states in 2005. Large-scale need for assistance followed as individuals, families, local governments, and other collectives sought compensation or other action from federal government. Because after-action reports and investigations showed flaws in governmental storm response, policy makers reviewed and subsequently reformed national emergency management guidance for all hazards, including weather hazards. As in this instance, chance events such as major storms can open a "policy window" of opportunity for change (Kingdon, 2011). In contrast, a motivating event might be small scale, even personal and singular. Following a child's death caused by a drunk driver, a parent formed the national nonprofit organization Mothers Against Drunk Driving (MADD) to influence law-enforcement standards for drunk driving.

Sometimes you choose the problem. Choosers vary. Inside government, elected and appointed officials have authority to decide what is and is not a problem and which problems will receive attention. In the budgeting illustration (Chapter 1), a governor and state legislative committees exemplify this kind of chooser. The milk-labeling illustration (Chapter 1) shows a state administrative agency head selecting a food product for regulation. A writing sample shows a federal administrative agency policy analyst choosing military health-care benefits for policy reform (Example 1, this chapter). Outside government, a chooser might be an advocacy group or a coalition of groups that brings a problem to legislators' attention, as when a coalition of farm groups advocates for changes in food safety bills (Scenario 2, Examples 3 and 4, this chapter).

To influence policy making, the perception of a wrong is not enough. If public policy is to be a solution, the wrong must be defined as one that policy makers can address. For example, you might perceive that obesity is wrong because it harms individuals, but individual solutions cannot be legislated. However, if you define obesity as a public health problem, you can relate obesity to public health standards or to medical research in the causes of disease. Those are problems with broad societal significance that can be addressed by policy makers.

Problem definition is important. As the logical first move in a policy process, problem definition sets the topics and direction for debate. Definition is predictive. Different definitions lead to different actions. No matter how messy a policy process becomes, your action is directed by your definition of the problem.

For example, although health authorities define obesity as a health problem, the numbers of overweight and obese people, especially in the United States, continue to rise. Why, you wonder, are people fat despite health warnings? Your question redefines the problem, thereby revealing different potential solutions. By focusing on the experience of people in everyday life, you expose another set of conditions relevant to obesity, behavioral issues such as eating habits, physiological issues such as genetics, cultural issues such as food preferences, economic conditions such as food costs, and economic interests such as food-industry profits. You point to intervention targeted to consumers, educators, businesses, and industries rather than health-care providers.

Problem definition takes differences of perception into account. To a large degree, problem definition is subjective. One constituency's problem is another's acceptable status quo. Narrow and exclusive problem definition freezes possibility and invites competing solutions. Broad and inclusive definition imagines change and invites solution by cooperation. In practice, problem definition is also rhetorical. Practical rhetoric is interaction between people or between organizations. The problem definer's awareness of rhetoric or interaction (Who am I? Whom do I address? How do I define the problem? How do others define it?) brings assumptions and values to light and exposes potential conflict or cooperation. Any problem description must go beyond its topic to recognize who cares and why they care.

How to Define a Policy Problem

Goal: Ability to recognize problematic conditions, to frame the policy problem they present as you see it, to be aware of your perspective and your purpose.

Objective: Purposeful description of the problem.

Product: A short (1 page) or longer (20 or more pages) document.

Scope: Individual or collective; local or broader in impact; well known or unrecognized; widely discussed or little considered; past, present, or anticipated.

Strategy: Provide information necessary for your purpose.

Expect to be flexible in the writing process. Problem definition is usually iterative. After completing a task, you might find that you must revise earlier work. Or, after defining a problem, you might find that you want to, or you must, redefine it because conditions have changed or you have gained more knowledge.

Get a Problem onto the Public Agenda

You want to bring public attention to a problem of concern to you. It might be known to others, but only recently familiar to you. Or you might be aware of an unnoticed aspect of a known problem. Or you might be aware of a not-yet-recognized problem. In any case, you must understand problematic conditions well. Also, you must know who cares and why they care.

To develop your knowledge, follow an approach of observation and inquiry. Do Tasks 1–4 listed here in sequence. Results of each task will help you perform the next. Note: this task outline assumes that you are a novice in problem definition.

Task 1: Describe the Problem and Identify the Interests

First, describe the problem and identify the interested parties. This involves recognizing problematic conditions, identifying the problem(s) that those conditions create and the issue(s) of most concern, and specifying individuals as well as collectives that have a stake in the conditions or the potential policy actions. To increase your awareness of problematic conditions and to recognize interests in it, you can proceed in any (or several) of the following ways:

- Work from observation of experiences, practices, effects:
  - Note likes/dislikes about your (or others') daily routine.
  - List good/bad aspects of your experience with problematic conditions such as your current or past job(s) or a family member's or a friend's job(s).
  - Sit for an hour in the office of a service provider to observe people affected by the problem and to observe the practices of policy implementers.
  - Visit locales affected by the problem to observe impacts.
- Work from subjective constructions:
  - Listen to or read or write stories (actual or imagined) that refer to the problem.
  - Describe the problem from a viewpoint and then describe it again from a different viewpoint.
- Work from unfinished business:
  - Reexamine a neglected need.
  - Revive a former interest.
  - Return to an incomplete project.

- Work from anticipation:
  - Imagine the consequences if things continue as they are.
  - Imagine the consequences if things are changed as you advocate.
- Work from ignorance:
  - Choose a matter that concerns others (but is unfamiliar to you) that you want to know more about.
- Work from knowledge:
  - Consider the concern technically, informed by your (or others') expertise.
- Work from values:
  - Consider the concern ethically or legally, informed by your (or others') ideals or commitments.

Task 2: Specify the Issues

When a problem has been identified, it is not yet a policy matter until its issues for policy are specified. Issues refer to stakeholders' concerns, political disagreements, and value conflicts. To recognize such issues, you might do the following:

- Think about impacts of the problem. Who or what is affected by it?
- Conceive the problem narrowly and then broadly. Is it individual and local or more widespread?
- Conceive it broadly and then narrowly. Is it widely distributed or concentrated?
- Think about attitudes. How do different stakeholders perceive the problem? What values (ideals, beliefs, assumptions) are expressed in their definitions?
- Think about authority. How do stakeholders want to address the problem? Do they see government action as a solution? Do they agree or disagree on government's role?

Task 3: Offer Solutions (If You Are Proposing a Solution)

Solutions typically rely on policy instruments that government can use (Bardach, 2011). These include actions such as spending more or spending less and starting or ending programs. If you already have a positive and feasible solution to suggest, do so. Generally, problem descriptions with a proposed solution get more attention. If you don't have a proposal, if you want to counter a proposal, or if you want to create alternatives, stimulate your thinking with any of these approaches:

- Review the problematic conditions with a fresh eye, looking for unnoticed solutions.
- Reconsider a tried-but-failed or a known-but-ignored solution to find new potential.
- Look at the problem from a different perspective (a different stakeholder's, for example).
- Assign it to a different governmental level or jurisdiction if government already addresses the problem.
- Consult with nonprofit groups and nongovernmental organizations that are concerned about the problem.
- Consider doing nothing (keep things as they are).

Task 4: Write the Document—Problem Description

Before you write, use the method (Chapter 2) to make yourself aware of the rhetorical framework (audience, purpose, context, situation) for your communication. Write with that framework in mind.

Problem descriptions in any form are expected to answer the following basic questions:

- What are the problematic conditions? What problem do they cause?
- What are the issues for policy?
- What is your concern? What is your intended reader's concern?
- Who else is concerned (on all sides)?
- What are the key disagreements and agreements among those concerned?
- What plausible and realistic solution can you offer? (optional)

Problem descriptions can be presented in varied genres or document types. If the genre is prescribed for you, use it in accordance with your rhetorical framework. If you are free to choose, use a genre that fits your audience, purpose, context, and situation. These are commonly chosen options:

- Letter, memorandum, or brief describing problematic conditions, possibly identifying causes of the conditions, and stating the problem.

- Letter, memorandum, or position paper conveying informed opinion, possibly advocating an approach to the problem.

In this chapter, next, you can see examples of problem descriptions in memorandum, report, position statement, brief, and proposal form. For more samples and other resources, go to these respected sources:

- *CQ Weekly Report, CQ Researcher Online, CQ Researchers Database* available in print (to users of subscribing libraries) or online at http://library.cqpress.com/ (by purchase).

- Opinion sections of national newspapers such as the *New York Times* (http://www.nytimes.com/), *Los Angeles Times* (http://www.latimes.com/), *Chicago Sun-Times* (http://www.suntimes.com/), or *Washington Post* (http://www.washpost.com/).

You must cite the sources to which your problem description refers. Use the citation style prescribed or choose the American Psychological Association (APA) style described at http://www.apastyle.org/learn/faqs/index.aspx/.

For further help with citing government sources, consult the standard text available in libraries: *The Complete Guide to Citing Government Information Resources* (Cheney, 2002). After you write, check your document's quality against the checklists in Chapter 2.

Five Examples

Writing samples of problem definition by advocates are presented here. They were written by professionals acting in administrative reform of military health care (Example 1) and legislative reform of food supply safety (Examples 2, 3, 4, and 5). Scenarios precede the samples to provide context.

Scenario 1

The Chief of Patient Information in the Surgeon General's Office, U.S. Reserve Armed Forces, is the subject matter expert for clinical policy questions relating to health-care eligibility and benefits, records administration, medical readiness, and associated Army policies and regulations. She conducts analyses to answer questions in her subject areas and she writes policy documents. Regarding health-care eligibility, a problematic condition has caught her attention. While doing routine research to answer an eligibility question, she finds that reserve component soldiers are not eligible for many of the medical and dental benefits available to active component soldiers. Senior administrative officers have long been aware of this condition and they know that increased reserve deployments are worsening it. Senior administrators have previously defined the benefits gap as a policy problem and recommended legislative solutions involving changes to the Department of Defense's health program, without success.

   In this context of inaction, the analyst has encountered a problem recognized by others but not, until recently, by her. With permission from her administrative superiors to revisit the problem, she makes the disparity in military health-care benefits a focus of her graduate coursework in professional communication undertaken for continuing education. She utilizes an assignment to write a preliminary description of the problem (Example 1, here) to develop her knowledge of problematic conditions and to practice framing the problem for policy action.

Example 1

MEMORANDUM

To: (Primary Audience—Still being determined)

Cc: (Secondary Audience—Still being determined)

From: (Author)

Date: (Date of publication)

Subject: (Expansion of Healthcare Benefits for Reserve Component Service Members)

Overview of the Problem

Three hundred thousand American citizens serve in the Reserve Armed Force (RAF), with the number increasing daily. Even though the Reserved Armed Force has devoted over 60 million man-days to the Global War on Terror, these Reserve Component (RC) Soldiers do not receive the same medical or dental benefits as their Active Component (AC) counterparts. Due to the different lifestyle of a RC Soldier compared to an AC Soldier and to the varying benefits, Reserve Armed Force units are struggling to meet medical readiness goals for worldwide deployments and operations.

Problematic Conditions

Current Operations Tempo: The current operational tempo of the United States military requires both AC and RC units to deploy on regular and frequent rotations. The RAF was established with a 5:1 ratio of training to operational years of service. Currently, most RAF units are barely meeting a 2:1 ratio. The lack of dwell time between deployments requires Soldiers to maintain a much higher level of constant medical readiness.

Lack of Outside Health Insurance/Financial Hardship: While the majority of RAF Soldiers have civilian employment, the percentage with personal health insurance drops to less than 30% of the force. Even though enlistment contracts require Soldiers to maintain their medical readiness, many do not have personal insurance or the financial means to procure healthcare.

Socioeconomic Status: RAF Soldiers have an average annual income that is 50% less than the average Air National Guard service member. While the "Hometown Recruiting" program has reached small communities and rural areas previously untapped for military service, the majority of the resulting force consists of blue-collar or farm-dependent citizens with a lower than average socioeconomic status.

The Problem

Too many RAF Soldiers are not medically ready for deployment or missions.

Impact of the Problem

With the RAF quickly developing into an operational force, the United States depends on its service members to maintain a high state of medical readiness in preparation for worldwide deployments and missions. The lack of consistent healthcare benefits for RC Soldiers results in a national average of 23% Fully Medically Ready (FMR) Soldiers across the RAF. As a result, units are deploying to combat theaters with 10–15% fewer Soldiers than missions require. The resulting holes in coverage in security forces, logistics support, and medical providers in combat theaters are devastating the war fight and endangering the Soldiers that are able to fight, as they do not have the support they require.

Potential Solutions

Maintain Current System: Maintaining the current policy of 90 days of healthcare benefits prior to arrival at mobilization station will alleviate a small portion of the medical and dental issues preventing Soldiers from deploying. The current system balances the cost of healthcare with the cost of "fixing" a Soldier. This system does not allow for the deployment of

Soldiers with issues that are treatable, yet require more than 60–90 days for optimum medical care.

Full Coverage for Alert: Soldiers currently receive full healthcare benefits 90 days prior to their arrival at the mobilization station. While this allows for them to receive care for minor illnesses and annual appointments, it does not allow enough time for Soldiers to receive treatment for more serious, yet treatable illnesses, such as hypertension, gum disease, or dental issues requiring dentures. Extending full healthcare coverage to Soldiers immediately upon alert of the unit will allow for the treatment of 95% of all dental issues, and the majority of illnesses which do not otherwise disqualify for worldwide deployment.

Full Coverage throughout Period of Service: Extending full healthcare benefits to RC Soldiers (which would mirror the full Tricare coverage AC Soldiers receive) would allow Soldiers to maintain a healthier lifestyle through regular medical and dental appointments. The potential gains of preventive medicine would, over time, reduce the cost of reactionary medicine for RC Soldiers, resulting in higher readiness rates. Additionally, if healthcare costs were covered, Soldiers could be held accountable for their individual medical readiness under statutes of the Uniform Code of Military Justice.

Next Steps

As the country continues to call upon our Reserve Component forces, it is critical that we establish a more thorough and dependable system of providing healthcare to RAF Soldiers. The discrepancy between benefits received by the AC and RC is monumental, despite the valiant service of both components on the battlefield. I challenge concerned citizens, leaders, and politicians to recognize the time and money being lost on professionally trained Soldiers who are unable to deploy due to preventable medical and dental issues. Disagreement with our country's position in the current war is unrelated to the benefits our Soldiers deserve for their service. Let us take care of the very men and women who are risking their lives for our country on the dangerous frontlines of the Global War on Terror by improving healthcare benefits regardless of duty status or military component.

WHAT THIS EXAMPLE SHOWS. Example 1 illustrates narrow problem definition focused on a single affected population. It provides expected information by answering required questions (Task 4, this chapter). It identifies problematic conditions, specifies a problem those conditions present, and proposes solution options. It makes no recommendations, except (perhaps inadvertently) in the draft memo's subject line. "Expansion of benefits" in the subject line is inconsistent with the "Potential Solutions" section of the document, where alternatives are described but not chosen. As a genre, problem description might appropriately either include or omit recommendations. However, the communication's purpose must be clear. If this document's subject line more accurately said "Healthcare Benefits Disparity Requires Attention" it would avoid introducing a solution.

The weakness of Example 1 is omissions. It leaves some basic questions unanswered (Task 4, this chapter). It does not identify other interested stakeholders or potential agreements and disagreements among interested parties. Perhaps stakeholders and interests are implied in the final paragraph subheaded "Next Steps." But that generalized paragraph does not pinpoint actors or their concerns. And, it does not specify steps to be taken. Finally, the document lacks credibility because it does not identify the writer or intended recipients. Explanation for this omission is that there is no policy action underway, so the purposes and audiences are not yet identifiable. Nonetheless, because it is incomplete and still a draft, the document is not ready for use in a policy process. However, it is instructive for the writer because it shows what remains to be done. It illustrates the demand for rethinking and rewriting as you iteratively define a problem. Omissions, even errors, can be instructive for writers.

To format this communication, the writer, who is a professional in government, appropriately chooses a written memorandum or memo (Viewpoint 4, Step 2, Chapter 2). This is a common workplace genre intended for quick reading, easy understanding, and efficient referencing in meetings. (In colonial America, it was called a memorial, meaning information to be remembered.) Modern memos are organized top down, with an initial overview followed by topical sections, like the inverted pyramid of news articles. This organization and the memo's compact form fit the time, attention, and accountability demands of governmental workplaces.

Unlike a news article with a single headline, a memo has a header or stacked items identifying the communication's who (sender and addressed recipient), what (subject), why (purpose), and when (transmittal date). Additional intended recipients might be specified in a "cc" ("copied on this communication") item placed either in the header or at the document's end. The memo's subject is identified in the "re" ("regarding") line, which serves as the memo's title. Content is chunked into sections with subheadings (like miniheadlines) cueing readers to the particulars covered in each section.

In Example 1, capitalization ("S" in "Soldier," for instance) reflects prescribed style in the writer's workplace and is retained here.

Scenario 2

Previously, you read a Congressional Research Service summary of the 2011 FDA Food Safety Modernization Act (Chapter 2). That act had a long prior legislative history. "Pure food" policy originating in the 1930s generated a steady stream of federal legislative and administrative reforms intended to assure the safety of food that Americans consume. Over decades, congressional committees, commissions, and taskforces worked with the endorsement of several presidents to create a body of laws, standards, and regulations, as well as federal agencies responsible for administering them. After 2001, the U.S. "war on terror" added food security or protection against tampering and deliberate contamination to food safety policy.

These precedents focused on food manufacturing and distribution. Food growing and handling on the farm were not addressed except for the initiation of a national system to identify and track meat animals. Opportunity to pull food growing and handling into the food safety net came between 2006 and 2011. At that time, random events, national elections, and political advocacy converged to enable reform. Illness outbreaks attributed to spinach (2006), eggs (2006), and peanuts (2009) renewed public perception of a food safety problem. National elections in 2008 shifted political power to a new majority in the legislature and administration. Citing illness outbreaks attributed to peanut processing, the newly elected president Barack Obama announced the creation of a new interagency food safety working group. "We all eat peanut butter, including my daughters. We need to fix this," he said.

Interest advocacy geared up to influence legislative and administrative initiatives. Legislative committees in the House and Senate drafted new bills, held public hearings, requested reports from research and investigative services, and received advocates' advice on bill provisions. Administrative agencies received advocates' petitions for new rules and held hearings to collect public comment on them. Intense activity in 2009–2010 resulted in the landmark FDA Food Safety Modernization Act passed by the 111th Congress in December 2010 and signed by President Obama in January 2011. Administrative rule making to set standards and create regulations for enforcement of the new law began in 2012 with proposed regulations and a call for public comment. Based on public comment received, the proposals were pulled back. Revised regulations were announced with a call for comment in 2014.

Sample communications in the 2009–2010 legislative process are shown next. Professionals in government or nonprofit organizations wrote these samples. Condensed versions are shown, along with information for accessing entire documents.

Example 2

FDA Has Begun to Take Action to Address Weaknesses in Food Safety Research, but Gaps Remain

GAO-10-182R, May 24, 2010
Additional Materials:
Accessible Text
Contact:
Office of Public Affairs
(202) 512-4800
youngc1@gao.gov

Summary

The United States faces challenges to ensuring food safety. First, imported food makes up a substantial and growing portion of the U.S. food supply, with 60 percent of fresh fruits and vegetables and 80 percent of seafood coming from across our borders. In recent years, there has been an increase in reported outbreaks of foodborne illness associated with both domestic and imported produce. Second, we are increasingly eating foods that are consumed raw and that have often been associated with foodborne illness outbreaks, including leafy greens such as spinach. Finally, shifting demographics means that more of the U.S. population is, and increasingly will be, susceptible to foodborne illnesses. The risk of severe and life-threatening conditions caused by foodborne illnesses is higher for older adults, young children, pregnant women, and immune-compromised individuals.

In January 2007 GAO designated federal oversight of food safety as a high-risk area needing urgent attention and transformation because of the federal government's fragmented oversight of food safety. The Food and Drug Administration (FDA) is responsible for ensuring the safety of roughly 80 percent of the U.S. food supply—virtually all domestic and imported foods except for meat, poultry, and processed egg products—valued at a total of $466 billion annually, as of June 2008. In 2007 the FDA Science Board, an advisory board to the agency, reported that science at FDA suffers from serious deficiencies. In addition, our prior reviews of FDA's food safety programs have identified gaps in scientific information, limiting FDA's ability to oversee food labeling, fresh produce, and dietary supplements. Further, as part of our recent review on the effectiveness of the strategic planning and management efforts of FDA, 67 percent of FDA managers reported, in response to a GAO survey, that updated scientific technologies or other tools would greatly help them to contribute to FDA's goals and responsibilities; however, only 36 percent of managers reported that FDA was making great progress in keeping pace with scientific advances. In written comments responding to our survey, some managers stressed the need to increase and stabilize funding, recruit and retain top scientists, and make decisions on the basis of scientific evidence.

In this context, you asked us to examine ways in which FDA may use science to more effectively support its regulatory work and to inform the public about food content and safety. This report focuses primarily on FDA's (1) progress in addressing selected recommendations identified by the Science Board; (2) incorporation of scientific and risk analysis into its oversight of the accuracy of food labeling, fresh produce, and the safety of dietary supplements; and (3) a new computer screening tool that may improve its efforts to screen imports using a risk-based approach.

FDA has begun to address selected Science Board recommendations. For example, FDA reported in May 2008 that it created the Office of Chief Scientist and, in May 2009, it added more responsibilities to the office to signal a new emphasis on regulatory science. According to the Acting Chief Scientist, his office plans to identify major scientific cross-cutting opportunities across FDA and to collaborate with other government agencies. However, gaps in scientific information have hampered FDA's oversight of food labeling, fresh produce, and dietary supplements. In addition, FDA's new computer tool—PREDICT—is designed to improve its risk-based import screening efforts by analyzing food shipments using criteria that include a product's inherent food safety risk and the importer's violative history, among other things, to estimate each shipment's risk. FDA has developed a draft performance measurement plan for evaluating the effectiveness of this risk-based approach.

(The full report can be found at www.gao.gov/products/GAO-10–182R/.)

WHAT THIS EXAMPLE SHOWS. Example 2 exhibits many of the qualities in public policy communication that this guide supports (Two Checklists, Chapter 2).

The Government Accountability Office (GAO) is a respected research, legal, and investigative agency of the Congress. Its reputation lends credibility to its reports. In addition, the document exhibits features of traceability and accountability that encourage readers to presume that the report's information is reliable. By stating (in a letter of transmittal not shown here) explicitly for whom the report speaks (GAO) and to whom it is addressed (a committee chairman) and by referring (in the full report) to review of this and prior reports by the agency concerned (FDA), this report is accountable.

The summary's organization anticipates the report's reception and use in hectic policy workplaces. It is compact. It is coherent, with transitional markers such as "first . . . second . . . finally." Key information is easy to find, an especially important feature if the content will be condensed for oral briefings or discussed in public hearings. Within paragraphs, the information is ordered top down or in general-to-particular logical order. Opening sentences summarize; following sentences elaborate. The summary's readers can rely on obvious transitions and repeated order of presentation to scan comprehendingly. Information hunter–gatherers can use these features to target their selections (Viewpoint 2 , Chapter 2).

The genre is a report. Government agencies such as GAO often require reports for specific communication purposes. GAO specifies formal written reports for communicating finished results of investigations requested by a Congress member. Institutions including government agencies sometimes also prescribe a house style of document design. GAO style for report summaries is illustrated here: there are three main sections (why the study was done, what was found, what is recommended). GAO style encourages the use of subheadings such as Why GAO Did This Study, What GAO Found, and What GAO Recommends. This summary does not use subheadings. If it did, the report's readability would be even better.

The reader who accesses this report via the GAO website on the Internet will see the 1-page summary that is reproduced here. Accompanying the summary, links go to the full 25-page report, to GAO contact information, and to an accessible version of the report. The latter version implements GAO's communication policy, which recognizes that many readers now seek governmental information via the Internet and that different readers have different Internet access capabilities. The reader selecting "Accessible Text" will find an accompanying explanation of GAO's compliance with the Federal Web Managers Council's guidance "Provide Access for People with Disabilities (Section 508)." The guidance is publicly available at http://www.howto.gov/web-content/. The explanation says, "This text file was formatted by the U.S. Government Accountability Office (GAO) to be accessible to users with visual impairments, as part of a longer term project to improve GAO products' accessibility. Every attempt has been made to maintain the structural and data integrity of the original printed product. . . . We welcome your feedback. Please e-mail your comments regarding the contents or accessibility features of this document to webmaster@gao.gov."

Scenario 2 Continued

As they developed a new bill in April 2009, staff members of the House of Representatives Commerce Committee met with advocates for sustainable agriculture. According to advocacy group mission statements, sustainable agriculture is farming that is ecologically sound, community supportive, and economically viable. Among topics discussed in the April meeting was advocates' objection to a one-size-fits-all approach to safety regardless of farm size, scale, or type of operation. Committee staff asked for alternatives to consider. In response, an advocacy group representative wrote a position statement laying out a logic for making exceptions. The statement is presented here.

Example 3

A Message to Public Officials on Food Safety

By Brian Snyder, Executive Director Pennsylvania Association for Sustainable Agriculture (PASA) May 22, 2009

It seems everyone in elected office these days wants to do something about food safety. . . . As a community of farmers, we must also come to terms with the fact that harmful pathogens occasionally present in food can originate on farms in various ways that at times defy easy explanation.
. . .

Now let us consider the desire folks in government have to devise a legislative solution for the problems of food safety. . . . It is the acknowledged job of government to protect us to the extent possible from negligence and preventable forms of injury and/or death. But it is distinctly NOT the job of government to attempt to eliminate risk in life altogether, nor to impose expectations that may impinge unnecessarily on the free enterprise activities of the citizenry without a clearly understood benefit.

More than anything else right now, we need some plain talk on the real issues involving the safety of our food supply. With good science available on all sides, there is widespread disagreement about what matters most and why any of us should care.

We at PASA believe quite simply that the most important thing anyone can do to reduce risk in the food system is to make it as locally-based as possible. A safe food system is built on trust, and trust is built on actual human relationships. Such relationships are harder to maintain the larger and more diffuse the food system becomes.

Furthermore, we contend that the greatest risks to food safety occur when two systemic factors are combined: a) "food anonymity" and b) geographically broad distribution patterns. The most basic strategies for achieving a safe food supply, therefore, are not only to keep the distribution patterns as local and/or regional as possible, but also to put the farmers' faces back on the food. In an ideal scenario, both strategies would occur. Whatever else is said about specific practices on a farm or in a food processing facility, these two factors should be acknowledged as priorities and properly rewarded by the regulatory authorities right up front.

With this in mind, the following three-tiered structure seems both to be the current reality in food production and marketing systems, and a necessary framework for any successful effort to further regulate food safety and security:

1. Farm-direct—This includes farm stands, farmers' markets, community supported agriculture (CSA) programs (e.g., subscription farms)

and other innovative strategies where the relationship between individual farmers and consumers is immediate and understood.

2. Identity-preserved—This involves distribution patterns on a regional scale where the farmer and consumer do not necessarily meet, but the identity of the farm is preserved on products all the way through the system, from field to fork.

3. Commodity stream—This represents sales where no direct relationship between farms and consumers exists. The farm identity is vague or lost altogether, sources are aggregated and distribution tends to be widespread, including food exported to other countries.

Taking them one at a time, we believe there should be minimal intervention by the government in regulating practices in the first tier, with respect to private transactions occurring between individual farms and consumers. . . . Problems arising here can quite naturally be traced quickly and addressed effectively without associated threats to any broad segment of the population.

With the second tier, it is most important to understand that the government has a tremendous opportunity to take advantage of the good things currently happening out there. The goodwill and positive business practices of farmers, processors and retailers who are already participating in local and regional food system initiatives are ensuring a significant degree of traceability that should be supported in any way possible.

Let me say this as plainly as possible. The government has every right to set reasonable standards for food quality and safe production practices. Nonetheless, farmers with their names—and reputations—listed on every package of food should have options to work on a voluntary basis with independent, third-party entities of their choosing in meeting such standards. Such partnering entities might include certifiers of organic, sustainable or natural products, farm cooperatives, breed associations and other trade organizations with a direct interest in supporting best management practices on the farms they serve.

The third tier represents the vast majority of food product consumed in this country and almost all that is exported to others. The need here for clearly stated and enforced quality and safety standards is obvious and should be a central priority of any food-related legislative agenda in the immediate future. . . .

The essential element here is not that there is some theoretical distinction between "good" and "bad" farmers. . . . This is also not fundamentally an issue of "big farms" vs. "small farms," though it appears unavoidable that vocal contingents on both sides of that divide will try to make it so.

The most pressing concern right now is that, in the rush to do something productive on the most public aspects of safety and security in the food supply, our public officials might take action that will a) do too little, for fear of offending some of the powerful interests involved, or b) do too much and thereby inflict real damage onto one of the most promising trends in agriculture to come along in at least half a century.

. . .

But if we can really get this right, a visionary and "fresh" approach concerning food safety at local, state and federal levels of government might lead to an agricultural renaissance in this country that will do as much for the economic health of our rural communities as it will for the physical health of our people.

(The complete statement can be found at http://pasafarming.org/news/policy-statements/.)

◄━• WHAT THIS EXAMPLE SHOWS. This statement illustrates broad and inclusive problem definition. One indicator is its inclusive language. Broad and inclusive definition combines topics and generalizes goals to expand the problem scope, to invite solution by cooperation, and to envision comprehensive change. Expanded scope is shown by combinations such as "food safety and security" and "growers and processors." Potential for cooperation is shown by "community of farmers" and "farmers of all stripes." Comprehensive change is represented by parallelism in the structure of sentences such as this one: "Do as much for the economic health of our rural communities as . . . for the physical health of our people." When characterizing actors in the process, the writer avoids stereotypes such as "agribusiness, large corporations, family farmers." He uses nonpolarizing, generic "farmers," instead. Similarly, the writer argues against thinking in simple dichotomies (e.g., "good" and "bad" farmers or "big farms" and "little farms").

Inclusiveness invites actors who disagree to work together. By framing the problem generally and using an approachable, reasonable tone (Viewpoint 4, Chapter 2), the statement invites consideration of alternatives.

A policy communicator's thinking is exhibited in the text (Viewpoint 3, Chapter 2). The writer states the organization's perspective ("We at PASA believe . . .") explicitly before acknowledging other perspectives. The organization's position is that, because the food supply system is complex, solutions to the problem of food safety should be flexible (Viewpoint 4, Chapter 2).

The statement answers all the questions a problem description is expected to answer (Task 4, this chapter.) It specifies causal conditions, the policy problem those conditions present as seen from the definer's perspective, and issues for policy consideration (e.g., risk standards, product traceability, compliance monitoring).

This advocate chose a written position statement to present the organization's advocacy. That genre is appropriate for addressing mixed audiences with both intended and potential readers (Viewpoint 3, Chapter 2). Legislators and staff on specific congressional committees are intended readers in this instance. Potential readers might be members of the writer's state-level organization, national partner organizations, and news media. For access, the advocacy statement appears on the "Press Room" page of the organization's website.

Organized as an informal opinion essay, the statement's style is nontechnical expression ("plain talk on the real issues") (Viewpoint 4, Chapter 2; Appendix A). The statement purposefully blends essay and memo organization at a key point. To present informal analysis of the food supply system to support a logic for exemptions, the writer switches from essay to memo form. The "three-tiered structure" that is "a necessary framework . . . for reform" is enumerated in a list. Listing and numbering distinguish individual items; indenting surrounds the entire list with blank space. All these devices pull attention to the analysis (Viewpoints 2 and 3, Chapter 2).

This advocacy statement does not make policy recommendations. For those, read the National Coalition of Sustainable Agriculture's position statement (Example 4, this chapter) and specific recommendations (Example 1, Chapter 4).

Example 4

Food Safety on the Farm: Policy Brief
October 2009
For over twenty years, the National Sustainable Agriculture Coalition (NSAC) has advocated for federal agricultural policies that foster the

long-term economic, social, and environmental sustainability of agriculture, natural resources, and rural and urban food systems and communities. NSAC's vision of agriculture is one where a safe, nutritious, and affordable food supply is produced by a legion of family farmers who make a decent living pursuing their trade, while protecting the environment, and contributing to the strength and stability of their communities. NSAC's work has resulted in federal programs that promote small and mid-sized family farms, increase new farming and ranching opportunities, invest in sustainable and organic research, reward conservation excellence, and expand local and regional food systems.

Over the last several years, the rise in major outbreaks of foodborne illnesses has called into question the sufficiency of the U.S. food safety system. Up until now, food safety regulatory oversight has focused mainly on processing, food handling, and manufacturing sectors—areas shown to be of highest risk for foodborne pathogen contamination. However, several food safety bills have been introduced into the 111th Congress that could directly or indirectly affect farms and ranches by expanding these authorities and making some on-farm safety standards mandatory. In addition, in the spring of 2009, the Obama Administration created an interagency Food Safety Working Group through which the Food and Drug Administration and U.S. Department of Agriculture are adopting new food safety standards and oversight, including on-farm measures.

While NSAC applauds Congress and the Administration for taking steps to decrease foodborne illnesses by strengthening federal food safety oversight and enforcement, in respect to farms it urges decision-makers to ensure that:

- Measures are risk-based, focus on risk reduction, and are justified by scientific research;
- FDA coordinates with other state and federal agencies and community-based organizations with food safety expertise or pre-existing standards or training programs for standard development and enforcement;
- Standards do not discriminate against, but rather encourage, diversified farming operations and conservation practices;
- Standards are appropriate to the scale of the enterprise;
- Fees of any kind, if they are imposed, are equitable to reflect different scales of production and ability to pay;
- Traceability rules for farmers should not require more than good, basic recordkeeping (one-up, one-down) of all sales;

- Marketing Agreements and Orders are not used to regulate food safety.

    NSAC members and food safety experts agree that the responsibility for ensuring that our food is safe is incumbent on all actors in the food supply chain: from farmers, packers, processors, and distributors, to the final consumer. It is our position, however, that proposals proffering one-size-fits-all solutions to food safety fail to acknowledge the diversity of agriculture and are inappropriate and counterproductive courses of action.

(The complete brief can be found at http://sustainableagriculture.net/wp-content/uploads/2008/08/NSAC-Food-Safety-Policy-Brief-October-2009.pdf/.)

➤ WHAT THIS EXAMPLE SHOWS. This policy brief has a two-part structure, an initial summary (presented in this chapter) followed by policy recommendations (presented in Chapter 4).

In the summary shown here, a policy communicator's thinking is evident (Viewpoint 3, Chapter 2). In the opening paragraph, the first sentence identifies the subject, long-term agriculture policy. The second sentence asserts the frame or perspective of the sustainable agriculture coalition. The third sentence justifies the frame by citing the coalition's authority based on knowledgeable experience and accomplishment in policy work.

The second paragraph initiates a problem description. Its first two sentences document causal conditions including triggering events, insufficient regulation, and inadequate policy responses. From the coalition's perspective, those conditions present a problem of governance. The solution to that problem is principled reform. A bulleted list of guiding principles adapted to the current problem, food supply safety, is offered. The list concludes with an assertion of the coalition's position that principled reform for the long term is better than short-term solutions. In two compact paragraphs, the summary efficiently represents all the elements of policy communication: knowledge, perspective, position, adaptation, and documentation.

Scenario 2 Continued

As versions of food supply safety legislation progressed through the House over the summer of 2009, splits developed in the sustainable agriculture community's attitude toward reform. Advocates divided primarily around the logic for exemptions from new safety requirements. Some wanted to exempt farms, including those offering value-added products, based on the size of the operation, while others were more interested in protections related to the style and geographic breadth of marketing programs. During deliberations on the companion Senate bill in the fall of 2009 and 2010, an amendment proposed by Montana Democrat Senator (and organic farmer) Jon Tester and North Carolina Democrat Senator Kay Hagan included a solution that would exempt certain producers based on combined considerations of size and geography. In its final form, the Tester–Hagan amendment allowed for limited exemption of operations with less than $500,000 in annual gross revenue and all sales within the state of residence or 275 miles (if out of state), as long as the farm of origin is made clear on a placard or label. The sustainable agriculture community's debate changed in reaction to the amendment. Some advocates argued strongly for this solution but others continued to push for total exemption from federal government scrutiny for all small farms. Opponents argued that state and local public-health standards were sufficient food supply safety guards.

The Tester–Hagan amendment was accepted in the Senate Health, Education, and Labor Force Committee's bill. Later it was incorporated in the enrolled bill passed by both the House and the Senate. Also incorporated were related requirements for the FDA to assist small businesses in complying with the new law. These incorporations respond to advocates' concerns and demonstrate advocacy's influence on legislation. To illustrate that influence, sections of the final bill are shown next.

Example 5
FDA Food Modernization Safety Act (H.R. 2751 ENR.)

Title I: Improving Capacity to Prevent Food Safety Problems
Sec. 102. Registration of Food Facilities
(b) Suspension of registration.

(2) Small entity compliance policy guide.—Not later than 180 days after the issuance of the regulations promulgated under section 415(b)(5) of the Federal Food, Drug, and Cosmetic Act (as added by this section), the Secretary shall issue a small entity compliance guide setting forth in plain language the requirements of such regulations to assist small entities in complying with registration requirements and other activities required under such section.

(c) Clarification of Intent.

(1) Retail food establishment.—The Secretary shall amend the definition of the term "retail food establishment" in section 1.227(b)(11) of title 21, Code of Federal Regulations to clarify that, in determining the primary function of an establishment or a retail food establishment under such section, the sale of food products directly to consumers by such establishment and the sale of food directly to consumers by such retail food establishment include—

(A) the sale of such food products or food directly to consumers by such establishment at a roadside stand or farmers' market where such stand or market is located other than where the food was manufactured or processed;

(B) the sale and distribution of such food through a community supported agriculture program; and

(C) the sale and distribution of such food at any other such direct sales platform as determined by the Secretary.

(2) Definitions.—For purposes of paragraph (1)—

(A) the term "community supported agriculture program" has the same meaning given the term "community supported agriculture (CSA) program" in section 249.2 of title 7, Code of Federal Regulations or any successor legislation; and

(B) the term "consumer" does not include a business.

Sec. 103. Hazard Analysis and Risk-Based Preventive Controls.

(l). Modified Requirements for Qualified Facilities

(1) Qualified Facilities.—

(A) In general.—A facility is a qualified facility for purposes of this subsection if the facility meets the conditions under subparagraph (B) or (C).

(B) Very small business.—A facility is a qualified facility under this subparagraph—

. . .

(C) Limited annual monetary value of sales.—

(i) In general.—A facility is a qualified facility under this subparagraph if clause (ii) applies—

(ii) Average annual monetary value.—This clause applies if—

(I) In the 3-years preceding the applicable calendar year . . .
(II) the average monetary value of all food sold by such facility (or the collective average annual monetary value of such food sold by any subsidiary or affiliate . . . was less than $500,000 adjusted for inflation."
(The full bill can be found at H.R.2751 ENR. *FDA Food Safety Modernization Act.* Http://thomas.loc.gov/cgi-bin/query/z?c111:H.R.2751/.)

◆— WHAT THIS EXAMPLE SHOWS. In a policy process, knowledge travels along communication channels. This example shows knowledge moving from advocates' position statements and policy briefs into legislation. Bill drafters appropriately transformed advocacy to legislative concepts such as risk-based hazard analysis and appropriately carried advocates' domain-specific wording such as "roadside stands" and "farmers markets" into the legislation. This example forcefully reminds us that problem definitions predict solutions, that problems are defined in words, and that word choices matter.

Summary and Preview

This chapter tells you that problem definition is fundamental and language awareness is important in policy work. "We talk of policy problems in words. How words are used to represent things is a subject usually treated in the domains of rhetoric and literature, but symbolic representation is the essence of problem definition in politics" (Stone, 2002, p. 137). Here you learned to define problems as an advocate with rhetorical awareness. In Chapter 4, you will learn to define problems as a policy analyst with political discourse awareness.

References

Bardach, E. (2011). *A practical guide for policy analysis: The eightfold path to more effective problem solving* (4th ed.). Washington, DC: CQ Press.

Cheney, D. (2002). *The complete guide to citing government information sources: A manual for social science and business research* (3rd ed.). Bethesda, MD: Lexis Nexis.

Kingdon, J. W. (2011). *Agendas, alternatives, and public policies* (2nd ed.). London, England: Pearson.

Stone, D. (2002). *Policy paradox: The art of political decision making* (Rev. ed.). New York, NY: Norton.

Further Reading

Coplin, W. D., with Sandefer, E. (2007). *The Maxwell manual for good citizenship: Public policy skills in action.* Lanham, MD: Rowman & Littlefield.

Stone, D. (2012). *Policy paradox: The art of political decision making* (3rd ed.). New York, NY: Norton.

Evaluation: Analyze and Advise

Key Concepts

- Frame the problem as an analyst
- Political discourse awareness
- Policy discourse awareness

Defining a problem does not solve it. Analysis and evaluation of alternative definitions and potential interventions are usually required. This chapter shows analysts using critical thinking and critical language awareness. "Words are . . . symbols . . . An astute policy analyst or political actor must understand and be able to analyze how symbols work" (Stone, 2012, p. 160).

As it is used here, critical generally means a questioning approach to discovery and a skeptical attitude toward conventional wisdom. Political discourse refers broadly to discussion, debate, news media reports, and (on occasion) procedural communications in government; it refers narrowly to communications of a particular policy initiative (Example 3, Chapter 3; Example 3, Chapter 7). Critical discourse analysis infers connections based on examination of language use (Fairclough, 1985). It discovers connections between texts and their contexts. It discloses ways that communication constructs authority and the exercise of power. For instance, by looking critically at the language of political argument, critical discourse analysis can uncover ideological perspectives, expose faulty or misleading arguments, and pinpoint information gaps.

"Policy analysts need to have well-developed critical abilities" in addition to technical abilities and people skills, says one analyst (Mintrom, 2012, p. 22). He remarks, "Policy analysts are at their best when they question the proposals being put forward by others, when they take time to discover why problems are being presented in specific ways, what their sources are, and why they have arisen at this time" (pp. 20–21).

Critical thinking functions throughout the formation of a policy communicator's knowledge, perspective, position, adaptation, and documentation (Viewpoint 3, Chapter 2). Primarily, it functions in the formation of perspective. In the visual arts, where the concept derives, perspective pulls together a viewpoint, features of objects, and horizon to frame a representation of reality such as a landscape. In language arts, perspective similarly frames the representation and interpretation of information. Written or spoken representations of reality generally come to us already framed or presented and interpreted in accordance with a perspective (Graumann, 2002). In policy communication, problem definition illustrates. As noted in Chapter 3, one constituency's problem is another's acceptable status quo. Perspective often makes the difference. Another illustration is policy analysis, where the questions and the analytic approaches are framed by perspective. For instance, market analysis and comparative institution analysis take different perspectives on a problem. Consequently, each represents the problem differently.

Perspective is substantive, intrinsic, built in. It is not (usually) consciously intentional. Sometimes, however, it is intentional, even unethical. Perspective can lead communicators to spin information or present it too selectively. Selectivity can result in deception.

Telling the difference between perspective and intentional deception can be hard. That's where critical analysis of discourse can help. For policy evaluators, recognition of perspective is basic work (Gee, 1999, p. 20). Critical thinking skills for recognizing perspective, whether your perspective or another, are taught throughout this guide. You will find critical thinking tips in tasks specific to each chapter. For instance, in Chapter 3, you recognize perspective built into problem definition by describing a problem from different actors' viewpoints (Task 1). Here in Chapter 4, critical thinking and language awareness are taught by several devices: a sketch of critical reading experience, an illustration of critical discourse analysis performed in a public hearing, a writing sample illustrating a student's use of viewpoint switching (Example 2), and commentaries highlighting features of samples that exhibit critical thought.

Here's a sketch of critical reading: Early on in reading a document, you begin to infer and to query the communication situation. You ask yourself, "Who is providing this information? To whom? Why?" You look analytically at text features, asking, "What is the message? How is it supported? Any gaps? Why?" You notice that you are attending to what the presentation says directly as well as indirectly. You ask, "What is this in reference to? Where is it coming from? What's its story? Why? Why now?" You might notice how you feel about the communication, asking, "Do I believe this? Do I trust it?"

Critical reading to connect a text with its contexts is different from reading to mine it for relevance (Viewpoint 2, Chapter 2). When you read critically, you don't simply hunt and gather. You probe. The sketch imagines workaday critical reading that any policy actor should do.

For an actual instance of critical discourse analysis communicated by a policy analyst testifying as an expert witness in a governmental public hearing, read the next illustration. Extracts from the hearing's transcript are provided, along with information on access to the full transcript.

Illustration: "Agroterrorism, the Threat to America's Breadbasket"

November 19, 2003, Hearing by the Senate Government Affairs Committee

Republican Senator Susan Collins of Maine chaired a hearing on proposed amendments to extend the 2002 Bioterrorism Act to cover agriculture and food industries. In her statement opening the hearing Senator Collins defines the problem as the vulnerability of the U.S. food supply chain. As evidence, she cites a paper trail of documentation that she says indicates terrorist intentions to attack the supply chain.

Opening Statement by Senator Collins, Committee Chair

" . . . Hundreds of pages of U.S. agricultural documents recovered from the al Qaeda caves in Afghanistan early last year are a strong indication that terrorists recognize that our agriculture and food industry provides tempting targets. According to a new RAND Corporation report, which will be released at today's hearing, the industry's size, scope, and productivity, combined with our lack of preparedness, offer a great many points of attack. Among our witnesses today will be the report's author, Dr. Peter Chalk, a noted expert in biowarfare. . . . A CIA report . . . confirmed that the September 11 hijackers expressed interest in crop dusting aircraft. . . . This horrific page is from *The Poisoner's Handbook*, an underground pamphlet published here in the United States that provides detailed instructions on how to make powerful plant, animal, and human poisons from easily obtained ingredients and how to disseminate them. It was found in Afghanistan. . . . Last spring, a Saudi cleric who supports al Qaeda . . . issued a fatwa, a religious ruling, that justified the use of chemical and biological weapons, including weapons that destroy tillage and stock" [*Agroterrorism*, 2004, pp. 1–2].

Testimony by Peter Chalk, Witness

The second witness, Peter Chalk, is a risk analyst for the research organization Rand Corporation. He authored the Rand report on biological warfare and agriculture cited by the committee chair in her opening statement. His testimony complicates the discourse she has initiated. Chalk makes measured acknowledgement of the validity of claims made by Collins. However, he qualifies the risk. "Now, although vulnerability does not translate to risk and there are few reported actual incidents of terrorists employing biological agents against agriculture, a realistic potential for such a contingency certainly exists" [p. 14]. He applies probabilistic reasoning to control inferences. "The problem is that you can't extrapolate [a single disease outbreak] to the general agricultural industry because the referent . . . experience is not there" [p. 22].

Chalk then draws attention to the constructed nature of the threat to food production by showing its inadequate risk assessment.

". . . I have only come up with two documented cases of the . . . use of biological weapons deliberately as a political strategy against livestock" [p. 31].

Chalk goes on to rank the risk comparatively. "Despite the ease by which agricultural terrorism can be carried out and the potential ramifications. . . . I don't think that it is likely to constitute a primary form of terrorist aggression. . . . However, I think [such attacks] could certainly emerge as a favored secondary form of aggression" [p. 17].

Without referring directly to the Rand report that he authored, Chalk effectively disassociates its findings from the paper trail in which Senator Collins places it. By resisting the committee chair's frame for the report, he controls the use of his knowledge, perspective, and position in this public process.

(The full transcript can be found at http://www.gpo.gov/fdsys/pkg/CHRG-108shrg91045/html/CHRG-108shrg91045.htm/.)

What This Illustration Shows.
The committee chair's opening statement shows faulty cause-and-effect reasoning and ideological bias (Smith, 2009). It purposefully perceives food production as vulnerable to hostile attack by terrorists. As member of the majority political party and committee chair at the time of the hearing, Senator Collins had the authority and power to frame a discussion of food supply safety. In this hearing, she framed it selectively in connection to terror.

She used five symbolic devices, metaphor, synecdoche, narrative, assembled meaning, and recontextualization, to build the frame. Metaphor is implied comparison; in her statement, food protection is compared to war. "Leaders declare war on social problems not only to signal their firm determination but also to create public support for increased funding. . . . The war metaphor sanctions draconian measures" (Stone, 2012, p. 176). Synecdoche represents a whole by one of its parts; Senator Collins represents total breakdown in food supply by hypothetical single threats in a narrative, a horror story of vulnerability. "Politicians or interest groups deliberately choose one egregious or outlandish incident to represent the universe of cases, then use that example to build support for changing a policy addressed to the larger universe" (Stone, 2012, p. 169). Assembled meaning is meaning by aggregation, or a constructed association of items.

This device relies on many-to-one reduction that sweeps unlike items into one category. Like all symbolic meanings, assembled meanings are not inherent. Rather, they are constructed by language choices. Senator Collins purposefully implies a commonality among unlike items. In the sample shown here, she groups agricultural aircraft, underground publications, and chemical weapons. Each item is given new meaning by association with the others. Although recontextualization, like symbolic representation, is inevitable in discourse, distortion is not inevitable or ethical.

Witness Chalk effectively deconstructs Senator Collins's rhetorical construction. His testimony critiques the chair's position and the terror perspective. Politely, he exposes misleading cause-and-effect association while agreeing that a problem might exist. He addresses the potential problem analytically, citing statistical evidence. His testimony and answers to questions—distinguishing between vulnerability and risk, measuring the probability of risk, declining to speculate beyond available evidence—show him critically analyzing the policy discourse. His critique draws attention to the terror perspective, making it visible and showing its limits. Politely and credibly, the witness constructs alternatives. Effectively, he makes room for argument.

How to Critically Evaluate Policy and Analyze Policy Discourse

A problem is recognized. Policy alternatives for addressing it are under consideration. You are asked or you wish to present a definition of the problem and a review of policy alternatives. Your intended audience might be policy makers, an interested community, or the general public. Your strategy is to analyze critically. (Note: The task outline of questions assumes that you are prepared to perform— outside the tasks listed here—appropriate technical policy analysis.)

Goal: Policy evaluation.
Objectives: Consider alternative problem definitions including influential contextual factors. Construct alternative policy responses. Analyze their likely impacts. Critique their descriptive representations. Draw conclusions and offer recommendations.

Product: Short or longer written document that can be easily summarized for oral presentation. Length may vary from 1 to 50 or more pages.

Scope: Local or broader in impact; widely discussed or ignored; past, present, or anticipated.

Strategy: Analyze the policy discourse. Analyze policy alternatives.

Task 1: Identify the Problem and the Interests

- What is the problem? What brings it to attention? Who brings it to attention?
- Why does the problem come to attention now? What conditions led to the problem?
- Whose behavior is affected, or whose concerns are relevant? Who will benefit by solutions to the problem? Who will pay? Who will implement policy to solve it?
- What stake does each interested party (affected groups, target beneficiaries, implementers of policy) have in the problem?
- How does each define the problem?
- What ideals and values (equity, liberty, efficiency, security, loyalty) or ideologies (vision of how the world is or how it should be) are expressed in each definition?
- What symbols or stories or metaphors are apparent in each definition?
- What conflicts of values or ideologies are evident among definitions?
- How does politics influence the problem?

Task 2: Specify Alternative Solutions and Relevant Criteria for Evaluating Them

- What are the goals/objectives of a public policy to solve this problem?
- What symbols or stories or metaphors are evident in the expression of goals/objectives?
- What policy instruments might achieve the goals/objectives?
- What are at least two (alternative) policies to meet the need?
- What are the relevant criteria for choosing the best one? How do stakeholders weigh the criteria? How appropriate are the weights? What are the trade-offs among criteria?
- What would be the outcome of each alternative according to criteria you consider relevant?

Task 3: Recommend an Alternative and Explain Your Reasoning (If You Are Making a Recommendation)

- Which policy option or instrument do you recommend? Why is it best? Why are other alternatives worse?
- What is the basis for your recommendation? What type of analysis supports it?
- What symbols or stories are apparent in the expression of your recommendation?
- How will your choice affect stakeholders?
- On what conditions (political, economic, organizational) does successful implementation of your choice depend?
- What are the constraints (political, economic, organizational, ethical) on implementing your choice?

Task 4: Write the Document: Policy Analysis with (or without) Recommendation

Before you write, consider your readiness to communicate (Viewpoint 3, Chapter 2). Do you have needed knowledge and awareness? Use the method (Viewpoint 4, Chapter 2) to consider the communication situation rhetorically and to plan your communication. After you write, use the checklists to assess the product and revise as needed.

Policy analysis is communicated in varied document types. If a particular type is prescribed for you, use it in accordance with your intended purpose and audience. Academic courses might prescribe a policy analysis memo, for instance. If you are free to choose, you might use a memo, a brief statement of position, or an extensive discussion paper.

Policy analyses in any form are expected to:

- characterize a problem according to its size, scope, incidence, effects, perceptions of it, and influences on it.
- identify policy choices available to address the problem and the criteria for choosing.
- identify perspectives and reasoning apparent in the choices made.
- show awareness of other perspectives, reasoning, and choices.
- specify the basis for selecting any proposed recommendation (the type of analysis performed), the effects for different groups, and the factors that will affect its implementation.

> You must cite the sources to which your policy analysis refers. Use the citation style prescribed or choose the APA style (http://www .apastyle.org/learn/faqs/index.aspx/). For more help, consult *The Complete Guide to Citing Government Information Resources: A Manual for Social Science and Business Research* (Cheney, 2002) available in libraries.

Three Examples

Example 1

Previously you read that a coalition of sustainable agriculture interest groups advocated principles to guide reform (Scenario 2, Example 4, Chapter 3). Here, you will read selected recommendations derived from those principles. (You may wish to review Scenario 2, Chapter 3, before reading the recommendations here.)

National Sustainable Agriculture Coalition Policy Brief and Recommendations
Food Safety on the Farm
October 2009

Principles and Policy Recommendations
There is no question that our food system needs to be safer. But if proposed food safety legislation and administrative actions are to have the desired effect of reducing pathogen risks and increasing agricultural innovation, long term sustainability, consumer choice, and availability of fresh, high quality produce, they should reflect the following principles and recommendations.

[Principle] I. Measures of safety should be risk-based, focused on risk reduction, and be justified by scientific research.

Proposed regulations and updated GAP guidelines should focus on the highest risk activities. Several areas of concern are highlighted here:
Centralized Processing: Attention should be given to the scale of the food production enterprise and its potential to distribute products to millions of people. In most of the recent outbreaks of food borne illness, the main source of the problem was centralized processing, distribution, and retail distribution, not growing and harvesting.

Centralized processing and distribution means that a single lapse can sicken a large, geographically dispersed set of individuals. Most documented cases of contamination of fresh produce can be traced to processing facilities where the products from multiple farms are commingled.

Leafy greens provide an example. The vast majority of "ready to eat" bags of salads, spinaches, lettuces, and lettuce hearts have unique risks associated with them. In the last ten years, 98.5% of all E. coli illnesses originating in California were traced to processed, bagged salad mixes, not to crops harvested as whole heads, bunched greens, or greens that are cooked.

Manure Use: Properly composted manure is an effective and safe fertilizer. A great volume of research has shown that judicious use of composted or aged manure is essential for maintaining the high soil microbial diversity and biological activity that is vital to soil quality. The buffering or exclusionary role of diverse microbial communities in soils richer in organic matter has been shown to accelerate die-off of E. coli 0157 and plant pathogens in soil. New safety guidelines, standards, and marketing agreements need not regulate all forms of manure use, but should focus on uncomposted or improperly composted manure, and biosolids, which pose a greater contamination risk. The food safety measures in the National Organic Program include rules for compost, uncomposted manure and biosolids, and may be used as an example.

Animals of Proven Significant Risk: Food safety guidelines, standards, and marketing agreements should use the term "animals of proven significant risk," instead of referring to all animals or all wildlife when managing risk. Wild animals do not present a significant contamination risk for produce. Preliminary results released in April from a two-year study by the CA wildlife agency, UC Davis, and USDA found that less than one-half of 1 percent of 866 wild animals tested positive for E. coli O157:H7 in Central California. Unnecessary control or elimination of wildlife could have devastating impacts on the ecosystems surrounding farms. Robust studies also document that deer are not a significant risk. Therefore deer should be eliminated from this list of potential vectors by the California Leafy Greens Marketing Agreement (LGMA).

Instead, new guidelines, standards, and marketing agreements should recognize the relative risk posed by cattle. Studies show that cattle are the primary source of E. coli H7:0157 with up to 50% of some herds being contaminated. This is particularly true for grain-fed cattle. More research is needed to provide scientific evidence for the sources and vectors of E. coli H7:0157 and other microbial pathogens to determine if other animals should be deleted or added to the list. Food safety standards should also encourage conservation measures such as perennial forage, buffer strips, and grasses to filter out contamination in overland water flows from livestock feedlots, loafing yards, pastures, and manure storage areas. Emphasis should be placed on halting avenues of contamination between animals and produce fields, including irrigation water contaminated by run-off from feedlots.

Human Transmission: Experts say that "deficient employee training" is the top food safety problem in the food processing industry.

If employees are not properly trained to implement food safety measures, and if hygiene standards are not enforced, unadulterated products will be at risk for contamination.

Water Quality: Quality of irrigation and rinsing water is intimately linked with produce contamination. Irrigation water can become contaminated by nearby large-scale livestock operations or by overflows from sewage systems. Contamination of produce can also stem from the water used to wash produce in processing facilities. FDA must set standards at the processing level to keep water baths from spreading microorganisms among different batches of produce.

Policy Recommendations:

- In developing guidelines and standards, the FDA and USDA should target critical [high risk] control points in the food system, including processing and packaging, the nature of the supply chain (e.g. the number of steps between the farmgate and end-consumer), that have been documented to increase risk.

- Target FDA and USDA research funding to the most critical [highest risk] points of risk in the food system for fresh produce and other raw agricultural commodities; in processing plants, on water testing of farms; on testing other vectors including animals, people, and dust; on the impact on risk of conservation and biodiversity measures; and on the environmental and social impact on farming of any proposed new food safety measures.

- Additional research should be conducted into the role of resource conservation and soil improvement practices, such as vegetated buffers, and maintaining high soil biological activity and diversity, in reducing on-farm risks of food-borne pathogens in produce fields.

- Protect wildlife and biodiversity by focusing on animals of significant risk, rather than indiscriminate animal control as the FDA and the USDA develop produce guidelines, standards, and marketing agreements.

- Focus safety guidelines, standards, and marketing agreements related to manure on biosolids and uncomposted manure, or improperly composted manure.

- Updated Good Agricultural Practices (GAP) should include recommendations for how to select and use water sources and guidance for producers on how to test water quality at specified intervals.

- Standards should encourage conservation practices that promote food safety.

. . .

[Principle] VIII. Marketing Agreements and Orders should not be used to regulate food safety.

Food safety should be treated as a pre-competitive area that is not subject to commercial competition. As such, it should not be regulated through the federal office in charge of "facilitating the strategic marketing of agricultural products in domestic and international markets"—the mission of the USDA's Agricultural Marketing Service. Marketing agreements and orders are industry-driven and do not have in place a democratic or transparent process for the development of standards and metrics that will ultimately impact all producers in the respective sector. The members of boards and committees in charge of developing the auditing metrics that are the basis of food safety inspections are appointed, not elected, so the producers signing onto a marketing agreement have to trust that the rules and metrics developed will not be prejudicial or preferential because individuals not necessarily representing them will be drafting laws that affect them.

Policy Recommendation:

- Oppose the proposed national Leafy Greens Marketing Agreement.

(The complete brief and all recommendations can be found at http://sustainableagriculture.net/wp-content/uploads/2008/08/NSAC-Food-Safety-Policy-Brief-October-2009.pdf/.)

———

WHAT THIS EXAMPLE SHOWS. This policy position statement illustrates critical thinking and clear writing. The recommendations express the perspective of a minority community, a coalition of groups representing sustainable agriculture farmers in the national industry of food growing and handling. The minority perspective advocates alternatives to the proposals offered by the majority or representatives of conventional agriculture. For instance, the coalition critiques and opposes a proposal made by an agriculture trade association to reform food supply safety by market management.

The coalition's recommendations manifest knowledge, position, adaptation, and documentation (Viewpoint 3, Chapter 2).

Dense detail referring to supporting documentation shows knowledge. The coalition's position is evident in language of sustainable agriculture taken from position statements and policy briefs (Examples 3 and 4, Chapter 3) and legislative bill language (Example 5, Chapter 3) and reused in this position statement. This recontextualization or language reuse is credible because it is logically argued; it is ethical because it is traceable.

Recommendations are adapted to the recipient's authority and power to act. In this brief intended for congressional committee members, recommended actions call for legislative intervention to fund and authorize programs and to oversee administration.

The coalition's position is stated explicitly and argued logically. Logic functions globally in this text to support coherence; it also functions locally to support specific claims. That is, when a thinker-writer claims that something is true, the reader expects supporting evidence. To be taken seriously, positional arguments must exhibit support for claims made. In this example, claims and evidence are tightly linked. Here is an instance:

> The vast majority of "ready to eat" bags of salads, spinaches, lettuces, and lettuce hearts have unique risks associated with them [*claim*]. In the last ten years, 98.5% of all E. coli illnesses originating in California were traced to processed, bagged salad mixes, not to crops harvested as whole heads, bunched greens, or greens that are cooked [*support*].

Presentation in this example has two strengths, global coherence of the whole document and clarity of individual sentences. Readers find written text coherent if it motivates them to read carefully and if it lets them know what to expect so that they can read knowledgeably (Williams & Colomb, 2012, pp. 107–108).

Multiple devices are used here to motivate and to guide readers. For instance, the tactic of listing aids memory. First introduced to a bare-bones list of principles in the brief's summary (Example 4, Chapter 3), readers reencounter the principles in the recommendations. Here, each principle, or "old" information, is listed again, followed by "new" information or recommendations. The old-to-new pattern within a list framework is repeated for eight principles, each having up to five related recommendations. Because the content is specialized and densely detailed with numerous key points, readers' attention might falter without strong guidance by the presenter. Here, readers are helped to attend carefully and knowledgeably by the listing framework and the recurring old-to-new pattern. Whether they hunt for target content or read the entire document, readers are likely to feel confident that the presenter wants them to understand and to care about the subject. Readers trust such presenters.

Presentation is clear at the level of individual sentences. The sentence is an important feature in this document's design for communicating. For instance, each principle is stated as a single sentence. Also, each recommendation is stated as a single sentence. If the sentence is long, its construction is (usually) understandable. Sentences are most clear when the main character is the subject, and the most important action is the verb (Williams & Colomb, 2012, p. 9). Other attributes of clarity are exhibited when there are no long introductions at the start of a sentence and no interruptions between the subject and verb. Clarity is enhanced, too, by varying the length of sentences. A short sentence offers relief. The following instance shows a clearly constructed long sentence and a short sentence following it. Underlining and italics are added for emphasis.

> Most documented <u>cases</u> [*subject*] of contamination of fresh produce <u>can be traced</u> [*verb*] to processing facilities where the products from multiple farms are commingled. Leafy greens provide an example.

In other instances, long sentences are less clear because they have too many characters and actions. They might also have a long introduction. Consequently, focus is weakened. Here is an illustration:

> **Original.** In <u>developing</u> guidelines and standards [*action*], the <u>FDA and USDA</u> [*characters*] <u>should target</u> [*action*] critical . . . control points in the food system, including <u>processing and packaging</u> [*action as character*], the <u>nature of the supply chain</u> [*character*] (e.g. the number of steps between the farmgate and end-consumer), that have been <u>documented</u> [*action*] to <u>increase</u> risk [*action*].

Readers might get lost in such action-packed sentences. As a remedy, this long sentence could be divided into two sentences, each with a single main character and action or subject and verb. The first sentence's introduction could be eliminated. The action of the first sentence could become the character of the next, for coherence. Here's how:

> **Revision**. <u>FDA and USDA guidelines and standards</u> [*character*] <u>should target</u> [*action*] critical . . . control points in the food system. <u>Targets</u> [character] <u>should include</u> [*action*] documented causes of risk such as processing and packaging, the nature of the supply chain (e.g., the number of steps between the farm-gate and the end-consumer).

For more instruction in revising sentences as shown here, see Appendix A as well as guides by Williams and Colomb (2012) and Smith and Smith (1987) referred to at the end of this chapter.

Example 2

For a course assignment, a graduate student in public policy communication wrote a policy brief with recommendation. At the time, she was also a career professional in a federal administrative agency. For the academic assignment, she chose to evaluate policies pertaining to a familiar subject from her professional work, aviation noise. To communicate her policy evaluation and recommendation, she adopted the persona of a concerned citizen representing a homeowner association affected by the problem. The homeowners live near a large airport. In her professional work, she often interacted with similar civic associations. She took that persona for the assignment to discover perspective, as an exercise in critical analysis. She wanted to see the problem from an affected population's viewpoint rather than from her own agency administrator's viewpoint.

MEMORANDUM

To: Representative Howard Coble (R-NC), Transportation and Infrastructure Committee

From: John Johns, Esquire, President, Ebenezer Homeowners' Association (EHA)

SUBJ: Briefing Memo to Define the Problem: Aviation Noise Pollution Poses an Increased Risk to our Nation's Health that Requires Immediate Federal Oversight

Date: March 14, 2011

cc: Armando Tovar, Noise Officer, Raleigh–Durham Airport (RDU) Authority

Greg Denning and Tim McBrayer, Wake County Members of the Raleigh–
Durham Noise Committee

OVERVIEW

Noise pollution presents an increasing danger to the health and welfare
of our Nation's population. One of the major sources of noise pollution is
the aviation industry. Air transportation has become the predominant
mass transportation system in the United States. As the aviation industry
expands so does the harmful impact of noise pollution on our
population.

Control of aviation noise primarily rests with state and local governments as a result of public law shifting responsibility away from federal
government. This has contributed to inconsistencies in aviation noise
control and abatement policies across the nation. As a result, major gaps
exist in protective coverage of all its citizens from noise pollution.

A study is needed now to determine the feasibility of assigning aviation
noise control and abatement to the federal level. The Federal Aviation
Administration (FAA) currently receives funding for aviation noise control
and abatement. FAA's role to support the economic expansion of the
aviation industry is in direct conflict with public protection from aviation
noise pollution. Specifically, consideration should be given to funding
the Environmental Protection Agency's (EPA) Office of Noise Abatement
and Control (ONAC) to set national policy and implement standards
uniformly.

POSITION

Studies Emerge on the Harmful Impact of Aviation Noise on Health
Our nation's health is at risk. According to the World Health Organization's Guidelines for Community Noise, noise is a major, increasing health
risk factor. Adverse health effects from noise include hearing loss; sleep
disturbances; cardiovascular and psycho-physiologic problems; performance reduction; annoyance responses; and adverse social behavior (1).

Public Awareness of Aviation Noise as a Pollutant
Aircraft noise first began to draw attention as an annoyance in the late
1960s. As the increase in aviation noise rose in the 1970s and 1980s, it
became a greater concern to those living in close proximity to airports. In
the 1970s, with the creation of the EPA's Office of Noise Abatement and
Control (ONAC) attention was brought to the fact that aviation noise was
a pollutant rather than simply an annoyance. The Quiet Communities Act
of 1978 mandated research in noise control, education programs and the

establishment of the Quiet Communities Program (2). This remains in effect today providing limited relief to select communities.

EPA and FAA Shared Oversight Ineffective

During the 1970s, EPA was to recommend noise standards to FAA based on consideration of public health and welfare. FAA was to determine if the proposed EPA standards were consistent with safety, economically reasonable and technologically practical to implement and enforce. During the 1970s, the FAA focused on a new problem in aviation, that of terrorists hijackings. In the 1980s, FAA dealt with the nationwide strike of Air Traffic Controllers with the demand to rebuild a new workforce. With the aftermath of September 11, 2001, the FAA worked to restore confidence in air transportation. Now, FAA turns its focus on the replacement of outdated air traffic control technology. All plausible reasons that the FAA did not aggressively tackle noise abatement as its top priority.

State and Local Oversight Applied Inconsistently

In 1981, under the Reagan Administration, EPA's ONAC ceased to be funded. The thought was that noise abatement would be best addressed at the state and local levels. This resulted in inconsistencies in the oversight of aviation noise and abatement from community to community. New technology exists for quieter aircraft, appropriate land use surrounding airports, sound proofing techniques, barrier construction and acoustical shields to reduce noise and they should be applied uniformly. Without national, uniform noise control and abatement standards, our entire population is not protected adequately against the health hazards of aviation noise pollution.

Noise Measurement to Assess Aviation Noise Inadequate

It is acknowledged that the Day–Night Level (DNL) is not the best tool to use since it uses an average of noise levels of all aircraft that land and depart in a 24-hour period. According to one FAA expert, "The DNL is really not a good metric but it is the best anyone has developed" (3). This tool should measure single event noise and sustained background noise levels. Studies indicate that noise is a hazard at 50 decibels and higher. The FAA uses 65 decibels and higher to monitor noise. FAA contends that only an estimated 500,000 people nationwide are directly impacted by aviation noise using the 65 decibels (4). Estimates by citizen's groups estimate the number of people at risk occur in the millions nationally based on citizen complaints. One estimate of the Chicago O'Hare Airport area alone, estimates that 1.6 million people are adversely affected by noise pollution (5).

Legislative History Indicates Limited Focus on Aviation Noise
The Noise Control Act of 1972 was an initial step to involve EPA in the regulation of aircraft noise. EPA recommended noise standards to FAA based on considerations of public health and welfare (6). EPA's mission for the protection of human health and the environment places EPA as the more appropriate agency for oversight. FAA focused on the promotion of the aviation industry and not on public health or welfare. This is evident in its criteria to restrict Stage 3 aircraft noise that mandates any airport restriction must:

- Be reasonable, non-arbitrary and non-discriminatory,
- Not create an undue burden on interstate or foreign commerce,
- Be consistent with safe and efficient use of navigable airspace,
- Not conflict with any existing federal statutes or regulation, and
- Not create an undue burden on the national aviation system (7).

VARIOUS VIEWPOINTS
The Ebenezer Homeowners' Association recognizes the economic value of the Raleigh–Durham (RDU) Airport. Annually, RDU generates revenue of $2 billion and supports 6,000 jobs (8). EHA also understands that noise is inherent in the operation of aircraft. The association thinks that existing measures currently exist to significantly reduce the adverse impact of noise in the surrounding area.

The aircraft and aviation industry view aviation noise control and abatement as an expensive cost of doing business. Costs are inherent in developing quieter aircraft technology or retrofitting current aircraft. The costs to citizen's health and welfare must also be considered.

The RDU Airport Authority attempts "to balance the demand for increased services with the concerns of communities around the airport" (8). However, aircraft are allowed to access the airport anytime of day or night. Communities nationwide require federal oversight to focus on measures that protect the population against dangerous levels of aviation noise.

The FAA points out that the worst levels of noise in the 70–75 DNL range have been removed. The removal of Stage 1 and Stage 2 aircraft contributed significantly to this reduction. However, the FAA uses noise at 65 DNL or higher, as its target level for noise reduction. This may have been a good initial target to reduce from 75 DNL but it does not come close to the 50 DNL or higher range that causes adverse health and welfare issues (9). The aviation industry is expected to grow along with the byproduct of increased noise pollution. The population remains at risk.

Sources Cited

1. World Health Organization (WHO), *Guidelines for Community Noise*, April 1999, World Health Organization, Geneva, Switzerland, http://www.who.int/environmental_information_information/noise/Comnoise6.htm (Edited by Birgitta Berglund, Thomas Lindvall, and Dietrich H. Schwela)

2. U.S. Senate, 95th Congress, 2nd Session (1978), S. 3083: *The Quiet Communities Act*, Online: Thomas.loc.gov. 14 February 2011. http://thomas.loc.gov/cgi-bin/dbquery/z?do95: SN03083:||TOM:/bss/do95query.html|, (Public Law 95–609).

3. Email dated 18 February 2011, Subject: *Noise*, from Scott Seritt, Manager, Atlanta Airports District Office (contact: Scott.Seritt@faa.gov).

4. Federal Aviation Administration's *2010 Business Plan*, October 15, 2009, (Flight Plan Target: Noise exposure) www.faa.gov

5. Public comment from US Citizens Aviation Watch Association and the Alliance of Residents Concerning O'Hare to the Federal Aviation Administration's public call for comment to revise the *1976 National Aviation Noise Abatement Policy*, October 20, 2000.

6. *Noise Control Act*, 42 U.S.C. § 401 et seq., (1972). Online: General Services Administration, 9 February 2011. http://www.gsa.gov/graphics/pbs/Noise_Control_Act_ of 1972.pdf, (Public Law 92–574).

7. Federal Aviation Administration's Federal Aviation Regulations Part 161, *Notice and Approval of Airport Noise and Access Restrictions* dated September 25, 1991, http://www.faa.gov

8. Raleigh–Durham Airport Authority, *RDU Aircraft Noise Program*, 10 March 2011. Online: http://www.rduaircraftnoise.com/noiseinfo/managegrowth.html

9. *Report on Noise*. U.S. Environmental Protection Agency, U.S. Government Printing Office, December 31, 1971, Washington, DC.

➤ WHAT THIS EXAMPLE SHOWS. Critical thinking is shown in Example 2 by the comparison of alternative viewpoints. Equal consideration is given to each viewpoint, demonstrating fairness. Detailed familiarity with the domain indicates a knowledgeable policy analyst. Information is adapted to the intended reader, a committee chair with authority to act. This memo might serve well to brief officials or their staff members (Chapter 8). It is written documentation that could easily translate to key points for oral briefing.

Critical analysis of policy discourse is evident here in the critique of positions taken by administrative agencies over time. Policy positions are described as products of their historical and political context, as a way of explaining their limitations. This critique of precedents' limitations leads to specification of needs for reform.

As documentation, the example skillfully uses organizational devices such as subheadings to motivate informed reading and to serve rapid reading. Typically, sentences are constructed well to bear their load of detail. Occasionally, the presenter misses an opportunity to use storytelling to motivate readers' understanding of the homeowners' position. Here is an instance:

> With the aftermath of September 11, 2001, the FAA worked to restore confidence in air transportation. Now, FAA turns its focus on the replacement of outdated air traffic control technology. All plausible reasons that the FAA did not aggressively tackle noise abatement as its top priority.

The final sentence occupies an important position in the paragraph. Recipients expect last sentences to cue knowledgeable reading by summarizing or repeating key points. If this final sentence were revised as follows, recipients would be reminded of the memo's recommendation to transfer noise abatement authority from the FAA to the EPA. "These shifting FAA priorities over a decade explain, but do not justify, its unaggressive approach to noise abatement." The revision would also silently remedy a grammatical error, the original fragmentary sentence's lack of subject and verb.

Example 3

This sample was originally written for a think tank as a report of academic research on taxation as social policy, with a focus on taxes paid by low-wage workers (Gitterman, 2003). The report was revised in 2007 partly at the request of a legislator. The revision is a policy brief for policy makers. Its recommendations focus on the earned income tax credit (EITC). The policy brief is publicly available on the authors' university research center website, and it is sampled here. A further revision is published in a scholarly journal (Gitterman, Gorham, & Dorrance, 2008).

The brief's evaluation of policy options and a recommendation are shown here. Other parts are shown in Chapter 5 (Example 3) and Chapter 6.

Expanding the EITC for Single Workers and Couples without Children (aka Tax Relief for Low-Wage Workers)

Daniel P. Gitterman, Lucy S. Gorham, Jessica L. Dorrance

A Discussion Paper prepared for the Center on Poverty, Work and Opportunity at the University of North Carolina at Chapel Hill

January 2007

. . .

Analysis and Policy Proposals
Policy options to expand the EITC for (or provide additional tax relief to) childless single and married workers

A number of policy proposals for expansion of the EITC for childless single and married workers have been offered over the past decade. . . . The primary motivations behind these proposals have been to: a) improve tax fairness by mitigating the disproportionate level of taxes paid by single low-wage workers, especially after the tax law changes of the last decade which in many cases have increased the regressivity of the tax code; b) increase this group's attachment to the labor market, as earlier expansions of the EITC have proven to do for low-wage workers with children; and c) reduce the likelihood that workers engaging in significant labor market effort will remain in poverty.

In addition, we discuss three other issues that an expanded EITC for childless single and married workers could potentially address: the need to provide stronger incentives for workforce participation for young workers entering the labor market; high health insurance costs; and the importance of helping all low-income workers build savings and other assets.

In this section, we highlight options for expanding the EITC for single and childless workers, each of which addresses a somewhat different purpose and several of which target specific subgroups of EITC recipients. . . . For each option, we describe its purpose, the policy change needed, the estimated budget impact if available, and complementary policy changes that are desirable.

1. EITC Baseline Expansion for Single and Married Childless Couples

The first proposed recommendation with the broadest impact . . . would increase the EITC to 15.3 percent of earnings to provide relief from payroll and other taxes, doubling the current level of 7.65 percent of earnings. According to estimates by the Center for Budget and Policy Priorities (Furman, 2006), these changes would have an additional budget impact of approximately $3 billion and would increase the maximum EITC benefit for single and married childless workers from $399 to $1,236. Fully offsetting payroll taxes requires an EITC pegged at 15.3 percent of earnings.

. . . However, we note that by selecting differing percentage figures for the share of earnings that would qualify and using different phase-in and phase-out thresholds, an almost infinite number of variations of this proposal could be designed resulting in higher or lower EITC benefit levels and a correspondingly higher or lower budget impact.

. . .

2. Increased Work Incentives for Younger Workers

In addition to the increased work incentives provided by the baseline EITC expansion proposed above in (1), a second policy recommendation would further increase the incentives for young workers to participate in the legitimate labor market by lowering the age limit at which workers without children can qualify for the EITC from 25 to 21. We view this proposal as an addition to the baseline expansion proposed in (1), which is of higher priority, but it could be instituted independently. . . . No such age requirement applies to workers with children—as long as they are not claimed as a dependent on another taxpayer's return, they may file for the EITC. . . . An analysis of this type of expansion for younger workers offered by Edelman, Holzer, and Offner (2006) includes an estimate of its cost at between $1 billion and $2 billion. . . .

3. Expanding available funds for monthly health insurance premiums or retirement plan contributions

A third policy recommendation would assist any worker eligible for the EITC to address the high costs of health care and/or to increase funds available for retirement plan contributions. The health insurance component is particularly relevant to single and childless workers because they are less likely to qualify for Medicaid or the State Children's Health Insurance Program (SCHIP). Workers could enroll in the Advance EITC, which pays low-wage workers an extra amount in their regular paycheck each month. They would then target that Advance EITC to pay a share of their health insurance premium. . . . A similar approach could be used for an employer-based retirement plan, such as a 401(k)). As was true for proposal (2) to make childless workers eligible for the EITC beginning at age 21, we view this proposal as working best if it were in addition to a baseline expansion of the EITC since this would increase the funds available for health insurance premiums or retirement contributions.

. . .

4. Helping Childless Workers to Save and Build Assets

. . . Because [the EITC] can represent a significant amount of money to receive in one payment, it is often used by low and moderate-income families as a way to save money over the year. As generations of experience with traditional welfare has shown, however, a marginal increase in income rarely ends the poverty cycle for a family without some accumulation of assets. Federal policies have long favored the development of assets through tax breaks for 401(k)s, mortgage interest, and small businesses, and initiatives like the GI bill. Unfortunately, most of these policies do not benefit low-income families, who may not earn enough to pay income tax or have access to tax-deferred retirement accounts.

. . .

An expanded EITC for childless workers has great potential to be an essential component of a more far-reaching initiative to reduce poverty and build assets if we are willing to experiment with and invest in innovative approaches. We propose that the matched savings account concept be expanded so that, in this case, single and childless workers could use the added income from an expanded EITC benefit to invest in savings vehicles such as Individual Retirement Accounts (IRAs), Coverdell Education Savings Accounts (ESAs), and college savings 529 accounts and that their contributions be matched.

. . .

Lastly, we consider three complementary policy recommendations that would assist savings and asset building initiatives linked to an expanded EITC. The first is to make the Saver's Credit, which Congress recently made permanent, fully refundable so that it is more advantageous to low-income savers. The second calls for Congress to appropriate funding to the IRS to fund community free tax preparation programs for low-income tax filers similar to the funds it has provided for free tax preparation programs for the elderly and military families. . . .

The third, and final, proposal related to expanding opportunities for asset building, is to increase, or eliminate, the asset limits that are attached to a range of public benefit programs and which have a dampening effect on the propensity of public benefit recipients to save. . . . This issue is of particular concern to workers with disabilities since they often must rely on social security and Medicaid.

Conclusions and Suggestions for Policy Reform
Putting an EITC for Singles in a Broader Federal Tax Policy Context

. . .

Distributional and fairness concerns have always emerged during debates on broader tax policy reform proposals. As part of large congressional reconciliation tax-cut packages, EITC expansions have been used to maintain distributional equity for tax policy reform as a whole. . . .

The simple conclusion of our work is that workers without children who live below the poverty line should *not* be subject to high federal income taxes and taxed deeper into poverty. We hope to begin a dialogue rather than recommend one way to policy reform.

. . .

The most significant challenge for policymakers, policy researchers and Washington DC think tanks concerned about federal tax relief for low-income single and married couples without children is to continue to generate thoughtful empirical analysis and policy conclusions that show how to make our tax code fair for those workers and non-custodial parents who also work hard and play by the rules. The politics of tax policy research will continue to pose major challenges for research on the distributional implications of tax reform. The key challenge is how the trio of federal individual income tax provisions—personal exemptions, standard deduction, and tax credits—together can shelter a certain amount of earned wages from federal tax liability and thus increase the amount of take-home pay of all low-wage workers. Certainly, the budgetary environment of the moment does not hold a great deal of promise for expanded EITC commitments. Yet, recent political history over the last three decades demonstrates that new or expanded work and family support efforts are indeed possible politically, even at times of budget and economic stress. . . . An expanded EITC for single and childless workers could emerge as a proposal with considerable political traction.

(The policy brief can be found at http://www.law.unc.edu/documents/poverty/publications/gittermanpolicybrief.pdf./

Also see Gitterman (2003) and Gitterman et al. (2008).)

☛ **WHAT THIS EXAMPLE SHOWS.** This publication history illustrates the flow of policy analysis between research and practical politics. As a policy communication, Example 3 demonstrates know-how, or awareness that policy analysts need the capability of adapting information to the purposes of varied users and of communicating in multiple genres.

This sample's analysis defines a recognized problem, the tax burden of low-wage workers, and recommends a recognized solution, expanding a tax credit.

As a policy communication, the sample demonstrates skill in authoritative argumentation to support the recommendation.

(See Chapter 6 for examination of the sample's argument.) Its argument exemplifies critical thinking to evaluate policy options, to explore values inherent in the recommended policy instrument, and to identify limitations as well as benefits of utilizing that option. Critical analysis of policy discourse is shown by the brief's claim that tax policy expresses political agendas. That claim is supported by a legislative history tracing policy changes to power shifts in government over time. (See Chapter 5 for the sample's summary of legislative history.)

Summary and Preview

Two kinds of analysis are important in policy work, analysis of alternative actions and analysis of discourse. You need skill in discourse analysis, not as an end in itself but rather as a forensic tool, a means of interpreting policy argument. To know how language constructs meaning enables you to argue, yourself, and to anticipate ways that others might use your argument.

To support your policy argument with evidence, the next chapters offer specific instruction in government records research (Chapter 5) and logical structure (Chapter 6).

References

Agroterrorism: The threat to America's breadbasket. (2004). A hearing before the committee on governmental affairs, U.S. Senate, 108th Congress, 1st session, November 19, 2003. Washington, DC: U.S. Government Printing Office.

Cheney, D. (2002). *The complete guide to citing government information resources: A manual for social science and business research* (3rd ed.). Bethesda, MD: LexisNexis.

Fairclough, N. (1985). Critical and descriptive goals in discourse analysis. *Journal of Pragmatics, 9,* 739–763.

Gee, J. P. (1999). *An introduction to discourse analysis: Theory and method.* London, England: Routledge.

Gitterman, D. P. (2003). *Tax credits for working families.* http://www.brookings.edu/reports/2003/08childrenfamilies_gitterman.aspx/.

Gitterman, D. P., Gorham, L. S., & Dorrance, J. L. (2008). Expanding the EITC for single workers and couples without children: Tax relief for all low-wage workers. *Georgetown Journal on Poverty Law and Policy, 15*(2), 245–284.

Graumann, C. F. (2002). Explicit and implicit perspectivity. In C. F. Graumann & W. Kallmeyer (Eds.), *Perspective and perspectivity in discourse* (pp. 25–39). Amsterdam: John Benjamins.

Mintrom, M. (2012). *Contemporary policy analysis.* New York, NY: Oxford University Press.

Smith, C. F. (2009). Public professional communication in the antiterror age: A discourse analysis. In G. F. Hayhoe & H. M. Grady (Eds.). *Connecting people with technology: Issues in professional communication* (pp. 90–117). Amityville, NY: Baywood.

Smith, J. B., & Smith, C. F. (1987). *A strategic method for writing.* http://www.cs.unc.edu/~jbs/sm/.

Stone, D. (2012). *Policy paradox: The art of political decision making* (3rd ed.). New York, NY: Norton.

Williams, J. M., & Colomb, G. C. (2012). *Style: The basics of clarity and grace* (4th ed.). Boston, MA: Longman.

Further Reading

Bardach, E. (2011). *A practical guide for policy analysis: The eightfold path to more effective problem solving* (4th ed.) Washington, DC: CQ Press.

Redman, E. (2000). *The dance of legislation.* Seattle, WA: University of Washington Press.

◦

CHAPTER 5

Legislative History: Know the Record

Key Concepts

- Record of legislative action
- Legislative intent

Many kinds of information are needed for policy making. To frame a problem, identify its issues, or propose interventions, you might need to know about influential social history, technological developments, and economic patterns. You might consult scientific research, public testimony, advice of expert consultants and lobbyists, statistical data, government agency reports, transcripts of legal proceedings, and more. But one kind of information is essential: the history of government action on the problem. To get that information, you must consult the legislative record; you must be able to conduct legislative research using government documents. This chapter shows you how.

Why is knowledge of the record important? There are three reasons. First, for policy making, precedent matters. Action builds on prior action. Knowledge of precedent helps you to frame problems and to find solutions. Second, context matters. The record shows deliberation and debate. Third, content matters. The preamble or the statement of purpose of a published bill or law enables you to discern original intent and the intent of amendments. If you are proposing new action, credibility and standards for good policy argument demand that you know the history of prior action.

Who conducts legislative research and for what purposes? Government staff members (and sometimes interns) consult the legislative record to help them frame problems and identify issues. Outside government, professional staff (and sometimes interns) in organizations of many kinds such as nonprofit groups, trade associations, and policy institutes consult the record. They do so to inform their advocacy or analysis. Similarly, active citizens consult the record as independent researchers. They might pursue a personal interest, or they might volunteer to investigate a record of action that is relevant to an organization's mission. For legal interpretation, court clerks, law librarians, and legal services professionals regularly consult the legislative record to know a law's intent as part of adjudicating disputes over a law's meaning.

Who writes legislative history documents? Often, the people who conduct the research also write the document that reports the results. Government staff or professional researchers on contract to a committee or agency or volunteers for organizations, as well as individuals doing independent research, might produce a legislative history tailored to a particular need to know.

Interns might be assigned legislative research and writing tasks. To illustrate, a supervisor in a health-care policy institute asks an undergraduate intern to specify unmet needs in elder health care for a position paper being written by the institute's director. The supervisor gives no instructions on how to gather the necessary information. The intern considers how to approach the task. She figures that to identify unmet needs, she must know what current law provides. As a strategy for getting started, she works from familiar experience. Her elderly grandparents experienced nursing home care, so she decides to start by collecting information on nursing homes.

She goes, first, to the institute's reports published on its website. She finds in-depth analyses of individual laws. Because the website has limited search capability, she cannot locate laws that refer to nursing homes except by reading all the reports. She then tries searching on the Internet using the all-purpose Google search engine and the search term "nursing home care." That yields advertisements for providers and websites of advocacy groups, but little legislation or public debate.

Stymied, she asks the institute's professional staff for help. A policy analyst tells her that the institute subscribes to a commercial database of government information, ProQuestCongressional (http://proquest .com/). It supports varied search techniques and has good user instructions. He suggests that she do exploratory searching. First, she spends time learning the capabilities of ProQuestCongressional by practicing with its user scenarios. Then, she queries her topic using basic and advanced search techniques. Building keyword strings and specifying date restrictions are most productive. Search results show that a good time to focus on would be the years in office of the previous federal government administration. She searches again in that time frame. She looks first for published legislative histories of nursing home law, and then she spends several hours reading summaries of current laws and proposed bills. She checks the final action taken on each.

By the end of the day, she writes a two-page legislative history of elder care. She defines the most pressing current needs as those that were recognized by the previous administration but left unresolved. She summarizes a list of unmet needs culled from a range of bills or amendments proposed but not passed or adopted. She identifies the most significant failures in elder health-care proposals (according to criteria that she provides) and summarizes the public debate surrounding them. In a concluding reference list, she cites these bills or amendments by bibliographic identifiers in the databases so that the institute director can quickly find the acts to read their language. Task accomplished.

How to Conduct Legislative Research and Write a Legislative History

Goal: Knowledge of U.S. proposed or enacted law regarding a defined problem based on consulting legislative records.

Objective: Credible reporting of government action.

Product: Written document tracing either history of a single law or history of laws on an issue.

Scope: Either a single law or an issue involving multiple laws. Relevant action might be at the federal, state, or municipal level or at several levels. In addition to legislative records, administrative records of rule making and regulation and judicial records of litigation might be needed.

Strategy: Multiple approaches are available. No single approach to government records research fits all; however, you will save time and frustration by planning before you start. Use the guidelines given in the following sections to select a strategy.

►— **KNOW WHY THE RESEARCH IS NEEDED.** Knowing the purpose for the research tells you what, and how much, to look for. Will the information be used to make new law (legislative) or to interpret existing law (legal)?

In either case, there might be a published history that meets the purpose. Or you might need to find the records required to write a specialized history. Knowing the purpose for the research can help you (or a librarian assisting you) to decide where to look first. Do you want to find a history or write one?

►— **KNOW THE USER AND THE USER'S PURPOSE FOR THE INFORMATION.** Who, exactly, will use the information, and what is his or her interest or need? The user might be you, gathering information for personal use or for an academic or internship assignment. Or the user for whom you are conducting the research might be a legislator who wants to amend an existing law. Knowing the user's purpose tells you what, and how much, to look for. Federal records only? State or municipal records also?

►— **SET THE SCOPE.** Will the research follow a single law through all its forms and related actions—bill, codified statute, administration, regulation, amendment, and (possibly) adjudication? Or will your research follow an issue through policy changes and across multiple laws over time? What is the relevant time frame? What is the relevant level of government?

■━● TAKE THE NECESSARY TIME AND MANAGE YOUR TIME. Records research can take hours, days, or weeks, depending on how much you already know, what you are looking for, where the records are, how well you have planned, and other contingencies. Prepare for the reality that legislative records research will take time, probably more time than you initially planned. What is your deadline for completing the research? What is your schedule for conducting the research and writing the necessary documents?

■━● USE EXISTING SKILLS AND ADD NEEDED ONES. If you have a well-defined problem, are willing to learn, are curious and persistent, and have basic research skills including the ability to ask questions, identify relevant sources, and search databases, you are basically ready to perform legislative research.

You might need to learn about the legislative process, government record types, and standard or new tools for researching government records. If so, review as necessary using the tools suggested next here.

Task 1. Review the Legislative Process

If you already know federal legislative procedure well or if you are tracing state law, omit Task 1 and go on to Task 2.

As you conduct research in government records, you can feel as if you are drowning in information, classification systems, procedure names, and document types. Also, if you start into records searching without knowing the underlying legislative process, you will quickly become lost. Use the following reviews of the process to revive your effort (bookmarking your favorite and returning to it as often as needed):

- The House: How Our Laws Are Made (by House of Representatives Parliamentarian), http://www.house.gov/content/learn/legislative_process/

- The Senate: Enactment of a Law (by Senate Parliamentarian), http://www.senate.gov/legislative/common/briefing/Enactment_law.htm/

- The Legislative Process, http://www.house.gov/content/learn/legislative_process/

- How Does Congress Work? (by Indiana University Center on Congress), http://congress.indiana.edu/how-does-congress-work/

Task 2. Conduct Research

Do you want to find a history or write one? Decide early whether your purpose is served by using an already published history or producing one. For single federal laws, commercial research services such as ProQuest publish legislative histories with varying levels of detail. Free public services also publish legislative histories. To look for a published history for a federal law, try these sources:

- Library of Congress, Federal Legislative History, http://www.loc .gov/law/help/leghist.php/

- Law Librarians Society of Washington, DC, http://llsdc.org/

  - Legislative Sourcebook

  - Federal Legislative History Research, A Practitioner's Guide

  - Legislative Histories of Selected U.S. Laws on the Internet: Free Sources

  - ProQuest Legislative Insight Basic Research Guide, http://www .law.sc.edu/library/libguide/images/proquest_legislative_in sight_basic_research_guide.pdf

You are unlikely to find published legislative histories for an issue. Typically, they are specially produced by, or for, users who want the information specialized to their purposes.

As a general rule, federal records are accessible online and in research libraries. State records are generally less available. An individual state's records might be online or, more likely, in the print archives of the state's library. Local government records are available by asking the government of interest how to access them. Few local governments put their records online.

Major tools for finding federal and state records are provided by government information services, either free or by subscription. Free services such as the Library of Congress (http://Congress.gov/) can be accessed using any Web browser. Subscription services such as ProQuest (http://ProQuest.com/) are accessed by authorized users of facilities provided by research institutes, some for-profit organizations, a university library, and large public libraries.

At home and in many public libraries, you can freely access federal records and link to online state records through the following sites:

- Library of Congress, http://www.congress.gov/
- Government Printing Office, http://www.gpo.gov/fdsys/

For excellent, comprehensive tips on accessing government records, the following are good sources:

- Library of Congress Frequently Asked Questions (FAQ), http://www.congress.gov/help/faq/
- ProQuest—Legislative Insight, http://search.proquest.com/legislative insight (by subscription or purchase)

Free access to numerous federal government websites that link to records is also provided by these sources:

- Clark Library Government Information Collection (University of Michigan), http://www.lib.umich.edu/clark-library/collections/government-information/
- Government Documents/Information (Mansfield University), http://mansfield.libguides.com/govdocs/
- Catalogue of U.S. Government Publications, http://catalog.gpo.gov/F/

For state legislatures and local government, these are good websites:

- State and Local Governments (Library of Congress), http://www.loc.gov/rr/news/stategov/stategov.html/
- Law Librarians Society of Washington, DC, Legislative Sourcebook: State Legislatures, State Laws, State Regulations, http://www.llsdc.org/sourcebook/

Libraries offer a valuable resource: librarians! For professional, skilled, and time-saving assistance in legislative research, always ask a librarian.

General Tips for Using Government Information Libraries

- Depository libraries have federal government records in all available forms—digital, print, and microfiche. Depending on what you want to know, you might need all three. Online access to digital records is convenient for recent records, but print and microfiche are still important, too, for several reasons. Some records are not yet available online, and some might never be. You can miss a lot of legislative history if you only search online. Also, print compilations are sometimes easier to use because they are well supplemented by indexes and other locator aids. When using a tool new to you, check first for finding aids and instructions. You will save much time this way.

- You should take detailed notes as you go. Jot down contextual information and target information. List names of people, committees, subcommittees, and bill or law citations mentioned in the target record. Why? If your first search method fails, these notes can restart your search; they give you alternative ways to search.

You can use what you know to find what you want. For example, if a student intern researching elder health care jots down key terms, citations, names, and dates as she works in a database of government records, she is prepared to search by any of these facets:

- By subjects discussed in the record (for example, elder health care);
- By citation (number and letter "addresses") of a particular legislative record in a system of citation (for example, H.R. 1091–106 for a particular House of Representatives bill); or
- By names, dates, committees, or other elements of a legislative process (for example, the name of the senator sponsoring a bill).

In other words, she could find legislation on elder health care by subject (elder health care, nursing home care, Medicare, and so on), by citation (H.R. 1091–106), or by names or titles in legislative process information (e.g., Senator Tom Harkin; hearing witness Kathleen Sebelius, Department of Health and Human Services; Senate Committee on Health, Education, Labor, and Pensions).

Task 3. Write the Legislative History Document

To write your legislative history, begin by using the method in Chapter 2. You can reuse your plan for searching (Strategy, this chapter) to remind you of your purpose and audience. Plan your legislative history document accordingly. Let your intended reader's needs for the information guide your choice of content for the history.

What is the message of a legislative history? It is your conclusion formed after consulting the record. The history's scope is set by the purpose (whether you are writing a law history or an issue history) and by the amount of information required to support your message. In any case, you must organize your information to support the message. Organizational options include chronology (to show developments over time), significance (to highlight influential legislation), and trend (to show a pattern).

If no form is prescribed for presenting the results of your research, you might choose to use the following standard reporting format for professional and technical communication:

- Overview that concisely summarizes both the message and the key information in the document;
- Subsections that provide summaries of information;
- Subheadings that label each subsection; and
- Citations that are provided for each subsection.

Citation is important in a legislative history. The history's credibility and the practical needs of the information user (and the researcher) demand that all sources be easy to locate for confirmation and referral. Citations are the means of doing so. A full citation provides three kinds of information about a source: what type of record it is, how it is classified in a system of documentation, and who publishes it (a commercial research service or government). For government records, a full citation includes all the elements that help to identify a source. In legislative research, a full citation, or government style, is preferred over a terse citation, or legal style, that provides only an abbreviated source identifier, number in a system of documentation, and date. If either the government style or the legal style is prescribed for you, use that style. If not, choose the appropriate style and use it exclusively. Do not mix styles.

Here is a list of the elements in a full citation, or government style, for citing federal or state legislation:

- Issuing agency (house, number, session, year)
- Title (document number and name; long name may be abbreviated)
- Edition or version
- Imprint (city, publisher, date of publication)
- Series (serial list of publications)
- Source (publisher if print or database if online)
- Medium (Web service, e.g., ProQuest)
- URL
- Accessed date (in parentheses)
- Notes (in parentheses, add anything not already included in the citation that helps to locate the document)

Following are two illustrations of government style:

1. U.S. House. 101st Congress, 1st Session (1989). H.R. l946, A Bill to . . . Authorize the Department of Veterans Affairs (VA) to Provide Home, Respite, and Dental Care. Washington: Government Printing Office, 1990. (GPO Microfiche no. 393, coordinate C13.)

2. U.S. House. 104th Congress. "H.R. 3, A Bill To Control Crime." (Version: 1; Version Date: 2/9/93). Text from: *Full Text of Bills*. Available from: ProQuest Congressional; Accessed: 7/04/05).

In the second illustration, the source is a database available only to subscribers.

If you need more help on citing, consult these sources:

- ProQuest Congressional Help—How to Cite, http://proquest.com/
- *The Complete Guide to Citing Government Information Resources: A Manual for Social Science and Business Research* (Cheney, 2002)
- Uncle Sam: Brief Guide to Citing Government Publications (University of Memphis Depository Library), http://www.memphis.edu/govpub/citweb.php/
- Chicago Citation Format, *Chicago Manual of Style*, 15th ed., sections 17.270, 17.295

Remember to check your final draft legislative history against the standard (Two Checklists, Chapter 2).

Two Examples

Example 1
Legislative History of Banning the Use of Cell Phones while Driving

MEMORANDUM

To: North Carolina General Assembly Senator Dannelly; Representatives McAllister, Adams, B., Allen, Harrell, Hunter, Jones, Luebke, Michaux, Parmon, Tolson, and Womble.

From: AARP Steering Committee (simulated)

Date: April 7, 2008

Re: Ban on Cell Phones While Driving: A Legislative History

OVERVIEW

Driver distractions lead each year to thousands of unnecessary and preventable deaths on our nation's streets and highways. One such distraction is the use of cell phones while driving. In his article analyzing legislative attempts to regulate cell phone use, Matthew Kalin cites studies that estimate "that six-hundred thousand collisions occur each year because of cellular phone use in vehicles" and that "ten to one-thousand deaths per year" occur as a result of cell phone use in vehicles (Kalin, 262, n 21). Other researchers have compared people talking on a cell phone while driving to drunk drivers. In a 2006 study of drivers in a driving simulator, professors at the University of Utah found that "people are as impaired when they drive and talk on a cell phone as they are when they drive intoxicated at the legal blood-alcohol limit of 0.08 percent" (Strayer, Drews & Crouch, 385–90). Lives can easily be saved by banning the use of cell phones while driving.

The North Carolina legislature has made a good start in this area. Current legislation protects our children from bus drivers distracted by their cell phones (N.C.G.S. §20–140.6) and inexperienced drivers are not allowed to use a cell phone while driving (N.C.G.S. §20–137.3). Unfortunately, your bills to amend Chapter 20 of the North Carolina General Statutes to ban the use of cell phones by all drivers have not yet been passed into law.

The following review of current legislation shows that the important work of making our streets and highways safer from the dangers posed by distracted drivers has begun. Unfortunately, current legislation falls dangerously short in the area of cell phone use by drivers. For now, current legislation only forbids a fraction of the millions of people driving while using their cell phones. Consequently, we can expect innocent motorists and pedestrians to continue to be injured and killed on our roads and highways by drivers too caught up with their telephone conversations to pay attention to their surroundings. Now is the time to resume your call to protect everyone on our roads and highways from the danger posed by drivers distracted by cell phone use. North Carolina can become a leader in protecting motorists from the deadly consequences of drivers distracted by their cell phones by banning the use of cell phones by all drivers.

Major Legislation–North Carolina
General Assembly of North Carolina, 2005 Session

Senate Bill 1289 (Third Edition): "Cell Phone Use by Drivers Under 18 Prohibited" (G.S. 20–137.3). This Bill makes it illegal for drivers between the ages of 15 and 18 years of age to use a cell phone while driving. Specifically, this bill

- Makes the use of a cell phone by a person between the ages of 15 and 18 years of age while driving an infraction

- Provides for a fine of $25 (but does not assess court costs or result in points against the driver's license or insurance)
- Further punishes a teenage driver by not allowing the driver to advance to the next level of licensure for an additional 6 months
- Includes a ban on the use of hands-free phones, Internet gaming devices, electronic music devices, and the like.

General Assembly of North Carolina, 2007 Session

House Bill 183 (Third Edition): "Ban Cell Phone Use by School Bus Drivers" (G.S. 20–140.6). This Bill created Section 20–140.6 of the North Carolina General Statutes, making it illegal to "engage in a call on a mobile phone or use a digital media device while operating a public or private school bus" (N.C.G.S. §20–140.6). Specifically, this bill

- Makes the use of a cell phone by a bus driver a Class 2 misdemeanor
- Provides for a punishment of up to 60 days and a fine of no less than $100
- Allows for emergency exceptions

While the above protections are an important start, the AARP agrees with you that more is required. We applaud the following two bills that all of you worked so diligently on and hope you will continue your good work and see them passed into law. In fact, we encourage you to go even further in the name of safety—consider banning all cell telephone use (with the current exceptions), *including* hands-free phones.

Senate Bill 1399: "Ban Mobile Phone Use While Driving." This bill was re-referred to the Committee on Judiciary II (Criminal) on May 24, 2007. If passed, it would ban the use of cell phones while driving, but allow drivers to use hands-free phones while driving. It also allows for emergency exceptions and use by police, firefighters, and ambulance drivers. The use of a cell phone would be an infraction, with a penalty of a fine of $25.00. There would be no point assessment to the driver's North Carolina driver's license nor any insurance surcharge assessed as a result of a violation of this section. Also, this infraction would "not constitute negligence per se or contributory negligence by the driver in any action for the recovery of damages arising out of the operation, ownership, or maintenance of a motor vehicle."

House Bill 1104: "Ban Cell Phone Use While Driving." This bill was re-referred to the Committee on Judiciary III on May 18, 2005. If passed, it would ban the use of cell phones while driving, but allow drivers to use hands-free phones while driving. It also allows for emergency exceptions and use by police, firefighters, and ambulance drivers. The use of a cell phone while driving would be an infraction, with a penalty of a $100.00 fine and costs of court. No points would be assessed to the driver's North Carolina driver's license as a result of this infraction.

Legislation in Other Jurisdictions

According to a 2004 review of traffic safety legislation, eighteen states and the District of Columbia have passed laws regarding the use of cell phones while driving (Savage, Sundeen and Mejeur, 2004). Here is a sample of the legislation currently in effect in other states:

California: Section 23103 of the California Vehicle Code makes it illegal to operate a handheld device while driving, and the fine is $20.00 for the first offense and $50.00 for each offense thereafter (Barmby, 345).

New York: Section 1225 of the New York code bans the use of hand-held cell phones while driving, and a violation of same is considered an infraction, punishable by a fine of not more than $100.00 (New York Consolidated Law Service).

New Jersey: Section 39:4–97.3 of the New Jersey Statutes makes it illegal to use a cell phone while driving unless it is a "hands-free wireless telephone." A driver in New Jersey can be cited for such a violation only if she is detained for another driving or criminal violation at the same time. A person who violates this law is to be fined "no less than $100 or more than $250" and no points are assessed to the driver's license or insurance (LexisNexis New Jersey Annotated Statutes).

In addition to state legislation, a number of towns and cities implemented their own bans on the use of cell phones while driving. Brooklyn, Ohio was the first municipality in the U.S. to ban cellular phone use while driving, and Hilltown, Pennsylvania, also banned the use of cell phones while driving (Kalin, 244). Fort Campbell military base in Kentucky banned hand-held cellular phone use while driving (Kalin, 245). However, as you know, municipality ordinances can be overruled by a state law, "preemption," if the state legislators think it appropriate.

Again, we hope North Carolina can become a leader in providing for safer streets and highways by banning both hand-held *and hands-free* cell phone use while driving.

Federal Response

On July 18, 2000, Congress began hearings to discuss possible legislative solutions (Cripps, 107). The House of Representatives introduced the Driver Distraction Prevention Act of 2000, a study implemented to explore the impact of driver distractions on highway safety (Cripps, 107).

However, to date, Congress has not implemented a policy to protect drivers from the hazards posed by drivers distracted by cell phone use.

Works Cited

Barmby, Erin. "Review of selected 2007 California legislation: Vehicle: Chapter 290: California's message to hang up and pay attention." *McGeorge Law Review* 38 (2007): 42–52.

Cripps, Jr., Jesse. "Dialing while driving: The battle over cell phone use on America's roadways." *Gonzaga Law Review* 37 (2001/2002): 89–119.

House Bill 183. "Ban cell phone use while driving." Online: North Carolina General Assembly homepage 9 April 2008. http://www.ncleg.net/gascripts/BillLookUp/BillLookUp.pl?Session=2005&BillID=H1104

Kalin, Matthew. "The 411 on cellular phone use: An analysis of the legislative attempts to regulate cellular phone use by drivers." *Suffolk University Law Review* 39 (January 2005): 233–262. Citing, Hahn, Robert & Patrick M. Dudley. "The disconnect between law and policy analysis: A case study of drivers and cell phones, *Administrative Law Review* 55 (2003): 127, 130.

New Jersey Statutes Annotated 39:4–97.3 (2004). Online: LexisNexis (TM) New Jersey Annotated Statutes 8 April 2008. http://www.lexisnexis.com/us [Subscription required] New York Vehicle & Traffic Law 1225-c (2001). Online: New York Consolidated Law Service, Matthew Bender & Company, Inc. 8 April 2008. http://www.lexisnexis.com/us/ [Subscription required]

Savage, Melissa, Sundeen, Matt, and Mejeur, Jeanne, "Traffic safety and public health: State legislative Action, 2004." National Conference of State Legislators' Transportation Series, (December 2004, No. 20). [Purchase required]. Online, 8 April 2008. http://www.ncsl.org/print/transportation/04trafficsafety.pdf

Senate Bill 1399. "Ban mobile phone use while driving." Online: North Carolina General Assembly homepage. 9 April 2008. http://www.ncleg.net/gascripts/BillLookUp/BillLookUp.pl?BillID=S1399&Session=2007

Strayer, David, Frank Drews & Dennis Crouch. "A comparison of the cell phone driver and the drunk driver." *Human Factors* 48 (Summer 2006): 381–391.

Stutts, Jane, Donald Reinfurt, Loren Staplin & Eric Rodgman. "The role of driver distraction in traffic crashes." AAA Foundation for Traffic Safety Report. (May 2001): 1–63. [Purchase required]. Online: 9 April 2008. http://www.aaafoundation.org/pdf/distraction.pdf

---

Example 2. Legislative History of the Earned Income Tax Credit

This legislative history is incorporated in a policy brief advocating reform of the Earned Income Tax Credit (EITC). Other sections of the brief are shown elsewhere in this guide. Refer to a policy analysis and proposals (Example 3, Chapter 4) and summary of findings (Example, Chapter 6) before reading this legislative history.

Policy Significance and Context: The EITC and Tax Policy

As currently structured, the EITC provides a tax credit for low-income households that is based on income and family status and is fully refundable.

. . .

The original political debates in the early 1970s over the EITC reflected some differences over its primary purpose: whether to provide payroll tax relief to all low-wage workers or to increase the labor force participation of less-skilled workers who might otherwise rely on public assistance benefits to support their families, or both. Ultimately, Congress structured the tax credit to do both, but only for families with children, thus placing more emphasis on its policy role in welfare reform. In this way, the EITC fulfilled its original tenets as set forth by Congress: "an added bonus or incentive for low-income people to work," and as a way to reduce welfare dependency by "inducing individuals with families receiving federal assistance to support themselves" (U.S. Congress, Senate, 1975).

The earliest proposals for an earned income credit emerged in response to ongoing debates about a minimum income for all Americans and increasing concerns about the impact of rising payroll taxes on low-income workers. . . . Traditional forms of individual income tax relief, either by reducing positive tax rates or raising personal exemptions, were of more limited assistance to those low-income workers and their families whose federal income tax liability was already zero. Policymakers began to explore whether federal income tax relief should be delivered only as an "exemption," a "deduction"—which would reduce the amount of *earned* income subject to tax—or as a tax credit that directly offsets tax payments or liability. Some elected officials viewed such tax assistance as part of a broader program to provide a basic social safety net and reduce or eliminate poverty—as well as a convenient administrative way to deliver cash benefits to low-income families. Others viewed this individual tax benefit more broadly as a way to offset the burdens of other taxes that all low and moderate-wage workers pay, regardless of family status, such as payroll taxes, excise taxes, state and local sales, property, and income taxes.

Under existing federal tax law in 1974, workers were not required to pay income taxes unless their incomes exceeded the amount of the minimum standard deduction plus the sum of available personal exemptions. The House Ways and Means Committee concluded in its 1975 report accompanying legislation creating the EITC: "If the problems of low-wage workers are the regressive effects of payroll taxes then the credit should be available to all low-income individuals, regardless of marital status or children" (U.S. Congress, House, 1975). The House version of the EITC covered 28 million taxpayers. In order to keep costs down, the House reduced the proposed tax credit from 10 percent to 5 percent. The one-year revenue loss was projected to be $2.9 billion, all of which would be received by workers whose incomes were below $6,000.

Whereas the House version depicted the EITC as payroll tax relief, the Senate Finance Committee's bill depicted the EITC as welfare reform. While the Senate adopted the general concept of the earned income credit, it revised it to improve "its impact on the low-income taxpayers with children" (U.S. Congress, Senate, 1975). Since many low-wage workers were from non-poor families, extending earning subsidies to all workers could be "expensive and inefficient in reaching the poor," and thus, the Senate plan restricted its subsidy to families with children and applied the subsidy to total family earnings. (U.S. Congress, Senate, 1975). This change involved a revenue loss of $1.5 billion, or about one-half of the House proposal (U.S. Congress, Senate, 1975). Congress, in the end, accepted the Senate position that the "most significant objective of the EITC should be to assist in encouraging people to obtain employment, reducing the unemployment rate and reducing the welfare rolls; more importantly, most federal welfare programs apply to married couples with dependent children and it is in this area that the EITC can be most effective in reducing any tax disincentive to work" (U.S. Congress, Senate, 1975). By limiting the credit only to low-income workers with families, Congress reduced the number of potential "beneficiaries" from 28 million to 6.4 million. When the tax credit was enacted in 1975, it generated little attention. The initial credit amount was equal to only 10 percent of total income up to $4,000 (providing a maximum benefit of $400) and then it phased out at 10 percent until income reached $8,000. . . .

The EITC continued to be offered to eligible workers for the next several years and was made a permanent piece of the Internal Revenue Code (IRC) in 1978. Since that time, it has undergone significant expansions with broad bipartisan support. The credit was expanded in 1986 under President Ronald Reagan, in 1990 under President George H. W. Bush, and again in 1993 under President Bill Clinton when the size of the credit was doubled and a small credit was added for workers without children. . . . EITC expansions also were used to offset the regressive effects of increases in payroll taxes and in gasoline, alcohol, and tobacco excise taxes for families with children. The 1986 Tax Reform Act explicitly cited this principle of eliminating income tax burdens for families with incomes near the poverty level as the reason for increasing the dollar amounts of standard deductions and personal exemptions. The Omnibus Budget

Reconciliation Acts of 1990 and 1993 (OBRA-90 and OBRA-93) increased the credit rate, introduced a larger EITC (with a higher credit rate and more earnings eligible for the matching credit) for families with two or more children, and introduced a small EITC for childless workers. Each of these increases was phased-in over three years. Consequently, the credit rates increased every year from 1990 to 1995.

. . .

The Rise of an EITC for Single Workers

In 1993, President Clinton urged making the EITC available to very low-income workers who did not have children; opponents warned that it would be difficult to broaden the EITC to wage earners without children "without breaking the bank." . . . As part of the final legislative agreement in 1993, the EITC was extended for the first time to workers without children. In addition to offsetting a portion of these various tax increases, the establishment of the EITC for poor childless workers partially addressed a piece of unfinished business from the 1986 Tax Reform Act. . . . One of those goals, often espoused by President Reagan, was to eliminate federal income taxes on workers below the poverty line so they would not be taxed deeper into poverty. . . . The EITC raised the income level at which these workers would begin to owe income tax, but that level still remains below the poverty line.

After the 1994 elections, Republicans proposed several new limits on eligibility to the EITC. . . . House and Senate proposals erased some of the expansion in the credit achieved by President Clinton as part of his 1993 budget plan. . . . Under the 2001 tax reforms, President Bush allowed more married couples to become eligible for the earned-income tax credit. . . . The president also proposed a permanent extension of EITC-related provisions enacted in 2001 as part of his 10-year tax cut bill.

Some reformers charge that one of the biggest challenges is the fact that the United States has become divided between a growing class of people who pay no federal income taxes and a shrinking class of people who are bearing the lion's share of the tax burden.

. . . Not coincidentally, the latest round of tax cuts follows on the Council of Economic Advisers' (CEA) Economic Report to the President, released in February 2003, which made the case that low-to-moderate income families do not shoulder a fair share of the income tax burden. The document lays the intellectual groundwork for policies that would greatly simplify the tax system, but that would arguably raise the federal tax burden on lower-income workers, while reducing that on the affluent. . . . In keeping with this, Treasury Department economists are drafting new ways to calculate the distribution of tax burdens among different income classes, and those results are expected to highlight what Bush Administration officials view as a rising tax burden on the rich and a declining burden on the poor. . . .

As part of the President George W. Bush's Advisory Panel on Federal Tax Reform, several proposals were advanced to address the needs of low-wage workers. Robert Greenstein, executive director of the Center on Budget and Policy Priorities, focused specifically on the role of the Earned Income Tax Credit in improving tax fairness when single workers begin owing income tax several hundred dollars *below* the poverty line. . . .

. . .

What Role for the States?

In the absence of federal reform, states have experimented with EITC reforms. As of January 2006, 18 states and the District of Columbia have adopted Earned Income Tax Credits. Most recently, Delaware and Virginia enacted new EITCs, Illinois and Oregon changed their state EITC from non-refundable to refundable, and several states and the District of Columbia, expanded existing EITCs. In addition, three local governments—Montgomery County, Md., New York City, and San Francisco—offer local EITCs.

. . .

(The full policy brief can be found at http://www.law.unc.edu/documents/poverty/publications/gittermanpolicybrief.pdf/. Also see Gitterman (2003) and Gitterman, Gorham, and Dorrance (2008).)

WHAT THESE EXAMPLES SHOW. These examples illustrate records research for advocacy and analysis purposes. Example 1 is an issue history; Example 2 is a single law history. They exemplify the two main motivations for writing legislative histories, either to chronicle actions on an issue across jurisdictions (Example 1) or to characterize a pattern of legislative intent for a particular law over time (Example 2).

In Example 1 an attorney representing a nonprofit organization (simulated) conducts records research to put the organization's advocacy into a context of precedents. In Example 2 policy analysts search the records of prior reform to support their recommendation of new reform.

The examples differ as documentation (Viewpoint 3, Chapter 2). Both exhibit knowledge that is expected in a legislative history. However, they communicate in different forms, illustrating the variety of functions that legislative history serves. Example 1 is a report in memorandum form. An attorney or a librarian or an organization staff member might prepare such reports for a user's particular interest or purpose. Research would have the limited objective of developing that user's knowledge. Example 2 has a broader objective. In Example 2 the legislative and administrative record is also interpreted, not only reported. The interpretation shows the direction, including changes of direction, of governmental action over time. Individual policy actions are recontextualized in a pattern of intent. This interpretive history is used as evidence supporting a recommendation. Thus, in Example 2, interpretive legislative history functions rhetorically to persuade. It says that the recommended action fits within precedent and is possibly achievable.

Example 1 and 2 are written for silent reading, not speaking. Sentence structure and length are indications. In Example 2, sentences, although long, are constructed understandably. In Example 1, however, excess words in many sentences strain a reader's attention. Readability would be improved by removing unnecessary repetition that causes wordiness in sentences and by varying sentence length. In the following instance from Example 1, repetition is italicized in the original. The revision shows less repetition, shorter phrases, and varied sentence length.

> **Original.** *Unfortunately*, your bills to amend Chapter 20 of the North Carolina General Statutes to ban the *use of cell phones by all drivers* have not yet been passed into law. The following review of *current legislation* shows that the important work of making our streets and highways safer from dangers posed by distracted drivers has begun. *Unfortunately, current legislation* falls dangerously short in the area of *cell phone use by drivers.* (71 words)

> **Revised.** Unfortunately, your amendments to Chapter 20 of the North Carolina General Statutes to ban the use of cell phones by all drivers are not yet law. The following review of current legislation shows that the important work of reducing risk posed by distracted drivers has begun. But it falls dangerously short. (51 words)

Summary and Preview

To ask persuasively for new government action, you must know what government has done, has not done, or has intended in regard to your concern. Legislative records research is essential to develop your knowledge of prior action. Chapter 6 prepares you to use your knowledge of the record in making policy arguments.

References

Cheney, D. (2002). *The complete guide to citing government information resources: A manual for social science and business research* (3rd ed.). Bethesda, MD: LexisNexis.

Gitterman, D. P. (2003). *Tax credits for working families.* http://www.brookings.edu/reports/2003/08childrenfamilies_gitterman.aspx/.

Gitterman, D. P., Gorham, L. S., & Dorrance, J. L. (2008). Expanding the EITC for single workers and couples without children: Tax relief for all low-wage workers. *Georgetown Journal on Poverty Law and Policy,* 15(2), 245–284.

CHAPTER 6

Position Paper: Know the Arguments

Key Concept

- Policy argumentation

Making public policy requires making arguments and understanding arguments. This chapter helps you to argue a position, to critically analyze your own and other arguments, and to recognize grounds for political cooperation as well as competition. "Politics is a process of argument and persuasion" (Stone, 2012, p. 385).

A policy argument supports a claim that something should or should not be done. Such arguments have two main components: a claim and its support. The claim asserts what should or should not be done or takes a position on a debated question. Support for the claim presents the evidence, interpretations, and assumptions that lead to making that claim. The argument's presentation should be intentionally constructed to convince others to accept the claim and to agree with the position.

Arguments are made both implicitly and explicitly. Implicit arguments are unstated elements of problem definitions. For example, to define cell phone use while driving as a public safety risk is to argue implicitly that government has a role in regulating drivers' risky behaviors. Implicit arguments are usually not intended to deceive. They are simply the unacknowledged structures of thought within a position. Position takers should be critically aware of their implicit arguments as well as their explicit arguments. They should critically analyze other positions for implicit as well as explicit arguments, too.

Why argue? In policy work, you argue to disclose what you think and what you want to accomplish. You do not argue to prove or disprove; you do not argue only for or against. The popular notion of argument as a quarrel between adversaries distorts argument's function and significance for policy purposes. Similarly, the legal notion of argument as contestation by opposing parties is inadequate. In policy making, there are always more than two interested parties. In democratic process, you engage ideas, not adversaries. You argue to add your position to the debate and to the possibilities.

To illustrate, an undergraduate student government representative wants to change the culture at her university to discourage drug and alcohol abuse. As a dormitory resident advisor, she knows firsthand that campus culture encourages recreational drug use and underage as well as binge drinking. Initially, she took the position that punitive action was called for. As a member of the Judicial Affairs subcommittee of the student assembly, she had accomplished revisions in the university judicial system to increase sanctions against drug and alcohol use as well as penalties for violations. However, the sanctions and penalties had little impact on the character of campus life. Consequently, her position has changed. In a report that she authors for the student assembly's Judicial Affairs subcommittee addressed to the Dean of Student Affairs, she now argues that judicial action is not enough. She cites evidence from dormitory life based on her resident advising experience. She claims that comprehensive action is needed to reduce dependence on drugs and alcohol for social interaction. She specifies needs to update university policy, to reorganize administration of campus life, and to design educational interventions. In her choice of proposed solutions, she has anticipated opposing arguments by other student government leaders and by some university administrators favoring either the status quo or increased sanctions and enforcement. Her purpose for arguing is to deepen the campus debate on drugs and alcohol by focusing on the central question of why campus life encourages their use.

At the same university, another undergraduate majoring in public policy studies serves as an officer of a national student association that advocates drug policy reform. In that role, she writes a policy memo to the director of a national drug control policy institute stating her association's position on recent legislation and asking the director to rethink the institute's support for recent amendments to the Higher Education Act (HEA) of 1965. (Proposals to amend typically refer to the original legislation being amended. Major acts such as the 1965 HEA are amended, often, over many years.) Those amendments barred students with drug-related convictions from receiving federal financial aid for education unless they undergo rehabilitation. The student leader presents the association's opposition to the amendments on two grounds, fairness and feasibility. On fairness, she argues that reducing eligibility for aid to higher education hurts working-class families and discriminates against people of color. Regarding the discriminatory effects, she elaborates with empirical evidence showing that 95 percent of imprisoned drug offenders in New York State are people of color, whereas the majority of drug users are not. She interprets this evidence as showing racial bias in drug law enforcement at the state level. On feasibility, she argues that the amendments cannot be implemented because they do not call for allocation of funds to pay for rehabilitation. She anticipates rebuttals by the director of the drug control policy institute but she does not respond to them in the policy memo. Its purpose is to represent the student association's perspective on a current drug policy reform proposal.

What does policy argument do? It displays the reasoning that underlies positions. In public deliberation, arguments disclose the universe of definitions of the problem. In practical politics, argument reveals commonalities and conflicts. These are the grounds on which a course of action can be deliberated. Commonalities among arguments can point to potential cooperation, perhaps compromise, co-sponsorship, or coalition. Conflicts give insight into competing interests and values that must be taken into account in negotiating a solution.

In another illustration, a farmer has applied to local government for a permit to operate a large-scale industrial farm called a confined animal feeding operation. In the rural municipality where the farmer lives, the zoning ordinance allows such operations only as a conditional use of land zoned for agricultural uses. Conditional uses require case-by-case decisions by local officials on whether to permit or not permit the use. The decision process includes a public hearing inviting residents and others to comment on the proposed use. In the hearing held on the farmer's application, arguments including the following are made:

- Farmers have rights to use and to benefit from their property; to deny this permit is to violate the farmer's private property rights.

- Nearby homeowners have rights to use and to benefit from their property; to grant this permit is to violate the neighbors' private property rights.

- Large-scale confined animal farming pollutes the environment and creates human health risks; to grant this permit is to fail to protect natural resources and the public welfare.

- Large-scale confined animal farming is regulated and better monitored for compliance with antipollution control than unregulated small-scale farming; to grant this permit will not harm local water or community health.

- Farming is an endangered occupation; to grant this permit will enable a local family-owned farm to succeed by expanding operations and will help to preserve farming in the region.

- Farming is an endangered occupation, and industrial farming is driving smaller farmers out of business; to grant this permit is to harm the local economy, which is still based on diverse types of farming.

If you were a local official, how would you decide about this request? Clearly, many arguable issues and competing positions are involved. You might permit or not permit the use, basing your decision either way on a single argument. Alternatively, you might focus on a commonality among the arguments, such as the wish to preserve rights or the wish to protect public health. Then you might ask the farmer and the neighbors to work out a compromise application. You might delay your decision until you have a revised application that takes specified risks to the community into account.

Argument has its limits in practical policy work, of course. "Arguments are made by all players all the time; as a result they have limited effectiveness. Although arguments are a necessary ingredient to any strategy, they never work by themselves" (Coplin & O'Leary, 1998, p. 107). As the local government illustration suggests, you might need to craft a political compromise along with arguing your position. Also, you must recognize political conditions that will determine your argument's effectiveness. How well an argument is received has more to do with majority control in a governing body than with the quality of the argument. In the local government illustration, the official who represents majority political power might have sufficient influence to force a compromise. The minority power representative might not, unless others can be persuaded to join the minority's position.

When is argument important? Argument can make a difference at several points in the process. Arguments matter before a policy process begins, as positions are being developed. They matter at the outset of a process, as stakes are declared and agendas set. They matter again at the end of the process, when a decision is being made.

How to Argue Policy

Goal: Critical awareness of your own position, critical understanding of other positions, and willingness to consider and to engage other positions.

Objective: Reasoned argument for a position showing awareness of alternative positions and reasoning.

Product: Written document that explicitly argues and aims to persuade. A genre commonly used by policy analysts outside government is the position paper (sometimes called a discussion paper, "white" paper, or policy brief). Products might run to book length in some circumstances or they might be much shorter, perhaps two to six pages.

Scope: Either a big picture of conditions, causes, or consequences relating to a problem or a little picture of significant particulars.

Strategy: To know your position in relation to others. To consider your position ethically and politically make a list of the known positions on the problem:

- Ask and answer the questions "What does my position have in common with others on this list?" and "How does my position differ from or conflict with others on the list?"

- Note specific commonalities, differences, and conflicts of values, assumptions, or ideas between your position and other positions.

Task 1. Outline Your Argument

If you are authoring a position paper for a professional association or for a nonprofit organization, make sure you understand its mission and how the position you are taking relates to the mission. Be clear on that relationship. Consult before deviating from the mission.

In most cases, you can use the following outline for informal arguments to construct the logic of a policy position:

- Problem
- Issue
- Question about the issue that has at least two answers and is therefore arguable
- Claim (the arguer's assertion or answer to the question)
- Support:
  - Justification
    - Reasons ("because," or the relevance of the assertion)
    - Assumptions ("basis," or the values, beliefs, principles, and licenses that motivate the assertion as well as the authority represented in the assertion)
  - Elaboration
    - Grounds (supporting evidence for the reasons and the assumptions)
    - Limits (constraints the arguer would place on the claim)
  - Anticipated reactions (potential responses from others holding diverse positions)
    - Cooperative or supporting assertions
    - Competitive or opposing assertions
    - Altogether different assumptions
    - Challenges to reasons or to grounds

The outline does not include rebuttal. Why? Rebuttal is best done during deliberation when opposing positions are disclosed. Your position paper should not use space for rebuttal. Rather, your reasoning should exhibit anticipation of reactions.

Task 2. Write the Position Paper

Review the method in Chapter 2 before you write to get the rhetorical framework for your document in mind.

By consciously thinking about your position in relation to others (Strategy, this chapter) and outlining the logic of your argument (Task 1, this chapter), you have already begun to plan the contents of the document. That does not mean that the document's contents should simply fill in the outline, however. Think of the outline as a skeleton. The contents are its body, clothed for a particular occasion. Content might vary, whereas the argument's outline stays the same.

The message is your claim or your answer to the issue question. When arguing in a policy context, you must be aware of your authority for making a claim. Authority in argument has two meanings, a practical, role-related meaning and a rhetorical, character-related meaning. Practically, authority means credibility and power derived from a role rather than from a credential such as specialized expertise, although that might be relevant, too. Any role carries its own kind of credibility and power, whether it's the role of holding elected or appointed office or the role of being a citizen or community member. Rhetorically, authority means persuasiveness. Authority in this sense is a function of evidence and analysis. Authority is communicated by the quality of support for claims and care for using information reliably. At their best, authoritative arguments are credible and persuasive, both practically and rhetorically.

The document must clearly show whose position it communicates. Yours? That of an organization that you represent?

You must anticipate reactions to your position. Go back to the list you made of positions alternative to your own (Strategy, this chapter). For each position on the list, note the reaction you might accordingly expect, and then rank the reactions in order of importance to you. Anticipate responses, but do not rebut them in the position paper (unless you are directed to do so). Keep the focus on your position, not that of your rebutters.

Condense greatly for now. You will likely have later opportunity to elaborate. However, keep this in mind: it will cost you credibility to ignore information your readers might deem important in light of other arguments. Possibly put detailed evidence in an appendix. Charts, tables, other graphics, or extended textual materials should normally be appended. However, the choice to append important details should rest on knowing the circumstances in which the position paper will be read and used. Writers especially should know whether all readers will see the entire document, including appendices. Use a standard citation style for identifying sources. American Psychological Association style might be sufficient or legal citation style might be appropriate.

If you are authoring a position paper that speaks for a group or organization, plan to allow adequate time for consultation. Are you the

> sole author, or do you have collaborators? Are you ghostwriting for someone else? Plan also to allow for review and revision, possibly multiple reviews calling for multiple revisions. Who will review drafts? Who will make revisions? Remember to check the final draft against expected standards (Two Checklists, Chapter 2). Check sentences for clarity (Appendix A). Revise further, if needed, before releasing.

Example

The policy brief sampled here exhibits, in the original, multiple communication subgenres within a single, lengthy (55-page) document. They are policy analysis, legislative history, critical analysis of policy discourse, and argumentation. Here, argumentation is shown. Other subgenres are shown elsewhere (Example 3, Chapter 4; Example 2, Chapter 5).

To illustrate argumentation, the brief's abstract, introduction, summary of findings, and overview of policy options are sampled here. Immediately following, an outline applies the logical organization suggested in Task 1 to show this argument's structure. The outline refers to the entire brief, not only to the parts sampled in this chapter. To recognize the argument's development and coherence throughout the original document, you must read the entire document in reference to the outline. There are two ways of reading it here, either outline first or brief first. You might first read the outline and the sample in this chapter followed by Example 3, Chapter 4, and Example 2, Chapter 5, referring back to the outline here as needed. Alternatively, first read the full brief (using access information provided at the end of the sample here) and then read the outline here, referring back to the brief as needed. Either way, your objective is to toggle between the outline and the brief to discern the logical structure of argument in an extensive written document.

Expanding the EITC for Single Workers and Couples with*out* Children (aka Tax Relief for Low-Wage Workers)

Daniel P. Gitterman, Lucy S. Gorham, Jessica L. Dorrance
A Policy Brief prepared for the Center on Poverty, Work and Opportunity at the University of North Carolina at Chapel Hill
January 2007

Abstract

The Earned Income Tax Credit (EITC), the nation's largest anti-poverty program, now provides tax benefits of roughly $39 billion dollars a year to over 21 million households. By supplementing the earnings of low-wage workers, the EITC "makes work pay." The EITC's popularity can be attributed to its providing both work incentives and tax relief. In 1993, Congress extended a small earned income credit to singles and childless couples; however, about 96 percent of EITC dollars still go to families with children. This discussion paper argues that, while the emphasis of the EITC on rewarding work for families with children deserves continued primacy, expansion of the EITC to childless single workers and married couples without children deserves greater attention for the following reasons:

- The disproportionate and growing income tax burden (payroll, sales, excise) faced by this group of workers;

- The growing segment of workers at the bottom of the labor market, particularly single men with low levels of education and training, who remain confined to low-wage jobs;

- The strict separation in our thinking between households with and without children requires reexamination, given the growing number of children with non-custodial parents; and,

- With a national savings rate below zero, the need to facilitate asset building for all low-wage workers, including those without children.

We recommend expanding the EITC for single workers and childless married couples with a range of policy recommendations, each targeting specific new subgroups of EITC recipients and addressing a slightly different purpose:

- Increase the EITC from 7.65 percent to 15.3 percent of earnings up to $8,080 in order to directly offset payroll taxes; and adjust the phase-in and phase-out ranges;

- Lower the age requirement for single and childless workers to qualify for the EITC from 25 to 21 to target greater workforce participation incentives to young workers just entering the labor market and making major decisions about work;

- Encourage single low-income workers to claim the Advance (monthly) EITC and use the increase in employee payroll earnings to contribute toward health care insurance premiums; and,

- Link the EITC to asset building options such as matched savings accounts for education and training, homeownership, retirement, and entrepreneurship. In addition, remove asset limits for other public benefit programs, particularly to assist those with disabilities to enter the labor market and build assets.

Introduction

The Earned Income Tax Credit (EITC) is a refundable federal income tax credit first enacted with bipartisan political support in 1975. The EITC encourages low-income workers with children to enter and remain in the labor market by supplementing the earnings of those working for low wages, thus "making work pay." . . . In this policy brief, we explore three questions:

1. What do existing policy research and current data tell us about whether the original two goals of the EITC—payroll tax relief and encouraging employment—are being met adequately for the sub-groups of childless single and married workers;

2. Are there additional rationales that would justify an expansion of the EITC for this sub-group; and,

3. What policy changes could accomplish all or some of these policy goals?

. . .

Summary of Key Findings . . . This brief argues that, while the salient effects of the EITC on reducing child poverty and rewarding work for low-income workers with children deserve continued primacy, the potential for providing needed economic support and greater federal tax relief to childless single and married workers deserves immediate attention for the following reasons:

The disproportionate tax burden faced by low-wage single workers, which has worsened since the EITC was enacted in 1975, make tax relief an even greater priority as an issue of tax fairness. . . . If any workers need a tax cut, we argue that these workers do.

A growing segment of workers at the bottom of the labor market . . . remain confined to low-wage jobs. . . . Leaving this group at the margins of the labor market undermines the strength of the workforce, communities, and families.

Policy Options for an Expansion of the EITC for Childless Workers . . .

Politically, at both the federal and state level, an expanded EITC could embody both progressive and conservative values by: (1) rewarding those who work with an earnings subsidy; (2) providing the greatest benefits to those with the greatest need; (3) offsetting the tax burden on working poor singles and childless married couples struggling to make ends meet; (4) providing incentives for people to enter the workforce who otherwise might not do so; (5) achieving these ends without increasing employer costs, without creating hiring disincentives and with minimal government bureaucracy; and (6) helping single workers and families without children, and potentially many more, to build assets for homeownership, education, and retirement when combined with other institutional supports such as matched savings programs. . . .

(The full document including tables, charts, citations, and references can be found at http://www.law.unc.edu/documents/poverty/publications/gittermanpolicybrief.pdf/. Also see Gitterman (2003) and Gitterman, Gorham, and Dorrance (2008).)

WHAT THIS EXAMPLE SHOWS. Thinking that the legislator who requested this brief might run for president, the authors used the policy brief as an opportunity to focus the potential candidate's attention on the small tax credit available to workers without children. Because the EITC had become a major instrument of antipoverty policy, the authors argued to extend some of its benefits. The brief illustrates authoritative argument. The outline presented next shows the argument's structure.

Outline of the Argument to Expand the Earned Income Tax Credit (EITC) in the United States

Problem: EITC eligibility limited to families with children.
Issue: Ineligibility of single workers and couples without children.
Question: Should EITC cover single workers and couples without children?
Claim: The EITC should be expanded to childless single workers and married couples without children.
Support: Justification, elaboration, and limits.

- Justification
    - Reasons
        - The disproportionate and growing income tax burden (payroll, sales, excise) faced by this group of workers;
        - The growing segment of workers at the bottom of the labor market, particularly single men with low levels of education and training, who remain confined to low-wage jobs;
        - The strict separation in our thinking between households with and without children requires reexamination, given the growing number of children with noncustodial parents;
        - With a national savings rate below zero, the need to facilitate asset building for all low-wage workers, including those without children.
- Assumptions
    - Original policy goals of the EITC are to provide work incentives and tax relief for low-wage workers;

- The present tax code is unfair to low-wage workers;
- Progressive and conservative values support a safety net for people who work hard and play by the rules.
- Elaboration
  - Evidence for reasons
    - Empirical research on tax burden, job patterns, household demographics, and assets of low-wage workers.
  - Evidence for assumptions
    - Legislative history showing intent of original EITC legislation and amendments from 1975 to the present (see Example 3, Chapter 5).
    - Policy analysis of tax code (see Example 3, Chapter 4).
    - Political analysis of values (e.g., equity, efficiency, role of government) (see Example 3, Chapter 4).
- Limits
  - Political climate at the time of introducing a proposal to expand EITC;
  - If adopted, speed of implementation (might impact other anti-poverty programs);
  - Coverage (recommended solution does not cover single workers who are noncustodial parents).
- Anticipated reactions:
  - Cooperative (others might propose compatible policy changes, such as providing incentives for businesses to offer infant day care);
  - Competitive (others might argue that there are more pressing priorities, that there are better policy instruments, or for a different solution);
  - Different assumptions (replace the present tax code with a flat tax);
  - Challenges (need more empirical research and policy analysis before concluding that the tax code is unfair to low-wage workers).

Summary and Preview

Persuasive policy argument is purposeful, critical, credible, and authoritative. This chapter tells you that positions supported by argument are more persuasive than unsupported opinion. It shows you how to argue policy positions logically and politically. It illustrates outlining to organize your position and to analyze positions other than your own.

As an experienced policy actor says, policy argument is a little like negotiation. "The process requires you to analyze your own arguments, anticipate all other arguments, and analyze them. You're not just looking for holes in other argument; you're looking for potential cooperation, for common ground. This has a lot to do with dynamics of negotiation. . . . The point is to . . . understand what the interests really are. Seldom are they simple and seldom are they direct" (Helfert, 2014). Chapter 7 applies argument to requesting policy action.

References

Coplin, W. D., & O'Leary, M. K. (1998). *Public policy skills* (3rd ed.). Washington, DC: Policy Studies Associates.

Gitterman, D. P. (2003). *Tax credits for working families.* http://www.brookings.edu/reports/2003/08childrenfamilies_gitterman.aspx/.

Gitterman, D. P., Gorham, L. S., & Dorrance, J. L. (2008). Expanding the EITC for single workers and couples with*out* children: Tax relief for all low-wage workers. *Georgetown Journal on Poverty Law and Policy,* 15(2), 245–284.

Helfert, D. (2014). *Policy position papers.* Instructional guide available from the author (dhelfert@verizon.net).

Stone, D. (2012). *Policy paradox: The art of political decision making* (3rd ed.). New York, NY: Norton.

Further Reading

Ramage, J. D., Bean, J. C., & Johnson, J. (2011). *Writing arguments: A rhetoric with readings* (9th ed.). White Plains, NY: Longman.

Toulmin, S. (2003). *The uses of argument* (Updated ed.). New York, NY: Cambridge University Press.

↜

CHAPTER 7

Petition, Proposal, Letter: Request Action

Key Concepts

- Getting government to act on your concern
- Requesting administrative action
- Proposing legislative action

Action requests and policy proposals may originate inside or outside government. While it is true that legislators or administrators originate most proposals, any citizen or group can petition for action or propose policy. This chapter shows you how to petition, propose, or write a letter to achieve change.

Nongovernmental actors might request action by petitioning. The First Amendment to the U.S. Constitution guarantees citizens' right to "petition for a redress of grievances." Over time, petitioners have come to include not only individual citizens but also groups, organizations of many kinds, and corporations. Petitioning now goes beyond redressing grievances to requesting varied actions.

To illustrate petitioning, in a case of injury experienced during air bag deployment in an automobile collision, three different petitions for government action might be made.

1. A victim of chemical burns or breathing disorders attributable to air bag deployment might petition his or her congressional representatives to amend the National Traffic and Motor Vehicle

Safety Act of 1966 to authorize medical training programs specific to air bags for emergency services personnel.

2. A company that has developed a new technology for increasing passenger safety without relying solely on passenger restraints, such as air bags or safety belts, might petition the National Highway Traffic Safety Administration to test the new technology.

3. A professional association of automotive engineers might petition the National Highway Traffic Safety Administration to amend a vehicle safety design standard to include warning systems in cars to encourage seat belt use.

Another common practice for requesting action is proposing policy. Internal proposals usually convey one governmental body's request to another. For instance, Example 3, this chapter, shows a city government commission advising a mayor and city council. Example 4, this chapter, shows a federal agency director requesting congressional action.

External proposals usually represent organized, or group, interest in solving a problem. The role of nongovernmental groups in North American public policy making has deep historical roots. In colonial America, before the United States or its government was established, voluntary associations flourished. Individuals formed associations to provide basic social services, to meet public needs, and to protect community interests. Voluntary fire companies, water companies, library associations, prison associations, school associations, landowner associations, and militias were so common in the America of the early 1800s that a visitor from France, Alexis de Tocqueville (1945), observed,

> Americans of all ages, all conditions, and all dispositions constantly form associations . . . Wherever at the head of some new undertaking you see the government in France, or a man of rank in England, in the United States you will be sure to find an association (p. 106).

Such group activism provides background for the Tenth Amendment regarding limitations on central government that states "the powers not delegated to the United States by the Constitution, nor prohibited to it by the States, are reserved to the States respectively, or to the people."

Nowadays, groups that perform a public good might be granted tax-exempt status as charities or nonprofit organizations. Their function might be religious, scientific, literary, educational, promotional, protective, political, charitable, or other, in accordance with Internal Revenue Service standards for 30 categories of tax-exempt activity (Internal Revenue Service). Many, perhaps most, nonprofit organizations are not concerned with public policy. However, significant numbers of advocacy groups are active. Their methods vary according to the limitations of their tax-exempt status. Groups limited to education and outreach might communicate by legislative alerts, editorials, letters, personal visits to lawmakers, witness testimony, and more. Others, with more restricted tax benefits, might campaign for candidates running for office, lobby, and draft legislation.

Legislators and administrators often appreciate the help of advocacy groups in educating the public about needs for policy. Additionally, government staffs appreciate informed, accurate, well-argued lobbying because it helps them to brief legislators on complex or controversial issues. And, legislation and regulation writers might also appreciate proposed wording. (Examples 1 and 4, this chapter and Example 1, Chapter 9, illustrate.) A positive example of public good resulting from such help might be the continued strengthening of legislation in the United States on smoking as a health problem. Legislation aimed to limit smoking was passed in large part because health care advocacy groups worked with responsive legislators at all levels of government and educated the public to support directed warning labels on cigarettes, nonsmoking restaurant sections, and smoke-free public facilities. A negative example is the influence of lobbying by corporations and advocacy groups to weaken laws on occupational health and safety or on environmental protection. The milk-labeling illustration in Chapter 1 exemplifies both positive and negative lobbying.

Grassroots organizations such as neighborhood or block associations, community clubs, workplace voluntary groups, and student organizations might also use petitioning, proposing, or letter writing to accomplish their advocacy, just as nonprofit organizations might.

Why are petitioning, proposing, and letter writing important? They sustain democracy. They are democratic ways of addressing public problems by institutional means. Whether by direct democracy (as with California's state referenda) or by representative democracy (as with Washington's federal legislation), self-governing society relies on procedures for public intervention in the process. Recall that public policy has far-reaching effects in the everyday life of society. Policy makers need and want in-depth information that can shed light on problems and build public support for action. Nongovernmental groups or individuals who are informed about problem causes and impacts or policy needs and consequences are excellent sources of information. Who petitions, proposes, or writes letters? Individuals can do so, but organized groups are likely to be more influential because they represent the power of collective interest or capacity to advise.

How to Petition, Propose, or Write a Letter Requesting Action on Behalf of a Group

Goal: Knowledge of the functions of nongovernmental advocacy organizations and governmental advisory commissions in your area of interest.

Objective: Requesting action on behalf of an organization or group.

Product: Brief written petition, policy proposal, or letter representing an organization's advocacy or advice. Length varies according to purposes and situations, but a short document (one to three pages) is preferred. Genre may be prescribed or chosen.

Scope: The group's charter, purpose, mandate, or mission will determine the concerns or issues you will address.

Strategy: Create a petition, proposal, or letter including the following information:

- Desired outcome: What do you want to accomplish? Can you describe it as if it were already accomplished in a future you want to achieve?
- Today's situation: What's wrong in the present? Why is the action you propose needed? What causes the need?
- Relevant background: How did the problem arise? What original assumptions are no longer valid? What conditions have changed?

- Available options: What are the alternative ways of meeting the need? Advantages and disadvantages of each? Costs (money, other) of each?
- Recommended action: What is the best alternative? Can you briefly argue as to why?
- Summary: What are the results (referring to the desired future) if requested action is performed?
- Action items: Who is asked to do what, when, where, and how?

Task 1. Name the Need, and Specify the Action and Agency

Identify a need for policy: If you already know the need you will address or the intervention you will advocate, proceed to the next step, specifying the desired action and the responsible agency.

If you do not know the need well, or if you have not decided on intervention or you are responsible for selecting among many competing needs and proposed interventions, pause. Step back to focus before you proceed. Start again wherever you need to start, whether it is to define the problem and pinpoint the issue (discovery), review the history of action or inaction (legislative history), review the arguments (the range of positions), or use the method in Chapter 2 to reconsider the policy context and the communication situation for your proposal.

Specify the action and agency: Determining the needed action—knowing what is possible, knowing whom to ask, and knowing what to ask for—is not simple. Much time and effort can be wasted in seeking unlikely action or making a proposal to the wrong recipient. The best way is to continually and iteratively ask and answer, "What am I trying to do?" and "How can I do it most effectively?" That will lead to further guiding questions such as "Should I start small (that is, local), or should I start big (national or international)?"

Consider the options for action; for example, choose government action. What do you want the government to do? Government can legislate, spend, regulate, and enforce, all within limits. Which type of action is needed for the problem you are concerned about? To which level of government—federal, state, local—should you direct your proposal? Which department or agency can do what you want to accomplish?

Now consider nongovernmental options. Does the solution require government action at all? For example, a citizens group might choose to organize a boycott or initiate a lawsuit to solve a civic problem rather than to ask for government action or propose public policy.

Similarly, a student group might choose a community solution rather than governmental action. For example, in response to a racist incident on campus, one student group developed a constructive plan for educating students about everyday racism in campus life. Rather than proposing it as a policy to the student governance or to the school's administration, the group circulated their plan among other campus organizations and sent it to national student associations. They communicated it by word of mouth and publicized it through news media. The strategy was to ask similar student groups nationwide to draw public attention to the problem of race-based harassment on their campus and to offer as a model the original group's plan for addressing it. In this example, change in human behavior was sought through organized community education.

Task 2. Identify the Nonprofit Organizations Active on Your Issue

Here are some ways of locating and identifying nonprofit organizations:

- Ask local volunteer services about local nonprofits or local affiliates of national and international nonprofits.

- Ask a librarian for print or online guides to nonprofit organizations. (Chapter 5 on legislative records research includes a reminder that research librarians are a real resource for communicators. A reference librarian specializing in management and business, for example, will know the latest print and online sources of information on nonprofit organizations.)

- Read the transcripts of congressional hearings on your issue to find witnesses who spoke on behalf of advocacy groups. (To find hearings, see Chapter 5 on legislative history and Chapter 9 on witness testimony.)

- Search newspaper databases for news articles on your issue that might refer to advocacy groups.

- Search World Wide Web portals to nonprofit organizations. The following websites offer free searchable lists of nonprofits:

  - Urban Institute National Center for Charitable Statistics Nonprofit FAQ

  - Nonprofit Yellow Pages

  - idealist.org

  - NonProfitList.org

- Independent Sector
- The Foundation Directory Online
- Guidestar

Why restrict your knowledge to that provided by nonprofit organizations? You should not necessarily limit your knowledge to a single kind of source. If, for example, you represent a health care organization and are advocating for the right to use a controversial drug, you may want to enlist the support of the pharmaceutical company that manufactures the drug. While the company has a vested interest, it also might have facts and figures that could bolster or undercut your arguments. As another example, if you are advocating for highway safety improvement, you might consult with for-profit experts in accident research, such as the petitioners in Example 2 (this chapter).

Task 3. Write

Provide only accurate, verifiable information. Anything else will destroy your or your organization's credibility and persuasiveness.

Use the method in Chapter 2 to prepare, plan, and produce a written petition or proposal. The document's contents should answer the questions listed under Strategy in this chapter. Compare the finished product to expected standards (Checklists, Chapter 2).

There is no typical format for policy proposals. If you are writing for an organization that prescribes a template for policy proposals, or if your intended recipient prescribes a template, you should use it. If no template is prescribed, choose a form that is appropriate for your situation. For any written document requesting government action, the conventions of professional communication will apply. Identify the presenter and recipient, summarize in an overview, and organize content in subheaded sections. The document type might be a letter, a memo, a full-page ad in print newspapers, animated ads in online newspapers, a public declaration dramatically delivered in historical costume, a YouTube video, or another form chosen for its effectiveness in the situation. See, for example, the websites of national nonprofit groups that sometimes express their advocacy in serious as well as funny and attention-grabbing ways.

Four Examples

These examples show petitioning, proposing, and letter writing by experts and advisers inside and outside government.

Example 1. Petition

CENTER FOR AUTO SAFETY
1825 Connecticut Avenue, NW #33a
Washington, DC 20009-5708 (202) 328-1770
www.autosafety.org
January 21, 2007
The Honorable Nicole R. Nason, Administrator
National Highway Traffic Safety Administration
400 Seventh Street, SM7
Washington, DC 20590

PETITION FOR RULEMAKING
Dear Ms. Nason:

The Center for Auto Safety (CAS) petitions the National Highway Traffic Safety Administration (NHTSA) to take action to restrict the availability of two-way communication features through in-vehicle telematic systems while a vehicle is in motion. The purpose of this petition is to make the driving environment safer by reducing the availability of devices that have been proven to be traffic hazards.

According to NHTSA spokesman Rae Tyson, "Our recommendation is that you should not talk on the phone while driving, whether it's a hand-held or hands-free device." It is time for NHTSA to put the results of extensive research and its own recommendation into action.

BACKGROUND
The automotive industry has long been aware of the dangers posed by talking on a cell phone while operating a motor vehicle. Cellular telephones are an important resource for drivers who encounter emergency situations and pull off the road to make calls. However, when cell phones are used while driving, they are a significant cause of highway crashes. Many existing in-vehicle technologies . . . are being expanded to offer cellular telephone service to drivers. What was once an essentially helpful technology is becoming a source of dangerous driver distraction by the addition of personal communication features that are available to a person while driving.

In search of new profit centers, major auto companies are marketing vehicle-in-motion telematic options that degrade the safety value of the Automatic Crash Notification (ACN) originally installed in motor vehicles. For example, General Motors, which was a leader in ACN with its OnStar system, began degrading safety by including personal cell phone use as an integral part of OnStar. GM once tried expanding the scope of in-vehicle telematic systems to allow drivers to receive email, movie listings, personalized news, sport reports and weather while driving. The potential distraction is similar to permitting television monitors in the front seats of passenger vehicles, a practice that is *not* permitted by state law in most, if not all states.

   . . .

RESEARCH STUDIES

Research has consistently shown that operating a motor vehicle while talking on a cell phone, whether hand-held or hands-free, increases the risk of an accident to three or four times the experience of attentive drivers. The general consensus of the scientific community is that there is little, if any, difference in crash rates involving hands-free versus hand-held cell phones. The two-way conversation on a cellular phone, not the task of holding the phone, causes a cognitive distraction. This distraction induces "inattention blindness," inhibiting drivers' abilities to detect change in road conditions.

STATE LEGISLATION

. . .

   The highest standard enacted by District of Columbia, Connecticut, New Jersey and New York prohibits the use of any handheld cellular phone but permits drivers to use hands-free wireless devices.

   . . .

   Many cities have encountered difficulty enforcing bans because of the high number of violations. . . . The total number of cell phone calls from 1996–2001, 326 billion, shows the enormous potential exposure of cell phone use in vehicles.

   . . .

EXEMPLARY VEHICLE CRASHES

No one can deny that cell phones have resulted in traffic crashes, deaths, and injuries. [Name] and [Name] were both killed when drivers talking on cell phones struck their vehicles while they were stopped at a stop light.

   . . . There are hundreds of cases like [theirs] . . . NHTSA has known from the time of the first head of the agency, William Haddon, MD, that the best public health strategy is one that is passive; in this case, not permitting cell phone technology to be so readily available.

CONCLUSION

. . .

   It is time for the government to intervene on this dangerous practice . . . As a first step, the Center petitions NHTSA to issue a notice of proposed rulemaking which would amend FMVVSS102 to add a new provision reading:

> *Any vehicle integrated personal communication systems including cellular phones and text-messaging systems shall be inoperative when the transmission shift lever is in a forward or reverse position.*

. . .

Sincerely,

Clarence M. Ditlow, Executive Director

Tyler Patterson, Vehicle Safety Intern

(The full petition can be seen at http://www.regulations.gov)
Docket ID: NHTSA-2007–28442
Document ID: NHTSA-2007–28442-0003
Date Posted: Sep 13, 2007)

Example 2. Petition

In the late 1990s, two professionals in auto safety created a for-profit corporation in the public interest to assist victims in litigation resulting from automobile accidents. Both are experts, one of them in highway safety policy and the other in automobile design for occupant safety. Concerned about the high rates of injury and fatality caused in part by drivers' and passengers' failure to use seat belts, the experts frequently petitioned the responsible federal government agency to amend the safety standard to require inducements in all vehicles to encourage seat belt use. Here, next, is a recent letter and petition to the agency head regarding a persistent problem. This letter refers to earlier petitions by these experts not shown here.

Letter

Carl E. Nash
(address)
(phone)
(e-mail)

February 11, 2002

The Honorable Jeffrey W. Runge, M.D.
National Highway Traffic Safety Administrator
Washington, D.C. 20590

Dear Dr. Runge:

As I promised at the Fuel Economy/Safety session of the Transportation Research Board meeting, I am enclosing copies of the petitions that

Donald Friedman and I submitted to NHTSA before you became Administrator. They asked NHTSA to address the question of safety belt use inducements or reminders. We believe you, as Administrator, have considerable flexibility in how you might address this important contribution to motor vehicle safety.

NHTSA could take rulemaking action to require effective belt use reminders, but you could more expeditiously use your bully pulpit and other means to get auto makers to install more effective reminders in their new vehicles. A small research and fleet test program—which the industry should conduct along with NHTSA—could determine the most effective means of getting occupants to buckle up.

You are probably aware that the Insurance Institute for Highway Safety (IIHS) evaluated the weak reminder that has been included in most new Ford vehicles since 2000 and found that it increased usage by about five percentage points. . . . Ford found no consumer resistance or complaints from this very innocuous reminder. A more effective reminder . . . could be developed with a modest research program. The safety payoff over the next decade would be quite substantial, not to mention the fact that it would free police resources now used to enforce belt use laws.

I am a strong advocate of non-regulatory approaches to automotive issues. In particular, the committee technical standards writing process of the American Society for Testing and Materials (ASTM) is highly democratic *(anyone with something to contribute can participate)*, effective *(it makes use of knowledge and expertise from all quarters)*, and fair *(it cannot be dominated by any specific interest and these committees must reach consensus)*. ASTM committees can produce consumer information standards that are objective, that meet the need for motor vehicle safety, and that are stated in performance terms. As an example, it would have been preferable to establish an (ASTM) committee to draft the side air bag standard last year.

. . . More comprehensive consumer information on motor vehicle safety can be an effective complement to NHTSA's minimum regulatory standards. . . . This market-based approach is more flexible for both the government and automakers, and can facilitate important choices by individual car buyers.

If you would like to discuss the possibilities of this approach further, I would be pleased to participate in such conversations and to recommend others with a similar interest in this approach.

With regards,
Carl E. Nash, Ph.D.
Enclosures

Petition

To Amend FMVSS 208, Occupant Crash Protection To Require Effective Belt Use Inducement

Carl E. Nash, Ph.D., and Donald Friedman
Washington, D.C., and Santa Barbara, California

SUMMARY

This is a petition to amend Federal Motor Vehicle Safety Standard 208 (FMVSS 208) to require effective safety belt use inducement systems in all new motor vehicles sold in the United States. This requirement should become effective no later than the beginning of the 2001 model year. The inducement systems should activate only if a person sits in either front outboard seating position and does not attach the safety belt after occupying the seat and would stop when the belt is buckled. The requirement must be consistent with the "interlock" amendment to the National Traffic and Motor Vehicle Safety Act of 1966 (15 U.S.C. 1410b), which prohibits ignition interlocks and continuous buzzers.

The inducements could include, but need not be limited to: (1) a continuous visual warning to buckle safety belts located prominently on the instrument panel, (2) an intermittent, repeating audible suggestion (such as with a synthesized voice) warning occupants to buckle their safety belt, and (3) disruption of electrical power to such non-essential accessories as the radio, tape or CD player, and air conditioning. We further recommend that NHTSA undertake a quick reaction project to determine the acceptability and effectiveness of various types of use inducements to ensure that the spirit of the interlock amendment is not violated.

BACKGROUND

. . .

RESTRAINT POLICY AND USE TODAY

. . .

AN AMENDMENT TO FMVSS 208

Therefore, we petition NHTSA to amend FMVSS 208 to require a reasonable and effective safety belt use inducement to be built into all new vehicles. Effective belt use inducements can be required without violating the "interlock" amendment (15 U.S.C. 1410b) to the National Traffic and Motor Vehicle Safety Act . . .

Safety belt use is widespread, generally accepted, and required by law in virtually all states. The design for comfort and convenience of safety belts in many new vehicles has improved since the days of the interlock. Thus, we doubt that many motorists would object to use of well-designed inducement systems. However, we recommend that NHTSA conduct quick reaction tests using panels and field tests to determine effectiveness and consumer acceptance of various types of use inducements. . . . We note that a policy of increasing belt use through an inducement built into new motor vehicles would be preferable to the present policy of safety belt use laws for reasons unrelated to safety. Civil rights organizations (most recently the Urban League) have objected to primary belt use laws because of their potential to give police officers an excuse to stop minority drivers. Having the inducement built into the vehicle takes away that issue and should be strongly supported by civil rights and civil liberties advocates.

Requiring a belt use inducement built into all new vehicles would be a major improvement in every way to FMVSS 208. As existing cars are retired from use, it would increase belt use to near universality (with the attendant reduction in fatalities and serious injuries in all crash modes) without further state laws or enforcement activities. In fact, states could sunset their safety belt use laws within the next decade or two. We estimate that a belt use inducement has the potential to save a minimum of 7,000 additional lives per year.

We urge that NHTSA give priority to both testing and simultaneous rulemaking in response to our petition.

(The full petition can be found at http://www.regulations.gov. Docket ID: NHTSA-1998–4405 Document ID: NHTSA-1998–4405-0062 Date Posted: Dec 17, 1998. For the agency's comment denying this petition see its *Federal Register* notice on advanced air bags: F.R. vol. 64, no. 214, page 60625–6. [The notice begins on page 60556]. The docket identifier is NHTSA 1999–6407-0001.)

►~• WHAT EXAMPLES 1 AND 2 SHOW. Example 1 on cell phone use is an external petition by a nonprofit organization of experts. No specific policy process is underway, which explains why the petitioners ask the agency to start the process by issuing a notice of proposed rulemaking on the subject, use of cell phones while driving, and a call for public comment. Example 2 on seat belt use is an external petition by a for-profit organization of experts.

Examples 1 and 2 illustrate in-depth presentation of information. They are written to be read silently, not spoken aloud. One cue to this intention is the length of sentences in both texts. Many sentences in Examples 1 and 2 would cause a speaker to run out of breath. Another cue is the extensive detail.

The amount of detail in Examples 1 and 2 is probably appropriate. For both petitions and proposals, as for funding requests, the contents and length of submissions might be prescribed by the receiving agency. If the agency prescribes the information and length it wants and the form it prefers, write accordingly. Otherwise, a petition or proposal, like a grant application, might go unconsidered.

Where to put all the details? Putting them in the main body of the document can be an unwise choice. Detailed explanation or historical background can bury the message. A potential choice for the writers of Example 2 on seat belt use is to put explanation, background, and critique in an appendix. The success of this option depends on the circumstances of reception. To decide whether to append supporting information, writers need to understand the readers' situation. If all readers will receive the whole document and if they are willing to flip between the main text and appendix as they read, writers can safely choose to append detailed information. However, in some policy work settings, readers are likely to receive not the whole document but only the parts that pertain to their jurisdiction or responsibility. Appended information might not reach them. It is perhaps for this reason that the writers of Example 2 knowingly chose not to use appendices.

Examples 1 and 2 are well organized for readability. Document structure aids rapid comprehension. Even so, the message could be emphasized more in Example 2. Within paragraphs, the petitioners' implicit message ("There is a better way") competes with the implied critique ("The agency's way is flawed"). Impatient readers might want a sharper focus on the message.

Example 3. Letter Requesting Action

Scenario

The City of Tucson Small Minority and Women-owned Business Commission [SMWBC] is made up of citizens representing for-profit businesses and nonprofit organizations. For months, tourism has been on the commission's agenda. As business owners or organization leaders living near the United States-Mexico border, commission

> members are aware that so-called shadow (unregulated) trade in-
> cluding tourism flourishes alongside sunshine (regulated) trade in
> the city of Tucson and Pima County. Consequences include both
> benefits and concerns.

The current commission chair, a bed-and-breakfast owner and operator with professional experience in international trade, acts on the
mayor's request to look into issues concerning short-term private
home accommodation rentals (less than 30 days) transacted by
homeowners and tourists via the Internet. The commission's intent is
to achieve equity in business—that is, if one business owner needs a
license, then all businesses conducting activities in accordance with
the city of Tucson's definition of business need licenses. To open the
SMWBC's discussion, the chair voices concern that online transactions for rental are untaxed and unregulated, in contrast to traditional tourism rentals.

After months of discussion, the commission writes a letter to the
mayor and city council recommending investigation with an attached
memorandum detailing objectives. The letter and memorandum are
shown next here.

COMMISSION LETTER AND MEMORANDUM

City of Tucson
Small, Minority and Women Owned Business Commission (SMWBC)
July 7, 2014

Mayor and City Council
City of Tucson
City Hall
255 W. Alameda
Tucson, AZ 85701

Dear Mayor Rothschild and Tucson City Council Members,

The Small, Minority and Women Owned Business Commission (SMWBC)
has recently formed a sub-committee to explore the issues surrounding
the rapid expansion of the unregulated short-term rental industry.

Our overriding concern is the protection of both vendor and consumer in rental interactions, ensuring a level playing field wherein proper business license, certificate of occupancy, insurance policies, and access to redress are standard.

The Commission asks you to consider our attached request to have City staff investigate this matter for further action. The attached memo outlines the purpose, benefits, research, regulations, and communication aspects of this proposal.

The Commission respectfully asks for your review and evaluation of this proposal.

Sincerely,
Marion K. Hook, Chair
Small, Minority, and Women Owned
Business Commission (SMWBC)

MEMORANDUM (ATTACHMENT)

To: City of Tucson Mayor Jonathan Rothschild and City Council
From: The City of Tucson Small Minority and Women-owned Business Commission
Date: July 7, 2014

SUBJECT: SHORT-TERM RENTAL (STR) PROPERTIES REGULATION

BACKGROUND/PURPOSE:

- To determine the extent to which the City of Tucson is regulating, monitoring, licensing, and collecting bed-tax revenue from all forms of short-term rentals (defined as 30 days or less). On any given day, there are hundreds of such properties for rent in Tucson. Advertising sites such as VRBO, Flipkey, Homeaway, Tripadvisor, and Airbnb had a combined total of over 1,700 listings for the Tucson region on June 12, 2014. . . .

- To create equity for Tucson short-term rentals who are currently obtaining licenses, certificates of occupancy, meeting health department requirements, safety requirements, obtaining insurance, and charging, collecting, and remitting bed tax revenue.

- To identify those short-term rentals not participating in these safety and business regulations in order to provide a safe environment for those who are on either side of this business relationship.

To identify those who are not participating in the collection and remittance of bed-tax revenue.

- To develop recommendations for Mayor and Council regarding all short-term rental properties in Tucson. Recommendations to include regulation, monitoring and licensing of short-term rentals; including business license, certificates of occupancy, safety inspections, insurance coverage, and payment of bed-tax revenue.

BENEFITS

- Level the playing field for all vacation properties, including hotels, motels, bed and breakfasts, and short-term rental properties as addressed above.

- Ensure the suitability of the STR with inspection, Certificate of Occupancy, health and safety requirements and insurance to protect both the owner of the property being rented and the renter.

- Collect and remit to the City the required bed-tax revenue, Certificate of Occupancy revenue, business license revenue, event permit revenue and $2.00 surcharge per room night spent in Tucson.* In looking at the math, Tucson collected $9 million in base (6%) bed-tax revenue last year, along with $3.5 million in surcharge ($2 per room per night) revenue for a total of $12.5 million. According to a survey done by Visit Tucson, 20% of Tucson's visitors indicate they stay in short-term rentals. That, applied to the revenue total above, is $2.5 million. It is not known how many of the approximately 1,700 current listings are in Tucson city limits, but one would think it would be proportional to the number of hotel rooms in Tucson vs. the rest of the region. Even with an ordinance, some people will not register and/or remit bed-tax revenue. That stated, it is still realistic to think that the City could expect to collect somewhere between $500,000 and $1 million in year one with that amount increasing in future years as the City becomes more familiar with monitoring the applicable web sites and enforcing the ordinance.

RESEARCH

Presentations by Brent DeRaad, President and CEO, Visit Tucson; Andrew Squire, Economic Development Specialist, City Manager's Office, City of Tucson; City of Tucson Finance Department; and City of Tucson Attorney

Internet research of various companies that participate in short-term rentals (such as Airbnb, VRBO, Home Stay, Craig's List)

Internet research of cities, such as Palm Springs, CA, Austin, TX, and Portland, OR, which currently regulate or are in the process of studying the creation of policies for STR

REGULATION PROCESS

All qualified STRs:

Complete application form

Obtain Business License

Obtain Certificate of Occupancy

Show Proof of Insurance

Post Compliance Documents

Collect and Remit Bed Taxes

COMMUNICATION

Communication of STR Licensing Program

City web site

City workshops

Media

Small and Women-Owned Business Commission (SMWBC) Newsletter

Visit Tucson accommodation listing

FUNCTIONS OF SMWBC COMMISSION

The SMWBC is tasked, among other things, to:

- Facilitate communication between the City and small business
- Evaluate City policies and regulations for their impact on small businesses and make recommendations to streamline and/or modify such regulation as deemed necessary
- Sponsor and conduct educational forums, hearings, and workshops on topics of concern to small, minority, and women-owned businesses
- Recommend that the Mayor and Council consider alternative measures of legislation to encourage small, minority, and women-owned business participation

SUGGESTED ACTION

- Assign an employee or an intern to collect data and enter into a database on short-term rentals currently operating within the City of Tucson limits including, but not limited to:

- Business name
- Owner
- Address
- Contact information
- Distribute gathered information to City of Tucson Finance Department for distribution to appropriate regulatory bodies with City government
- Inform such short-term rental business of the need for proof of business license, certificate of occupancy, knowledge of parking regulations, event licensing, alcohol service limitations, proof of appropriate insurance, business transaction tax payment, and any other information the City deems necessary
- Institute a city-wide education program via the City's web site which will inform current and future short-term rental owner of the current regulations and taxes owed

While the commission studies the matter and before it sends its request to the council, a local news reporter attacks. The report frames potential council action as likely to restrict homeowners' liberty and rights. It misstates revenue implications for the city. Thus, city and county readers are given a biased characterization of the action before the city council has considered it. The news report is shown next, here.

SHORT TERM RENTALS MAY GET REGULATION

Posted: May 09, 2014 8:46 PM EDT Updated: May 23, 2014 9:52 PM EDT
By Bud Foster
TUCSON, AZ (Tucson News Now) -
There are thousands of homes in Tucson which are unsold and the future doesn't look bright right now.
The owners of many of those homes have found a way to make a few extra dollars while waiting for a buyer to come along.
Short term rentals.
A day, a weekend, a few days, a few weeks.
"We all understand trying to make a buck especially when times are down," says Marion Hook, owner of the Adobe Rose Bed and Breakfast near the University.
But that is only one of two hats she wears.
The other is chair of the Small, Women and Minority Business Commission for the city of Tucson.
For the past three months, the commission has been discussing whether short-term rentals should be regulated.

The conclusion is it should be, and the commission is drafting a letter which will be sent to the Tucson mayor and council in the next few weeks.

"Let's make the playing field as level as we can for small businesses," she says.

According to Visit Tucson, the short-term lodging business makes up 20% of Tucson vacation and business stays.

That's 100,000 room nights which don't pay bed taxes, a major source of revenue.

The loss is estimated to be "in excess of $2 million," says Brent DeRaad, CEO of Visit Tucson.

But it's not just the revenue that has tourism officials concerned.

"You want to make sure you have a safe experience for all involved," he says.

DeRaad believes an unregulated industry means there are too many unanswered questions about insurance, liability and personal responsibility.

He believes the concern is more widespread than Tucson.

"This is an emerging issue that states are taking a look at," he says. "And even at the federal level they are looking at what they may want or need to regulate the industry."

But that regulation may run afoul of personal property rights, which Arizona voters have said are important.

There will likely be some pushback on that.

"We know it's coming," says Hood. "It's something we should probably hear."

She says the goal is not to put anyone out of business but to ensure everyone in the industry has a business license and a certificate of occupancy.

After study, the city council unanimously agrees to investigate and calls for recommendations. The council's meeting minutes are shown next, here.

CITY COUNCIL MEETING MINUTES
Action item: Discussion to Review Unregulated Short-term Rentals (City Wide) SS/SEP09-14-179

Introductory comments were provided by Council Member Kozachik.

Information and presentation was provided by Marion Hook, Small, Minority, and Women-Owned Business Commission Chairperson, and Brent DeRaad, Visit Tucson President/Chief Executive Officer.

Discussion ensued with questions fielded and answered by Ms. Hook, Mr. DeRaad, and Martha Durkin, City Manager.

It was moved by Council Member Kozachik, duly seconded and CARRIED by a voice vote of 7 to 0, to direct staff to begin outreach with the Small, Minority, and Women-Owned Business Commission, Visit Tucson, the unregulated short-term rental industry, and Pima County, and return in 90 days with recommendations.

Citizens reading news reports about the council's vote reacted by sending email to the commission's chair. A sample follows.

"I'm withdrawing my offer of help and support for this venture. The more information I've turned up concerning city and state leads me to believe that there is no way to avoid reminding the city that most of the B&B's in Tucson and Arizona as a whole, do not pay [are exempt from] state or local taxes. When they delve into whatever it would take to make maverick renters ante up, the rest of us will be endangered. I've had long conversations with two other B&B's and they would be extremely put out should the city begin digging for new opportunities within the transient rental population...Please let sleeping dogs lie or you will make a bus load of enemies, including me. I'm sorry; in theory I agree with you but the city and state are so broke they would grasp at any foothold."

➥ WHAT THIS EXAMPLE SHOWS The commission's request asks city government to deal with ambiguity. The share economy in which people use web sites to rent their houses or spare rooms for tourist lodging or event space is the problematic situation. There are concerns about safety, liability, health, labor, and trade competition. Sharable housing is an undefined business category. How electronic or online commerce relates to traditional commerce is open to interpretation. Government's authority to intervene is ambiguous. Since the 1998 Internet Tax Freedom Act (continually renewed, most recently in 2014), Congress has restricted federal and state authority to tax or to regulate electronic commerce. Municipalities lack authority regarding electronic commerce, according to the National League of Cities' 1999 adopted resolution advocating fair treatment of local retailers in the regulation of electronic commerce. Despite unclear authority, some cities have initiated sharable housing policy. San Francisco, for instance, embraced concerns as opportunity. As Mayor

Edwin M. Lee said as he signed a Residential Rentals Ordinance in October 2014, "As the birthplace of the emerging, more sustainable economy, San Francisco must be at the forefront of nurturing and regulating its growth by modernizing our laws and confronting emerging policy issues and concerns" (http://www.sfmayor.org/index.aspx?recordid=691&page=846).

In the Tucson example, a news report and citizen email reveal polarized politics surrounding a policy issue. A clue to the political discourse is the use of metaphors to frame the issue. The commission, the news writer, and the citizen argue by means of commonplace metaphors. In traditional rhetoric, commonplaces are general claims, observations, or descriptions that can be used on many occasions (Lanham, 169). In the Tucson example, proponents of regulation use sports metaphor ("playing by the rules" and "level the playing field") to image an orderly, secure world. Opponents use taking and climbing metaphors ("tax grab" "grasp any foothold") to image a disorderly, insecure world. These expressions evoke different visions of society, one cooperative and the other coercive. As rhetorical devices of persuasion, commonplace metaphors can bring people together or push them apart.

Tip to communicators: Be aware of familiar metaphors that occur intuitively as you write or speak. Use them consciously, deliberately, or don't use them. Keep in mind that local political culture powerfully influences perception of policy problems. Tucson's political culture is casual. The mayor and council could misinterpret a more formal rhetoric as pretentious and find it off-putting, so the commission chose to use informal, familiar sports metaphors.

The commission's initial task ended when its recommendation went to council. Having fulfilled its advisory mandate and respecting political protocol, the commission left next steps to the mayor and council. Those steps included convening stakeholders and getting in-depth economic analysis from the city's Finance Department.

Tip to communicators: For controversial topics, create a communication strategy, not only communication products. Make a plan for implementing your strategy that is sensitive to political protocol.

Example 4. Proposal

Scenario

Senior officers in the Surgeon General's Office have decided that another attempt to increase Reserve Armed Force eligibility for health care is justified. More frequent, longer lasting active deployments, increasing injury rates, and depleted state budgets for reservists' benefits motivate the new effort. The Chief of Patient Information has been persuasive, too. As anticipated, she is now tasked to write the necessary legislative documents. Collaboration with other specialist staff will be necessary. For example, as specialist for eligibility, she will gather dollar information and other numbers from the medical budget staff. When all information is in hand, she drafts a prescribed strategic planning document called a Unified Legislative and Budgeting Initiative. Before it can be submitted to her immediate supervisor, all the peer specialists in her office with whom she has consulted will review the draft. Upon submission, it will be reviewed by an eight-level chain of command beginning with her immediate supervisor, going on to the Secretary of the Army and all applicable staff experts, congressional liaison, and legal opinion to conclude, if necessary, with the Secretary of Defense. Any level of review may request changes, which she will make and then re-submit to the requesting reviewer.

FY 2011 Legislative Initiative
(Unified Legislation and Budgeting)
TITLE
Increase the Early Eligibility (EE) Period for TRICARE Benefits for Members of the Reserve Components

SHORT PROPOSAL DESCRIPTION
To initiate a Unified Legislation and Budgeting (ULB) proposal to enable Reserve Components to address the Secretary of Defense's changes to mobilization policy. Under this proposal, the effective date for the entitlement to early TRICARE benefits for members of the Reserve Components receiving alert orders to active duty would be the date of the issuance of

the alert order. Current law only provides 90 days of early TRICARE benefits for members of the Reserve Components. The current 90 day authorization does not provide sufficient advanced notice to allow Reserve Component members to take advantage of this benefit. This ULB does not propose a change to TRICARE coverage for military dependents or family members.

APPROXIMATE FULL YEAR COST ($M)

The current cost of this benefit to the government is $−− per service member, per year.

. . .

DISCUSSION OF REQUIREMENT AND RELATIONSHIP TO HR STRATEGY

After a member is identified, screened and determined to be qualified for deployment, on average, he or she has a short time to take advantage of the Early Eligibility Period for TRICARE Benefits. If a member of the Reserve Components is identified as non-deployable due to a medical issue, the current 90-day TRICARE benefit does not provide adequate time for the medical issue to be treated. Additionally, the current benefit does not allow a service member adequate time to rehabilitate after medical treatment, thus eliminating a pool of otherwise deployable resources. As a result, the Reserve Components are overrun with service members who are unable to mobilize, leaving unit readiness diminished dramatically.

Providing an early TRICARE benefit upon the receipt of an alert order to active duty would allow for the treatment, rehabilitation, and successful mobilization for countless service members. This benefit will enable the fullest utilization of the service member's training and experience, to ensure higher levels of unit readiness. Extending this benefit will also solidify unit cohesion and allow the Reserve Components to be more responsive to wartime requirements.

This proposal would allow Reserve Component service members the maximum use of Early Eligibility for TRICARE. Increasing the eligibility period in coordination with other Reserve Component initiatives for earlier alert notification will result in higher unit readiness and higher retention of service members.

BUSINESS CASE

Reserve Component service members do not currently have adequate time to utilize this benefit to identify, treat, and rehabilitate medically disqualifying issues prior to mobilization. This has a tremendous adverse impact not only on service members and their families, but more importantly, on unit readiness and national defense.

This proposal directly supports the Army Legislative Objective to reset the Force to ensure readiness for current and future challenges with full funding to restore units to levels of readiness required to successfully execute programmed operational deployments, future contingencies, and homeland defense missions.

This proposal will enable the reserve component service members to receive preventive care and treatments necessary to become fully medically ready. Extending this benefit to alert to mobilization will allow ample time during the Reset/Train Pool of the ARFORGEN cycle to increase the readiness percentage and bring the RAF force to a green status. In addition, this will allow leadership to focus on training, mobilization activities, increase unit readiness and most importantly increase the quality of life for the service member. DOD has a high interest is seeing a fully deployable RAF force.

All seven Reserve Components have a direct stake in seeing a change in the legislation for this benefit. The Army National Guard, the Air National Guard, the Army Reserves, the Air Force Reserves, the Marine Reserves, the Coast Guard Reserves, and the Naval Reserves would be greatly impacted.

Number of Personnel Affected

	Army	Navy	Marine Corps	Air Force
Number	54,000	6,000	4,000	12,000

RESOURCE REQUIREMENT ($M)

The Early Eligibility for Medical Benefits (EE) is funded by the Defense Health Program Association Fund. Due to limited resources, the RAF does not have funding for this proposal.

. . .

Note: This proposal requires a corresponding appropriation of funding for implementation.

COST METHODOLOGY

Cost factors include 76,000 Reserve Component service members mobilized annually. The current cost of this benefit to the government is $—per service member. (This data is based on the GAO TRICARE Reserve Select report 08-104, December 2007.) Currently there are 38,700 Soldiers deployed and eligible for this benefit. The estimated funding impact to provide twelve months worth of the EE benefit is $—M.

LEGISLATIVE LANGUAGE

Current Public Law 108–136, National Defense Authorization Act for Fiscal Year 2004, section 703 states "a member of the Reserve Components who is issued a delayed-effective date active duty order or is covered by such an order for a period of active duty of more than 30 days, in support of a contingency operation, as defined in 10 U.S.C. 101(a)(13)(B)., shall be eligible, along with the member's dependents, for TRICARE, on either the date of issuance of such an order, or 90 days prior to the date the active duty prescribed in the order, whichever is later."

This proposal will change Public Law 108–136 section 703 to read " . . . the effective date of active duty for purposes of entitlement to active duty health care of members of the Reserve Components of the Armed Forces receiving alert order anticipating a call or order to active duty in support of a contingency operation, shall be the date of the issuance of the alert order for the member's unit in anticipation of the mobilization of the unit for service for a period of more than 30 days in support of a contingency operation or the date of the issuance of the order providing for the assignment or attachment of the member to a unit subject to an alert order. The member's dependents shall be eligible for TRICARE 90 days prior to the date of active duty prescribed in the order."

This proposal does not impact any other section of the law.

SECTIONAL ANALYSIS

Pros

The proposal will dramatically improve medical readiness by allowing maximum time to identify and treat medical issues that may affect unit readiness and deployability.

Service members will have an increased ability to use the TRICARE Benefit throughout the entire alert period to identify and treat medical issues and to fully rehabilitate after medical treatment. This will ensure that Reserve Component units will be at a higher state of readiness and ensure the full use of each service member's skills and training.

Cons

The cost of this proposal is over $–– million over a five-year period. The RAF does not have funding for this proposal.

―――――

WHAT EXAMPLE 4 SHOWS. This internal proposal by a professional in government shows use of a prescribed template for proposing legislation. Example 4's pared-down style effectively utilizes tables of numbers. This communication's style fits its purpose and cultural context.

People familiar with unified legislative and budgeting initiatives as well as soldiers' health care needs will read and discuss this proposal in meetings. Consequently, it does not explain specialized terms such as TRICARE (current military health plan) or abbreviations such as FY2011 (fiscal year 2011).

The argument in Example 4 is strongly supported by evidence of need, examination of assumptions, legislative analysis, political analysis, and cost estimation. It is credible. However, it does not provide accountability by naming the presenter and intended recipient in the document shown here. Likely, an accompanying cover sheet or other tracking sheet did name them.

Summary and Preview

Requesting government action is an art. Artful know-how includes language awareness, especially of semantics, especially of metaphor. It also includes narrative awareness, especially of the story that calculations tell. Chapter 8, next, shifts the focus from language awareness to audience awareness when policy makers are the intended audience.

References

Internal Revenue Service. 2014. http:// www.irs.gov

Lanham, Richard A. 1991. *A handlist of rhetorical terms*, 2d edition. Berkeley: University of California Press.

Tocqueville, Alexis de. 1945. *Democracy in America*. Vol. 2. New York: Alfred A. Knopf. [Originally published 1840]

CHAPTER 8

Briefing, Opinion, Resolution: Inform Policy Makers

Key Concepts

- Brevity
- Politeness
- Values

Policy makers need information for making decisions. They usually prefer it in short, summary form. This chapter helps you to write three common genres of summary: briefing memo, opinion statement, and resolution. This chapter also shows a nonprofit organization's process of developing a policy position, expressed as a resolution, to inform advocacy.

Policy makers receive large amounts of unsolicited information and advice. They ignore most of it. Instead, they directly seek the information and advice they need. Active citizens and issue advocates can be good sources.

What kinds of information or advice do policy makers typically need? For consideration of a problem, general information might include assessments of events or conditions; arguments and critical analyses of arguments; reviews of policy options and technical analyses of the options; specialized topic reports; investigative reports; summaries of laws germane to the issue; legal counsel on interpretation of laws; and summaries of expert opinion, public opinion, and political advocacy. Beyond these general types of information, any single issue demands its own particular and detailed information.

For example, a municipality that is developing a comprehensive plan for land use will need general assessments of area conditions (environmental, economic, historic, and cultural factors), reports on current costs of providing services in the area (such as roads, water, and sewage treatment), summaries of relevant state laws (such as regulations governing municipal planning), and more. To apply general information to a specific municipality, its elected officials might ask county or state government agencies for local population statistics, economic projections, or environmental data. They might ask legal counsel to examine land-use planning tools, such as zoning ordinances in nearby municipalities, or to review case law on legal challenges to ordinances. To prepare for public discussion of draft plans and ordinances, the officials will seek political advice. They will want to know the opinion and advice of organized groups and individuals living in the municipality.

Who provides information to policy makers? It varies by level and branch of government. In federal and state legislatures, professional staff might produce much of the needed information. The staff might consult experts, analysts, and informed issue advocates or lobbyists. Knowhow, or familiarity with the policy process and understanding of the political context and interested actors, enables staff to gather information and inform legislators usefully. Staff members typically summarize their findings in briefing memos. In federal and state administrations, agency professional staff follows mandated procedures for collecting stakeholder and public comments to inform regulatory decision making. Chapter 10 provides examples of the federal and state process.

Municipal government differs from federal and state government in the size of staffs. Whereas large municipalities might be well staffed, smaller ones have small staffs or no staff. Consequently, local elected officials might do their own information gathering. They might utilize a range of information providers including experts (representing subject knowledge), advocacy and stakeholder groups (representing organized interests), legal counsels (representing rules and procedures), other officials and associations of elected officials (representing politics), and citizens (representing the opinion or experience of individuals or groups). Any of these providers might write an opinion or a briefing memo to inform an official's work of representation.

A briefing memo or opinion statement or resolution should be terse and targeted. They communicate pointed information to people who have too much to do and not enough time. Whether its topic is narrow or broad, a briefing memo offers only essentials targeted to a particular reader's need to know. Briefing memos are more compact than policy analysis memos or policy briefs, which are longer and include discussion, possibly with detailed appendices. Memos and opinions only summarize. The expected length is one to two pages. Resolutions might be even shorter. Writers should design content for quick comprehension and easy referral. Pages should have a header that rapidly identifies the document's contents; an opening summary (not an introduction); sections with subheadings to direct attention point by point; shorter sentences with one main idea per sentence; and only necessary words.

How to Inform Policy Makers in a Briefing Memo, Opinion Statement, or Resolution

Goal: Recognition of meaningful information in a mass of details and representation.

Objectives: Capability of distilling, relating details to context, interpreting details accurately in context, and selecting details according to relevance. Capability of efficiently stating informed opinion that is aware of and responsive to other opinions.

Product: One- to two-page written briefing memo or one- to two-paragraph opinion or one- to two-sentence resolution, possibly with attachments.

Scope: Only relevant topics in a specific context targeted to meet a particular information need.

Strategy: Use guiding questions to help you develop the document's contents. Apply all of the questions in the method (Chapter 2).

Task 1. Develop the Information

From meetings:

- Attend relevant public or private meetings; take full notes; get copies of the agenda and related documents; get contact information for participants.

- Jot (in the margins of the agenda) your own notes and questions about the proceedings, and capture (as nearly verbatim as you can) the significant questions asked by others.
- Contact participants, government staff, topic experts, or knowledgeable citizens for answers to questions or referrals to other sources immediately after the meeting.

From experts:

- Conduct information searches for relevant research and analysis.

From informed reflection and analysis:

- Update original questions and reframe the issues as information develops.
- Specify your own relevant experience.
- Pause periodically to summarize your understanding and to critically examine it.
- Continue to consult as needed to improve your understanding of the process and context.

Task 2. Write the Memo, Opinion Statement, or Resolution

Before you write, review the method in Chapter 2. Tailor your answers to its questions for your purpose and audience. Choose your genre of communication accordingly.

Craft the document's contents for quick comprehension and ready use. Do not include everything you know; include only what the user needs and what the purpose requires. You can provide more information later if necessary.

Choose the right presentation medium. If you are representing an organization, use its template (if it has one) for memos or policy statements. If you are free to design the communication, fit it into one or two welldesigned pages. If the situation demands, you might also use a cover letter or attachments. Note: before attaching anything crucial, consider the circumstances of reception, or how the document will be read and used. Attachments sometimes get detached when the document is circulated.

After drafting the communication, review and revise as needed (Two Checklists, Chapter 2). If you are pressed for time, revise only the overview to focus the message sharply. From the reader's perspective, that is most important.

Three Examples

A briefing memo and e-mails by active citizens (Examples 1 and 2) communicate opinion to local policy makers. A resolution by a national nonprofit (Example 3) articulates an advocacy position.

Example 1

Scenario

Local government officials anticipate a farmer's request to operate a concentrated animal feeding operation (CAFO) in the municipality. It will be the first request of its type made since the municipality adopted a comprehensive plan for land use and a zoning ordinance. In that ordinance, although it is ambiguous, CAFOs may be considered conditional uses of agricultural land to be permitted only if they meet site-specific conditions.

In preparation for reviewing the anticipated request and making a decision, the municipal official who chairs the planning commission begins to self-educate regarding CAFOs. His first objective is to become familiar with state law governing local authority to regulate CAFOs. He browses county and state government listservs; identifies technical and legal experts for possible consultation; attends relevant workshops, public hearings, and meetings; searches databases maintained by the state association of municipal officers and state government agencies; and searches municipal archives of public comment during the process of zoning adoption.

In a public meeting, he offers a preliminary interpretation of state law setting boundaries on municipal authority regarding CAFOs. A resident attending the meeting questions his interpretation. After the meeting, she offers to research the matter further. Given his lack of staff and the limited time he can devote to any single problem, he accepts her offer.

She locates the relevant state law and regulations online and reads them. She telephones state officials involved in authoring and implementing the regulations to ask about interpretations. They refer her to current case law on CAFOs and municipalities. Following up with the help of librarians in the state law school, she reads synopses of relevant current and pending cases.

Several days after the meeting in which she raised questions, she composes a one-page summary of findings and includes her interpretation of them. She e-mails the summary to the local official.

The sample briefing memo that follows was attached to an e-mail message.

E-MAIL MESSAGE

Doug,

I recognize that the township supervisors and planning commissioners are trying to operate within state law on CAFOs. It's a complicated task, and I appreciate the careful thought you are putting into it. My intention is to help by getting good advice on interpreting state regulations so that we rightly know what authority Gregg Township has regarding CAFOs.

You raised two concerns in the July meeting of township supervisors. In the attached memo, I report what I've found and what I think regarding those two concerns. Basically, I find and I believe that the township has the necessary standing and authority to regulate CAFOs. You might want to talk to Douglas Goodlander (my source in Harrisburg). I'll call you later this week to see if you want to talk about any of this.

Catherine

ATTACHMENT: MEMORANDUM
Summary
Gregg Township has zoned in the possibility of CAFOs, and it may regulate them within the limits of state law.

The Prohibition of CAFOs
You say, "You can't zone concentrated animal feeding operations out [prohibit them by means of zoning]." *Reference*: Pennsylvania State Association of Township Supervisors. See July issue of *PA Township News* for article "Avoiding Controversy: How Townships Can Minimize Conflicts between Residents and Intensive Ag Operations."

I say: Gregg has provided for the possibility of CAFOs operating in the township by making "feedlots" a conditional use in the agriculture zone. If "feedlots" can be construed to include CAFOs, then Gregg has "zoned in" the possibility. The zoning ordinance has a procedure for permitting, or not permitting, conditional uses based on case-by-case review for specified criteria. ***Source***: Gregg Township Zoning Ordinance, Article 3, Agricultural Zone, Conditional Uses, C.4 Feedlots (p. 10), and Article 9, Conditional Uses, C. Criteria (pp. 3–4).

Municipal Regulation of CAFOs

You say, "I read the state regulation as taking the wind out of our sails in regulating CAFOs." ***Reference***: The "pre-emption of local ordinances" provision of the Rules and Regulations, 25 PA Chapter 83 Subchapter D, 803.25 (b) for the Nutrient Management Act (3 P.S.1701 et seq.) published in the ***Pennsylvania Bulletin,*** Vol. 27, No. 26, June 28, 1997.

I say: municipalities can regulate CAFOs. The next section of 83.205 (part c) states that "nothing in this act or this subchapter prevents a municipality from adopting and enforcing ordinances or regulations that are consistent with/no more stringent than the state act." Beyond nutrient management [antipollution measures to prevent excess nutrients in animal manure from entering water sources], other issues presented by CAFOs such as odor, noise, air pollution, and road use can be locally regulated. ***Source***: Douglas Goodlander of the Pennsylvania Conservation Commission. Goodlander is an author of 25 PA [nutrient management regulations] who has been involved in CAFO court cases in PA. He cautions that he can provide interpretation but not legal counsel. He encourages you to call him if you want (telephone number provided).

━● WHAT EXAMPLE 1 SHOWS. Two characteristics of this communication are especially noteworthy: its e-mail form and its reliance on context for intelligibility. E-mail is typically more informal and personal and often has less regard for spelling or grammatical correctness. In a public process, if taken out of its original context, e-mail might embarrass the sender or recipient or it might compromise the action.

The intelligibility of this message relies on context. The sender and receiver have worked together before. They generally agree on the importance of local control in governance, but they might disagree on regulation of CAFOs. In the limited context of a policy process underway, they had been meeting and talking about this particular issue before this e-mail was sent. When the e-mail and its attachment are read together, they can be accurately understood in that general and limited context. However, if they are read outside the context or if the two documents are separated and one is read without the other, the communication might be misinterpreted.

Why does this matter? Correspondence with an elected official is open to public scrutiny. In addition, the e-mail and its attached memo will become part of a permanent public record. The elected official in this example is obliged to archive all communications on public matters and to make them available to anyone with a right to public information now or in the future. You may have seen cautionary evidence, such as the following notification at the end of a town officer's e-mail:

> Pursuant to North Carolina General Statutes Chapter 132, Public Records, this electronic mail message and any attachments hereto, as well as any electronic mail message(s) that may be sent in response to it, may be considered public record and as such are subject to request and review by anyone at any time.

Context affects intelligibility in another way, too. Tone, or attitude conveyed, depends on context. Without familiarity from prior experience working together, the memo's brisk tone might seem unfriendly to its recipient. (General Method, Chapter 2, advises you to consider the attitude a communication conveys.) How might this happen? Contrasting viewpoints are summarized in efficient parallelism ("You say, I say"). Only necessary words are used. Citations and contact information are strategically included to save time for the recipient, a busy official who does much of his own research. There is a downside to this efficiency, however. Although its intention might be to help, the briefing memo's terse style lacks the sympathetic tone of the covering e-mail that acknowledges the difficult problem the official must resolve. If the two documents are received separately or get filed in the wrong folder, the reader's reception might be affected as he quickly refers to the memo to prepare for a meeting.

Communication is more than an information exchange; it is also a social interaction. Empathy or writers' awareness of readers' circumstances affects readers' receptivity. Additionally, tone or the perceived attitude of a text can affect its reception and improve or damage a working relationship. (A wise communicator once said, "People might remember what you write or say to them. They will remember how you make them feel.") Recalling that policy makers receive lots of unsolicited communications and have too little time to absorb needed information, you should be aware that tone explains why some communications are ignored. Memos or statements that are expressly hostile or that seem closed-minded are not likely to be read, to receive a response, or to be useful to the process.

Example 2

Several more communications illustrate good tone and bad tone in statements of opinion. Citizens e-mailed these messages to an elected official in county government regarding a proposed merger of city and county schools.

Good tone. The following three opinion statements got the policy maker's careful attention and received a substantive reply.

A. You currently face a difficult decision regarding the proposed merger of [Town and County] Schools. I am writing to suggest a public referendum on this matter given the significant impact that the results of your decision will have on your constituency. Thanks for taking time to consider this request.

B. The merger discussion is heating up quickly, and I'm hoping the real issue of the disparate funding for the two systems doesn't get lost in the commotion. The push for a referendum, called for by so many [Town] parents, seems a veiled attempt to simply stifle discussion, allowing the real issue to again get swept under the rug, still unfixed.

C. Here are a few questions I'd love to have answered. I know you're busy and probably receiving hundreds (??!!) of emails daily on this issue. I hope you can fit me in.

1. Do you see a funding imbalance between the two systems?

. . .

We need a solution. Thank you for considering my questions.

Bad tone. In contrast, the following three opinion statements (like many similar ones generated by a letter-writing campaign) got little attention and received no reply.

A. I understand that the [County] Board of Commissioners is evaluating a merger of the [Town and County] School Systems. I would like to communicate that:

• I, along with most of my local colleagues and neighbors, are vehemently OPPOSED to a merger.

• I request that a public REFERENDUM be held on this issue ASAP.

- Unless proper procedure is followed throughout, a proposed merger will be challenged in the [State] and Federal courts to the extent necessary.

- The voting records of the entire board will be well remembered and publicized in time for the next ELECTION.

B. I am greatly disappointed in your decision Wednesday night to short circuit democracy in our county. None of you ran last November with a position on school merger. You have suddenly sprung it on the citizens of the county. Since you would not face voters on the issue, you should allow a referendum on the issue in the county. Otherwise, you should delay the issue until an election year, and run on your beliefs. The idea that you can have a "stealth" merger of school systems and avoid the will of the citizens of the county, as some of you seem to believe, is not in keeping with the traditions of transparency and progressive politics in our county. I voted for you all last November. But I did not vote for school merger. Now I feel that your election was as much a sham. I would like a chance to vote on school merger or to vote again on your positions on the county commission.

C. I am very concerned about an article in the *Herald* which indicates that the schools in [County and Town] may merge. I don't understand what the advantage of such a move would be. If there is an advantage to the move please let me know what it is. If there is no advantage to the move, please let me know by ignoring this message.

WHAT EXAMPLE 2 SHOWS. These emails teach communicators to make careful choices. A public policy communicator must make many competing choices. Purpose, contents, presentation style and tone, medium of delivery, and concern for immediate reception and use as well as the permanent record all must be considered and choices made. The choices are important because the consequences are significant. The outcomes of policy affect real people and places.

Examples 1 and 2 show active citizens attempting to influence local policies. In Example 3, a nonprofit organization empowers its members by articulating a policy position they can advocate. The development of that organization's policy position is described. It starts with an individual member who cares deeply about the issue.

The scenario shows the process he followed to achieve a consensus and craft a policy statement at state and national levels.

Scenario

After years of working in finance and international banking in Tokyo and New York, an economist returned to farming and political activism in his home state, Wisconsin. With his wife and family, he now sells cattle as a cash crop and vegetables as value-added farm products for local markets. Distressed by the continued worsening of farm economics in which wealth from farms is transferred to agribusiness and subsidizes U.S. consumers, he tries in various ways to invigorate support of family farming by the Wisconsin Farmers Union (WFU). He works to strengthen advocacy by the National Farmers Union (NFU) for structural changes to revitalize agriculture. As a WFU director and NFU policy committee member, he regularly draws on his experience in banking, finance, and farming to draft policy positions. He writes issue analyses for farming publications and he proposes resolutions to the state WFU and the NFU. He shepherds the resolutions through the NFU's hierarchical, deliberative policymaking process.

Here's how the NFU policy process works: Members submit draft policy proposals to the NFU resolutions committee, preferably through a state chapter president or delegate, sometime before February prior to the annual national convention in March. The proposals may have been already adopted by a state chapter of the NFU or they may originate at the national level. Alternatively, a member may submit a proposal at the annual national convention by going before the resolutions committee with draft copies and persuading the committee to bring the proposal to the convention floor. Or, a member may bring a proposal to the floor directly (best if presented by an official delegate) with enough copies to distribute to all delegates in attendance.

On the floor at the appropriate time that delegates are reviewing and voting on outstanding policy, amendments, and addenda according to procedure stated in the NFU policy manual, the proposer is given two or five minutes to explain and advocate the policy proposal. Delegates may respond, question, or criticize the proposal. The proposer is then given two minutes to respond. Under Robert's rules of order, the proposal can then be motioned, seconded, and openly discussed. As the proposer in this example remarks from experience at state and national conventions, contentious discussion might carry on for an hour or more until a vote is called.

In 2014, this proposer offered five resolutions. The NFU adopted one, a resolution advocating reduction of profit taking by agricultural manufacturers. That resolution is shown here in proposed and adopted forms.

Example 3

RESOLUTION. PROPOSED WISCONSIN FARMERS UNION POLICY
"Excessive Profit-Taking by Manufacturers of Farm Inputs"

- Whereas the manufacturers of fertilizer and seed in the case of grain farming have benefitted excessively from historically cheap cost of production and high net sales prices;
- Whereas these manufacturers have generated over the past five years gross margin ratios in excess of 40% and returns on equity exceeding 20% while farmers earn on average historically equity returns of two to six percent;
- Whereas major farm equipment makers over the past five years have shown returns on equity between 20 and 30 percent;
- Whereas our farmer cooperatives have roughly demonstrated returns on equity around 10 percent;
- Whereas we as farmers are increasingly transferring wealth off our farms with time-risk factors far greater than manufacturers of farm inputs and we are effectively subsidizing and padding the bottom lines of these manufacturers and agri-business;
- Whereas the growing phenomenon of concentration of wealth and income in the US in the hands of a few to the detriment of the majority, particularly the middle and lower classes, is demonstratively witnessed in increasing profitability of farm input manufacturers;
- Whereas if profits are not raised for farmers, there will be increasingly a concentration of farm production in fewer producers and force more small and mid-size traditional farmers from the industry;

The Wisconsin Farmers Union hereby calls for pressure and influence to be placed on manufacturers of farm inputs by our members and our member-controlled cooperatives to reduce manufacturers' level of profitability at the expense of farmers with their diminishing returns and to advocate that our congressional representatives reduce or eliminate tax benefits and credits afforded by Congress to companies earning enormous return ratios.

ADOPTED NATIONAL FARMERS UNION POLICY
"Profit-taking by Manufacturers of Farm Inputs"
   We call for all farmers and member-driven and -controlled cooperatives to place pressure and influence on manufacturers of farm inputs to reduce the manufacturers' level of profitability at the expense of farmers. (http://www.nfu.org/policy-nfu/current-nfu-policy/)

WHAT THIS EXAMPLE SHOWS. In governmental communication, resolutions are substantive as opposed to procedural. Resolutions express a body's approval or disapproval of something that it cannot vote on because it lacks jurisdiction or because the matter is being handled by another body. Resolutions identify applicable principles, but they do not address methods and means of enforcement. Proposing a resolution is an appropriate way to articulate values, whether or not they are actionable.

As political expression, the WFU proposed resolution strategically uses symbolic representation in the form of naming, narrative or causal story, and numbers. The writer names the issue excessive profit-taking to connote extremity, lack of balance. That problematic extremity contributes to a problem, decline of family farming. In the causal story, excessively profitable manufacturers and subsidized consumers are the bad guys; farmers are the good guys. Numbers or percentages of profitability are the details that tell readers how the bad guys' profits depress the good guys' profits. In this story, traditional family farms are the victims, and manufacturers along with subsidized consumers are the villains. Naming and narrative are deliberately used for their emotional power in this example. They show a skillful interpreter of agricultural economic conditions defining a problem as he sees it in compelling terms. They imply threat to values of fairness and balance. In summary, the WFU proposed resolution uses multiple devices to express a perceived need for action.

Notably, the NFU adopted resolution omits these devices and shrinks the scope of recommended action. Emerging from the national organization's policy process, the final resolution is terse. In few words, the NFU states its consensus on the issue. NFU's intended impact is large, however. By adopting and publishing the resolution in its policy manual, the NFU authorizes members nationally to pressure manufacturers of farming supplies. As added value for political communication purposes, the policy statement's simplicity and brevity make it useful for referral when NFU members lobby elected representatives. In face-to-face meetings with legislators and their staff, NFU members can fill in the picture with details of their personal experience as farmers.

Summary and Preview

Opinion and information are vital to policy making. Information for a purpose and for targeted readers is characteristic. This chapter focuses on three common ways of informing policy makers in a pointed manner. A briefing memo is the written equivalent of a one-minute "elevator speech" or a one-minute oral summary of testimony. A written statement of opinion is the equivalent of a voicemail message. A resolution is the equivalent of a public announcement. The tone of such communications should be professional. Politeness is highly valued in the cultural context of public policy making. Concision is highly valued, too.

In Chapter 9 you'll learn about another way of informing policy makers, testifying as a witness in public hearings. Politeness and concision matter there, too, as witnesses and elected officials interact face to face.

Further Reading

Stone, D. (2102). Symbols (Chap. 7) and Causes (Chap. 9). In *Policy paradox: The art of political decision making* (3rd ed.). New York, NY: Norton.

Testimony: Witness in a Public Hearing

Key Concepts

- Write to speak
- Prepare to answer questions
- Argue by storytelling

Witnesses in governmental public hearings offer valuable knowledge to policy makers and administrators. Public hearings are a rare opportunity for elected officials to question witnesses in-depth and receive informed response. For witnesses, hearings are opportunities to influence policy outcomes. Witness testimony adds information and insight to political decision making. This chapter prepares you to testify as a witness in a public hearing.

In the U.S. federal government, "sunshine" or public access laws mandate open hearings for all legislative functions—making law, appropriating funds, overseeing government operations, investigating abuse or wrongdoing, and approving nominations or appointments to office. Hearings are held in executive and legislative branches of federal government. In state and local governments, public deliberation is mandated, but public hearings are not commonly held except for specific actions that require public comment. Adoption of a local ordinance requires a hearing, for example.

In government bodies organized by a political party structure such as the U.S. Congress, the majority party (the party in power) chairs committees and thus sets the agenda for committee work, including public hearings. Committee chairs (with their staffs) decide whether to hold a hearing on a topic within their jurisdiction, what the purpose of a hearing will be, and who will be on the witness list. Topics and purposes of hearings reflect the committee's jurisdiction and the chair's political agenda. The agenda might or might not reflect cooperation between the majority and minority interests of members on the committee.

Several committees might hold hearings on different aspects of the same topic, especially if the topic concerns a hot issue that crosses jurisdictions. Hot issues are those that are currently in the news, controversial, or especially significant in some way. Most hearings are not about hot issues, however. Most hearings are workaday sessions to oversee government operations, to decide on appropriations of funds, to reauthorize programs, and so forth. They do the routine work of governance.

Public affairs television usually does not broadcast these routine hearings. Selected daily hearings are summarized on the government page of newspapers and some advocacy group websites. Some congressional committee websites broadcast hearings in progress.

In the executive branch, departments or agencies hold public hearings on issues within their regulatory responsibility. Some are held in the field, in geographic areas or political districts directly affected. Executive branch hearings vary in format from informal public meetings to formal deliberative sessions.

In principle, anyone might be invited to testify who can provide information that lawmakers or administrators seek. In reality, witnesses testify at the federal level only by request of the committee. At state and local levels, the witness list is more open. There, you may be invited, or you may ask, to testify. If you wish to testify, you contact the staff of the committee or the agency holding the hearing.

In the communication situation of a typical hearing, witnesses testify as spokespersons for an organization or a government agency.

Occasionally, individual citizens testify on their own or their community's behalf. Witnesses must relate their special concerns to a policy context and their agendas to other agendas. Policy makers and witnesses interact face to face, and exchanges might be polite or confrontational. Questioning might be focused or loose.

Questioning is always political, and sometimes it is bluntly partisan. The atmosphere might be orderly or hectic. The time limits are always tight—typically one to five minutes for each witness to present testimony and five minutes for each member to question all the witnesses. There might be multiple rounds of questioning. Hearings can last for hours or days if the committee or the witness list is large.

Legislative hearings are characteristically more freeform than legal hearings in the administration of justice. In legislative hearings, generally, there are no prescribed rules for disclosing evidence or for objecting to questions as there are in law court hearings. Exceptions are investigative hearings in which witnesses might testify under oath. Even then, questioning is not constrained by rules. Consequently, witnesses for legislative hearings must prepare well for anticipated and unanticipated developments in the question-and-answer session that follows presentation (Smith, 1993).

Everything communicated in a hearing goes (via a legislative stenographer) into a transcript. This transcript is the official public record of the hearing. There are actually two public records, unofficial and official. Unofficially, the hearing might be broadcast and reported by news media followed by commentary in all media. These influential accounts shape public discourse and the perception of problems; however, they are not authoritative. They would not be included in a legislative history, for example. For the authoritative and official record of a hearing, a stenographer records the statements, questions, and answers verbatim, exactly as they are given. In current legislative reporting practice, the verbatim transcript cannot be edited, except to correct factual errors.

The transcript is later (sometimes months later) printed and published by the superintendent of government documents through the government printing office. This is the official, or legal, record of the hearing. Published hearing records are important for democratic self-governance because they give continuing public access over time to the accurate and full information produced by a hearing. That information is useful for many purposes. Journalists, law clerks, academic researchers in many fields, legislative staff, lobbyists, advocates, and active citizens use hearing transcripts as sources. Published hearings are primary sources for legislative history research, for example. They are also major sources for determining a law's original intent when the law is being adjudicated.

In the overall significance of government hearings for democracy, witness testimony is most important. For witnesses, it is an opportunity to bring concerns to the table, to talk directly with policy makers, and to make personal or professional knowledge useful for solving problems. For policy makers, hearings offer a rare opportunity to talk directly with knowledgeable witnesses and to question them. Policy makers appreciate that interaction. Most information they receive is filtered through staff or advisors. They like having the chance to interact with other sources of information and perspective.

How to Deliver Oral Testimony Based on a Written Statement

Goal: To speak authoritatively and to answer questions responsively in public deliberation.

Objective: Skill of writing speakable text, skill of speaking easily from written text, and readiness to answer anticipated and unanticipated questions.

Scope: Pinpointed topic pertinent to a hearing's purpose and the witness's role.

Product: Two expected communication products are as follows:

- Short oral summary, either a list of talking points (outline for speaking) or a one-page overview (to be read aloud).

- Full written statement, possibly with appendices, to be included in the record of the hearing.

Strategy: Confident and useful public testimony resulting from advance preparation.

Develop a Testimony in Context

Obviously, witnesses must know their subject and their message. Equally important, witnesses must understand the purpose(s) of the hearing and their own role and purpose(s) for testifying. Effective witnessing is achieved by presenting concisely and by responding credibly to questions. Responding to questions effectively is most important. If you are on the witness list, you are acknowledged as having something relevant to say. You do not need to impress people by showing how much you know about the topic. Focus strongly on your purpose and your message in relation to the hearing's purpose.

> *Know the context.* To what policy process does the hearing relate? To what political agenda? Who's holding the hearing? What is the stated purpose of the hearing? What is the political purpose? Who else is on the witness list? What are their messages likely to be?
>
> *Know your message.* Distill your message into one to two sentences that you can remember and can say easily. How does your message relate to the purpose of the hearing? How does it relate to other witnesses' messages? Anticipate committee members' responses and questions. What are you likely to be asked?
>
> *Know your role.* Are you speaking for an organization? For yourself? Why are you testifying? What do the organizers of the hearing hope your testimony will accomplish?
>
> *Know the communication situation.* Will the press attend the hearing? Are you available for interviews after the hearing? Will the hearing be televised? How is the hearing room arranged? Do the arrangements allow you to use the charts, posters, or slides? Are those visual aids a good idea if the room lights cannot be dimmed (because of televising the hearing)? What is the location for the hearing? If you are using charts, posters, or slides, how will you transport them? Who will set them up in the hearing room?
>
> *Rehearse your delivery.* Will you read your statement or say it? Generally, saying it is preferred. Be ready to do either, however. Rehearse by reading the full statement aloud and by speaking from an outline. You'll discover which way is easier for you and which you need to practice more.

Task 1. Write the Testimony

Use the method (Chapter 2) to plan testimony in both oral and written forms. Some witnesses prefer to outline the oral summary first and then to develop the full written statement from that outline. Others prefer the opposite way. They write the full statement first; then they outline an oral summary based on the written statement.

The key to both? Preparation. Write out your oral summary, even if it is simply a list of talking points on an index card. The written list will provide confidence and control as you testify. Recall that everything said in a governmental public hearing is recorded and that the record is made publicly available. Do not plan to wing it or to testify extemporaneously. If you do that, you risk exceeding time limits, which committee chairs do not like. And you might forget important information, say more or less than you intend to have on the public record, or find yourself being asked questions (about something you said) that you are not prepared to answer.

If you are free to organize your testimony, you might want to use the following template. Use it in outline form for the oral summary, and expand it appropriately for the full written statement. Put extensive support in appendices, not in the main statement. (Both the oral and the written versions will be included in the transcript of the hearing.) Here is the template:

- Title page or header to identify the organization and the witness, the agency holding the hearing, the topic, the date, and the location of the hearing;

- Greeting to thank the organizers for the opportunity to testify and to state why the topic is important to the witness;

- Message to state the main information the testimony provides;

- Support (evidence, grounds) for the message;

- Relevance of the message to the hearing's purpose;

- Optional: discussion or background to add perspective on the message (only if relevant or if specifically requested by conveners of the hearing); and

- Closing to conclude the testimony and invite questions.

Task 2. Write the Full Statement

The written statement might use the same organization as the oral summary. The written statement may be longer, include more details, and be accompanied by appendices. It can be any length, but it should be no longer than necessary. Even if the written statement is lengthy, it must be organized and concise. Good organization enables you to condense on demand. If, for example, you are asked by the committee chair to limit your remarks, you should only present your message, state its relevance to the hearing's purpose, and conclude by saying that you will be glad to answer questions. During the question-and-answer period, you can add content omitted from your summary.

Task 3. Present the Testimony

The following tips are important.

- Summarize. During oral delivery, whether reading a document aloud or speaking from an outline, state only the essentials. Save the details for the question-and-answer period.

- State the message early and emphatically. Whether reading a text or speaking from an outline, state the message up front.

- Stay within time limits. Usually, the chair of a hearing will tell you the time limits. If not, assume that you have two to five minutes for a summary. Do not go over the limit.

- Listen. Closely attend to the opening statements by the committee chair and the committee members. Opening statements cue the questions that you might be asked. Or they might include content to which you want to respond later, when it is your turn to speak. Listen also to other testimonies. Committee members might ask you to comment on other witnesses' remarks.

- Answer credibly. The question-and-answer time is often the most important part of a hearing. Committee members and witnesses alike agree on this. For committee members, it is a chance to interact directly with knowledgeable people. Members usually ask prepared questions to get important concerns, as well as witnesses' responses to the concerns, on the record. For witnesses, the question-and-answer time is a chance to connect their message to varied agendas represented in the questions or to pinpoint the usefulness of their knowledge to the committee. Witness effectiveness depends primarily on the witness's credible (honest, accurately informed, relevant) responsiveness to questioning.

When you have presented your testimony statement, you are not finished. Shift your attention to questioning. Follow these important guidelines:

- Listen to the questions asked of other witnesses. Do not daydream or otherwise lose focus while others are being questioned.

- Make sure you hear each question correctly when you are being questioned. If you are not sure you heard the question correctly, ask to have it repeated.

- Answer the question that is asked, not some other question that you half heard or that you prefer.

- Stop when you have answered a question. Wait for a follow-up question. Postpone details, elaboration, or qualification on your original answer until a follow-up question allows you to provide them.

- Do not lie or invent information. If you hear yourself fabricating an answer (perhaps out of nervousness), stop. Politely ask to have your answer removed from the record and begin again.

- Handle these situations especially carefully:

  - You are asked for your personal opinion. When you testify as spokesperson for an organization, be careful to present the organization's viewpoint. Avoid giving a personal opinion unless specifically requested, and then only if you appropriately can do so. If you do, be careful to distinguish your own view from that of the organization.

  - You don't know the answer. Depending on the dynamics at the moment (neutral or friendly or confrontational) and considering the effect on your credibility of not answering, you might choose among these options: simply say you do not know, say you are not prepared to answer but can provide the answer later, ask whether you might restate the question in a different way that you can better answer, or defer to another witness who can better answer the question.

  - Your credentials are challenged or your credibility is attacked. Do not get angry. Politely state your or your organization's qualifications to speak on the topic of the hearing. Restate why you are testifying or why the hearing topic is important to you or your organization. Maintain your role in the hearing as a source of information and perspective not offered by others. Maintain your composure.

Two Examples

Many examples of written testimony can be found on the websites of respected nonprofit organizations, public policy institutes, and government agencies. For instance, see U.S. Government Accountability Office Reports and Testimonies (http://www.gao.gov/). Example 1 on military health-care benefits was written by the professional in federal government shown previously (Example 1, Chapter 3; Example 4, Chapter 7). She wrote the statement for oral presentation by her supervisor as witness. Example 2 was written by a law student intern for a nonprofit organization to be submitted for the hearing record. Scenarios remind you of the context for Example 1 and introduce the context for Example 2.

Example 1

Scenario

The Office of the Chief Surgeon, Reserve Armed Forces, is asked by interested congressional offices to justify the request for increased health-care benefits for Reserve Component Soldiers. The House Armed Services Committee asks for a witness to testify in an upcoming hearing, specifically to justify increased dental-care benefits. Senior officers are unavailable to write the testimony. The Chief of Patient Information is asked to draft a statement making the case for more dental care. A senior officer will orally deliver the testimony as witness. Delegation of writing or "ghost-writing" is characteristic in her workplace, as in others. The work of many professionals may be present, unidentified, in a document that carries only the organization's name and perhaps the name of the head administrator.

This action officer has not previously written congressional testimony. She is uncertain about the genre. Also, she does not know the committee's political agenda and related purpose for this hearing. She has little experience in writing for congressional audiences. She has not attended a hearing. There are no guidelines for writing congressional testimony and there is no template for a witness statement in the Army manual of procedure or style. As an astute professional communicator, however, she knows that context, genre, purpose, and audience are as important as message. So, despite a hectic schedule, she makes the time to prepare for writing. She consults textbooks on policy writing and government writing. She searches the Internet for samples of testimony by government witnesses. Reading actual samples gives her a feel for the expected form. Asking experienced peers about the committee gives her a sense of the context. She drafts a statement and circulates it in her office for specialist review of content. She also sends it to a friend in another office, an experienced staff member for a senator who serves on relevant committees. The friend provides informal contextual review. Once formal review by staff is completed, the document comes back to the action officer. She makes all changes, and then she gives the document to the senior officer who will be the witness. He reviews and requests changes, which she makes. She briefs the witness on the testimony's topic. Before the committee hearing date, a "mock"

> hearing will be held involving key participants from all agencies who
> reviewed the statement.

Unclassified
Statement by Colonel Michael Flynn
Chief Surgeon of the Reserve Armed Forces of America
Before the House Armed Services Committee
Subcommittee on Oversight and Investigation
Second Session, 110th Congress
on
Dental Readiness in the Reserve Armed Forces of America

May 17, 2008

Chairman Smith, Ranking Member Clay, as the Chief Surgeon of the Reserve
Armed Forces of America, I am here today to answer your concerns about
the dental readiness of the Soldiers in the Reserve Armed Forces of America.

The interest of the subcommittee on this issue is well placed. Dental
readiness of our Citizen-Soldiers is a critical element in their capability to
meet Department of Defense requirements for deployment.

Current Situation
The transition from a Strategic Reserve to an Operational Force has placed
tremendous strain on the Reserve Armed Forces of America. Historically,
as a strategic reserve, Soldiers and leaders of the Reserve Armed Forces
addressed dental readiness issues at the mobilization station. The implementation of the Department of Defense's twelve month mobilization
policy in February 2007 forced units to address dental readiness at home
station in order to maximize collective training at the mobilization station.

The Reserve Armed Forces Medical Team, in conjunction with our
Armed Forces Dental Command partners, has successfully managed this
transition to an Operational Force. Since the beginning of the fiscal year,
our units have prepared seven Brigade Combat Units (BCUs) for deployment, with each unit sending their units to the mobilization station over
90% dentally ready. These incredible readiness rates are a tremendous
improvement over their previous mobilizations in 2003, when the average dental readiness rate was 13%. This significant decrease in the number
of training days lost to dental treatment at mobilization station has

enabled commanders to focus on collective training and maximize boots-on-ground time in theater.

Due to the low level of baseline dental readiness in the Reserve Armed Forces—currently only 40% of the force is dentally ready to deploy—truly herculean efforts must be applied by our units once a unit is alerted. Dental activities compete for the time of leaders, Soldiers, and families as a unit prepares to go to war. Soldiers that are cross-leveled to a ready unit dilute that unit's readiness and lengthen training timelines.

In order to improve the baseline readiness of the Reserve Armed Forces, the same programs, policies, and procedures that have been used to successfully prepare these BCUs need to be applied to our force as a whole.

Actions Taken

The Reserve Armed Forces, in conjunction with the Office of the Surgeon General and the Armed Forces Dental Command, has developed a multifaceted plan that has been approved by both the Army and Reserve Armed Forces leadership.

The cornerstone of this plan is the ability to provide dental treatment to our Soldiers outside of alert.

. . .

The Armed Forces Selected Reserve Dental Readiness Program (SRDRP) will enable units to provide dental treatment to soldiers through local contracts or utilizing the Reserve Health Readiness Program (RHRP).

The Reserve Armed Forces is a true reflection of our nation, and very few of our Citizen-Soldiers have private dental insurance. The participation rate in the TRICARE Reserve Dental Program has hit a plateau at 8%. The ability to provide treatment to our soldiers through the Armed Forces Selected Reserve Dental Readiness Program will have a tremendous impact on the readiness of the Reserve Armed Forces.

This program will also enable the Reserve Armed Forces to maximize the benefits of the Armed Forces Dental Command's initiatives.

. . .

With treatment programs in place, we must also address barriers to compliance with readiness requirements. Active component soldiers do not take unpaid leave to go to the dentist, nor should a Reserve Armed Forces soldier. The ability to provide two medical readiness days per soldier would be a powerful incentive for the soldier to complete readiness requirements, as well as a tool for our commanders to ensure compliance.

. . .

In addition to treatment and incentives, there must be enforcement as recommended by the Commission on Reserve Affairs. As alerted units prepare to go overseas, dental readiness is consistently the main reason for soldier ineligibility for deployment. The Armed Forces have multiple systems which provide unit and senior leaders the capability to track a unit's progress as they prepare for deployment. . . . These tools must be applied and dental readiness enforced by leaders at all levels throughout the Reserve Armed Forces to improve the readiness of our soldiers.

Lastly, in order to execute these programs and sustain an increase in the dental readiness of the Reserve Armed Forces, we must have the appropriate staffing. The Reserve Armed Forces dental corps is currently less than 70% strength, and the majority of remaining providers are eligible for retirement. This committee is considering the Department of Defense's request to increase the retirement age of Reserve Armed Forces healthcare providers from age 65 to age 69. This would create the same standard for all three components of service. I would ask that this committee support that request and make that adjustment to the law.

. . .

Likewise, as a reserve component consisting largely of part-time warriors, the Reserve Armed Forces relies heavily on its cadre of full-time personnel to do the administration, maintenance, and training preparation required to produce a ready force. The president's budget request currently before Congress seeks an increase in the level of full-time manning in our force. This is critical. We urge Congress to support this increase.

Conclusion

This is a very exciting time to be in the Reserve Armed Forces. We have deployed over 300,000 dentally ready soldiers in support of the nation since September 11th 2001. Even so, we can do better. The Army and the Reserve Armed Forces are committed to our Citizen-Soldiers, by caring for them and improving their dental readiness.

I am grateful for this opportunity to appear before this subcommittee and look forward to answering your questions.

► **WHAT THIS EXAMPLE SHOWS.** The testimony writer's consideration of semantics, or word meanings, is noteworthy. "It is surprising how easily the right words can improve understanding and the wrong ones can mire us in confusion" (Bardach, 2011, p. 133). Sensitivity to politics surrounding Reserve Armed Forces health care in general, and dental care in particular, is shown here by careful word choice, such as "dental readiness" and "successfully managed transition" and "tremendous improvement." These wordings characterize achievement under difficult working conditions. Careful choice of organization is also evident. The testimony is organized narratively to tell a story of good management in a trying situation. These presentation techniques, deliberate word choice and storytelling, are not deceptive. They are not spin. Rather, they are ethical (accurate, demonstrable) and rhetorically effective (credible) ways to characterize the organization's definition of the problem and message. Implicit meaning fits explicit statement well. The example illustrates an important aspect of policy writing: care for the meaningful interpretation of policy language. The words used to characterize a problem influence perception and action. "Political fights are conducted with money, with rules, with votes, and with favors, to be sure, but they are conducted above all with words and ideas" (Stone, 2012, p. 36).

Example 2

Scenario

A rural county of a southeastern state has a dwindling population living in or near small, scattered towns. The historically agricultural region is characterized by diminishing wooded wetlands near rivers, large commodity crop farms, corporately owned industrial livestock farms, and meat-processing facilities. Farming, meatpacking, a state prison system, a public school district, and service facilities along the region's only major highway offer low-wage employment. There is little to encourage many residents to stay, former residents to return, and developers to come. In response to these conditions, a significant number of the county's African American residents have become community advocates and political activists. Postwar migration in the 1940s and 1950s motivated by New Deal agriculture policy and federally subsidized mortgages for affordable land and homes brought urban families to take up farming this rural area. Among the successful farmers, African American leaders achieved rural electrification, farm financing parity, voting rights equity, community-based schools, community centers, and businesses un-related to farming.

A descendant of these leaders entered postgraduate training to become an attorney. In the The University of the District of Columbia David A. Clarke School of Law, he acted as student attorney to meet clients' varied needs for legal assistance. With other student witnesses, he testified in a District Council public hearing about conditions in District public housing.

Between semesters, he interned for the nonprofit Rural Coalition with headquarters in the District. As a Legal Fellow of the Coalition representing U.S. and Mexico farmworker organizations and indigenous communities, he developed congressional hearing testimony on various topics. For the example shown here, he coordinated staff contributions and editorial assistance to produce the Rural Coalition statement for the record of a Senate Judiciary Committee hearing on reform of the Voting Rights Act. Extracts from that statement follow.

Statement of
Gary R. Redding, Legal Fellow
On behalf
of the Rural Coalition
for The United States Senate Committee on the Judiciary

For inclusion in the record for the hearing entitled,
"From Selma to Shelby County: Working Together to Restore the
Protections of the Voting Rights Act"

Washington, D.C.
July 24, 2013
Assuring Voting Rights for Rural and Farm Communities

For forty-eight years, the Voting Rights Act has been a historic law benefitting the masses of U.S. citizens in their quest to participate equally in America's democratic political process. The current and potential threats to citizens' voting rights inform us that the Act is necessary even today. We must now modernize the Act to reflect the realities of today's political landscape. This statement provides a brief overview of past and present voting conditions and limitations in rural and farm communities and the implications of Section 2 of the Voting Rights Act in the wake of the *Shelby County, Alabama v. Holder* U.S. Supreme Court decision. Our statement provides conclusions and recommendations for updating Section 4 of the Voting Rights Act and making the process for reporting voting rights violations more straightforward and practical.

The Voting Rights Act, a codification of the Fifteenth Amendment to the U.S. Constitution, prohibits states from requiring any "voting qualification or prerequisite to voting, or standard, practice, or procedure . . . to deny or abridge the right of any citizen of the United States to vote on account of race or color" 42 U.S.C. § 1973(a). . . . Thanks to workers in the Civil Rights Movement and citizens particularly in rural communities, many of whom are still active in the Rural Coalition, the Voting Rights Act was enacted in 1965 and has been continually reauthorized, most recently in 2006.

Yet in 2013, many residents in rural and farm communities across America continue to face many of the voting challenges in local, state, and national elections that people in 1965 faced when the Voting Rights Act was passed. Even today, a high percentage of people remain who have difficulty acquiring information about the candidates and the issues. Factors that impede their participation include poor and often-times still segregated education systems that have left them unable to fully read and comprehend information about candidates and issues. Lack of access to electricity, computers, and the Internet in their homes and communities also limits their ability to follow news, watch political debates, and otherwise acquire critical information. Senior citizens, especially, still struggle to find transportation to and from voting precincts, which can sometimes be thirty or more miles away from their rural homes. Furthermore, the political process that is supposed to promote voter turnout often discourages or prevents people from voting.

In 1993, the U.S. Congress enacted the National Voter Registration Act (NVRA) to make voting more convenient and accessible by providing a NVRA form for prospective voters to register to vote, update their registration information, or register with a particular political party.

. . .

Despite these federal provisions and protections, proponents of restrictive voting requirements at the state level have in recent times proposed numerous laws to make voting even more difficult. Though each state differs in the particulars, the overall effect reduces voter participation. Opponents of these restrictive voting requirements and others also argue that they disproportionately target communities of color, the elderly, and youth.

. . .

In addition to . . . widespread attempts to weaken federal voting rights protections with new or excessive requirements and restrictions, some states are trying to nullify it altogether. *Shelby County, Alabama v. Holder* is the most recent case to come before the Supreme Court. Shelby County, a mostly white suburb of Birmingham, sought to invalidate Sections 4 and 5 of the 1965 Voting Rights Act by claiming they were being punished unfairly for decades old discrimination. Section 5 requires all or parts of sixteen states with a history of racial discrimination in voting to get federal approval before implementing changes to their voting laws. It applied to all or part of the following: Alabama, Alaska, Arizona, Georgia, Louisiana, Mississippi, South Carolina, Texas, and Virginia; forty counties in North Carolina, five in Florida, four in California, three in New York, two in South Dakota, as well as ten towns in New Hampshire, and two townships in Michigan. Congress chose all or parts of these sixteen states using a formula in Section 4 to identify where racially discriminatory voting practices had been more prevalent. In 2006, Congress reauthorized Sections 4 and 5 of the Voting Rights Act for another twenty-five years.

Shelby County argued that Sections 4 and 5 should be discontinued because its current political conditions are no longer racially discriminatory.

. . .

Reporting on voting rights violations poses special challenges for the estimated "46.2 million people, or 15 percent of the U.S. population, [who] reside in rural counties." Hope Yen and Hannah Dreier, *Census: Rural US loses population for the first time,* Yahoo News (June 13, 2013), http://news.yahoo.com/census-rural-us-loses-population-first-time-040425697.html.

The following hypothetical situation is based on a composite of actual experience encountered by our members in rural communities. It features Larry and is used to illustrate the barriers and challenges to voting faced by people who live in rural communities, and the impact on someone who is denied his rightful chance to vote.

Larry, 38 years old, married, father of ten-year-old twin boys, and a minimum wage factory worker, drives with his family twenty-five miles from his rural community to his polling place to vote. On the way, Larry stops for gas and pays $3.67 a gallon for regular unleaded gas, the current national gas average. After purchasing $25 for gas for only 6.81 gallons, the family proceeds to the polling place.

It is now 10:00 AM. Larry and his wife decide to each take a child into their respective voting booths. His wife goes into hers but before Larry can make it to his, a poll worker stops him. The poll worker tells Larry that his name is not on the voter roll. Unbeknownst to him, his name had been removed because his voter identification card was returned as undeliverable (as happened and was ruled unconstitutional in *U.S. Student Ass'n Found. et al. v. Land et al.*). Larry and his wife registered to vote last year during a door-to-door registration drive in their rural community.

Unable to vote or convince the poll worker that he is eligible to vote even though his wife was able to, Larry and his family return home, having driven fifty miles round-trip, only to have one of two votes counted for the family.

Larry and his wife sit at the kitchen table and ponder what to do. They are unaware that a Section 2 complaint can be filed with the United States Department of Justice. The United States Department of Justice's website instructs people to "contact the Voting Section at Voting.Section@usdoj .gov to make a complaint concerning a voting matter." The "Voting .Section@usdoj.gov" link is an email address. Even if they were aware, they could not send the email from their home.

The rural area Larry's family lives in does not have Internet access. Why?

National private cable providers are either refusing to provide Internet service to rural areas or planning to install it for one or two roads a year . . . Some communities have attempted to establish their own public Internet companies and have seen their efforts thwarted or complicated by cable companies working in tandem with state legislatures.

. . . Rural communities who want to build an infrastructure themselves cannot or will be hindered by the law's geographical or rate restrictions.

A few hours later, Larry and his wife try to recall a local community citizen's organization that could possibly help but one does not exist in their community. It is now 2 PM and both have to work in the morning at the local factory, so they scratch the idea of driving to an organization in a neighboring county. Besides, it would require more gas to drive the sixty miles to reach the organization's office.

His wife suggests they call a neighbor who lives two miles away and has dial-up Internet or travel twenty-five miles to the closest library. They decide to call the neighbor and Larry is invited over. Larry sits down at the computer and the dial-up connection fails to connect. The neighbor tells Larry to give it five or so minutes and the connection is slow.

Once online, Larry doesn't know where to go.

If Larry did, he would have to go to http://www.justice.gov/ or use a search engine to find the site. Once there, he would have to first find on the homepage where the link to "submit a complaint" is under the "Department of Justice Action Center" section. Second, he would have to know to click on the link. Third, he would have to scroll down to find the "voting rights discrimination" link and know to click on it. Fourth, he would come to a page titled "How to File a Complaint" and either click on the "Voting Section" link at the top of the page or have to scroll down to the very bottom to find the "Voting" section. Fifth, Larry would read that he "can register a complaint [by sending] an email message to the Voting Section at Voting.Section@usdoj.gov." Even for a computer savvy person, successfully completing all these steps might prove to be daunting.

Let's say that Larry completed all the aforementioned steps. Larry may see the word "complaint" and believe he is unprepared to compose a formal email explaining why he was denied the right to vote. Furthermore, he may not have an email address because it hasn't made sense to have one since he does not have Internet access at home and therefore no computer.

So, Larry heads back home. It is now 5:00 PM.

Larry decides to call a local attorney to ask for assistance in filing a complaint. The attorney's office is thirty-five miles away and his law firm specializes in local civil and criminal law, not civil rights law. Despite this fact, the attorney invites Larry to his office but informs him that he will be charged $75.00 an hour for the consultation and drafting of the complaint.

Larry gives up. He also decided not to vote in the local school board election that occurred ten days later.

These are typical situations faced by our diverse rural, farm member communities in rural areas around the country.

Although Chief Justice Roberts acknowledged in *Shelby* that "voting discrimination still exists; no one doubts that," some members of Congress appear to be against working in a bipartisan effort to update the Voting Rights Act. *Holder*, 133 S. Ct. at 2620. Senate Minority Leader Mitch McConnell (R-KY) called the Voting Rights Act "an important bill that passed back in the '60s at a time when we had a very different America than we have today." Susan Davis, *Congress unlikely to act on voting rights ruling*, USA Today (June 25, 2013), http://www.usatoday.com/story/news/politics/2013/06/25/congress-reacts-voting-rights-rulling/2456477/. Rep. Goodlatte (R-VA), chairman of the U.S. House Judiciary Committee, said that even though Section 4 has been ruled unconstitutional, "it's important to note that under the Supreme Court's decision in *Shelby County (v. Holder)* other very important provisions of the Voting Rights Act remain in place, including Sections 2 and 3." Tom Curry, *Conservatives not keen on effort to revise key section of Voting Rights Act*, NBC-News (July 18, 2013), http://nbcpolitics.nbcnews.com/_news/2013/07/18/19540938-conservatives-not-keen-on-effort-to-revise-key-section-of-voting-rights-act?lite. Section 3 also requires judicial intervention to impose preclearance requirements on a jurisdiction that enacts discriminatory voting procedures or laws. What Sen. McConnell, Rep. Goodlatte, and others fail to consider, however, are the geographical distinctions that create different challenges for voters in urban and rural areas.

. . .

Conclusions and Recommendations

While Section 2 may provide tools to remedy discrimination for those with the resources to access legal assistance and the courts, it is not sufficient to prevent discrimination and other tools must be provided to assist communities such as those mentioned here.

. . . Below are some of our recommendations and we urge the committee to seek additional input and work quickly to renew this important section of the law.

A new preclearance formula for Section 4 of the Voting Rights Act should be created by the U.S. Congress. . . .

Section 4 should mandate that citizens who believe their voting rights have been violated based on race, age or other factors, may file a petition either on paper or online, and the U.S. Department of Justice should be required to invoke preclearance based on the receipt of such petition. . . .

The U.S. Department of Justice should create an ombudsman position to solely investigate and address complaints of maladministration or voting rights violations. . . .

A "Voter Bill of Rights" should be created and posted in all registrars' offices and in each polling place that includes what a citizen can do if he or she is denied the right to vote. . . .

The U.S. Department of Justice should keep records of the locations from which all complaints, whether by phone, mail or electronically, and be mandated to investigate and invoke preclearance in areas where complaints exceed a set level that should be specified in the revision of the law. . . .

☛ WHAT THIS EXAMPLE SHOWS. This testimony exemplifies "actionable realism" (Wagenaar, 2011, p. 278). Its interpretation of law is fitted to advocating voting rights policy reform. Qualitative evidence including description of actual conditions, legal cases, and legislative records supports the advocacy.

When defining the problem, this testimony keeps in view the real conditions or the "life-world of everyday" (Wagenaar, 2011, p. 296). As the testimony's author remarked elsewhere ". . . Hearings usually feature experts or scholars, not the people experiencing the problem first-hand" (Redding, 2014). Consequently, he deliberately included the viewpoint of the affected.

To look at how those features of this testimony are constructed, pay particular attention to storytelling. Larry brings policy-affected people into the hearing, and his experience realistically details the needs for action. For instance, Larry's difficulty with reporting a voting rights violation via the Internet can be restated as a premise: rural communities lack adequate Internet service. The premise leads to the conclusion that rural access to communication technology must be remedied if voting rights are to be protected. That conclusion leads to recommendation of action to create an ombudsman position with capability of 24-hour Election Day violations reporting by telephone or by mail.

The example shows the "normative leap" from description to prescription (Stone, 2012, p. 171). This occurs where everyday experience is described purposefully to inspire intervention by a reader with authority to intervene. This testimony claims, with support, that the Supreme Court decision regarding the Voting Rights Act is misguided, thereby justifying corrective congressional action.

Skillfully using creative writing techniques to represent a policy problem realistically for a policymaker audience, this testimony meets two criteria of effective policy communication, credibility and usefulness. *Tip*: To connect a need, relevant data, and a recommendation, think narratively. Tell a story to show why action is needed and what action to take. Keep analysis close to the empirical evidence of causal conditions revealed by the story. Fit recommendations tightly to the story's insights.

Another strength of this statement is its handling of complexity. Policy problems are always complex. Complexity can be defined as internal intricacy or the number of moving parts and part–whole relationships. Interdependencies between policy problems also create complexity (Roe, 1994, p. 2). This statement exposes a previously unrecognized moving part or condition causing voting difficulty in rural areas, inadequate Internet service and access, and points to policy interdependencies. Particularly, it shows connection between protecting voting rights protection and providing communication infrastructure. In doing so, the testimony writer expands an older narrative that attributes voting rights violation primarily to racism. While not discounting the older narrative (indeed, arguing that it still applies), the testimony adds other dimensions or geographic, economic and infrastructural gaps in networked society.

Any policy communicator selectively represents the intricacies of a given topic in accord with a viewpoint and a message. This writer's selections disrupt taken-for-granted understandings of the societal problem, support the testimony's message that the Supreme Court ruling got it wrong, and advocate remedies to the Court's mistake. As an aside, the writer challenges the assumptions of experts and analysts who take access to the Web for granted. More to the testimony's point, he asks the Senate Judiciary Committee, which has power to create federal Internet policies and administration, to recognize geographic and economic factors in the problem of Internet access. Particularly in rural areas, low-performing service providers put poverty-affected populations at a disadvantage.

Summary and Preview

Testimony in a public hearing is a highly visible way of getting your knowledge, perspective, and message into the legislative public record. Chapter 10 introduces an equally important although less visible way of influencing policy, providing public comment during administrative rule making.

References

Bardach, E. (2011). Semantic tips: A summary. In *A practical guide for policy analysis: The eightfold path to more effective problem solving* (Appendix C, 4th ed.). Washington, DC: CQ Press.

Redding, G. (2014). Personal correspondence.

Roe, Emery. (1994). *Narrative policy analysis: Theory and practice.* Durham, NC: Duke University Press.

Smith, C. F. (1993). "Is it worth fixing this plane?" The rhetorical life of information in a congressional oversight hearing on the B-1 bomber. In B. Sims (Ed.), *Studies in technical communication: Selected papers of the 1992 CCCC and NCTE conferences* (pp. 111–146). Denton, TX: University of North Texas Press.

Stone, D. (2012). *Policy paradox: The art of political decision making* (3rd ed.). New York, NY: Norton. As cited in Schon, D. (1980). "Generative metaphor: A perspective on problem setting in public policy." In A. Ortony (Ed.), *Metaphor and thought*. Cambridge, UK: Cambridge University Press.

Wagenaar, H. (2011). *Meaning in action: Interpretation and dialogue in policy analysis*. Armonk, NY: Sharpe.

CHAPTER *10*

❧

Public Comment: Influence Administration

Key Concepts

- Your voice in government
- Plain language

In federal government, after a law is enacted an executive branch agency begins rule making to implement the law. This involves developing standards and regulations for administering and enforcing the law. As required by the Administrative Procedures Act as well as other laws and executive orders, the agency must seek public comment on the proposed standards and regulations before they can be put in force. Sometimes, oral hearings are held; typically, written comments are requested. This chapter shows you how to write a formal public comment in rule-making procedures.

Do comments make a difference? Yes. Agencies regularly pull back a proposed rule for revision based on comments received. Do carefully prepared comments make a bigger difference than mass e-mails or letters? Yes. Agencies systematically review substantive comments to collect useful perspectives and information. Does the method of delivery matter? Yes. All written comments are reviewed, whether submitted electronically or mailed. Telephone responses to formal calls for comment are not reviewed.

What happens after written comments are submitted? Agency-contracted external reviewers who are specialists in the subject matter read each comment. For instance, air quality specialists in the Research Triangle Institute (RTI) review EPA public comments on air quality regulation. In a human process minimally assisted by information management software, reviewers first sort comments that might number a million or more into categories such as general opposition or support, substantive, or out of scope. The majority (95%) of comments go into general opposition or support. A minority go into out of scope. The remaining substantive comments are read line by line. Reviewers fit substantive contents to a preconstructed outline of the call derived from the preamble, sections of the rule, and the agency's questions stating what it wants to learn from public comments. The outline also includes statutory and executive orders that relate to the call, agency remarks on changes in the rule language, and special categories for incorporate-by-reference comments that support other comments without added content and for duplicate comments submitted more than once. The outline will change if review shows that more or different sections are needed.

Within the substantive category, comments that offer new, unexpected, or should-be-considered information are sorted separately. Substantive comments are clustered by topic. Clusters are summarized and synthesized by the RTI reviewer before passing them on to a technical expert at RTI or in the requesting agency to confirm accuracy. Finally, reviewers (sometimes in collaboration with agency experts) draft recommendations that account for comment patterns and specifics. Overall, the process of reviewing public comments at RTI is iterative, shared, and human-performed. It is not automated (Bullock, 2014). Probably, this is typical of current public comment review. However, some federal agencies are experimenting with digital rule making or e-rule making to include computer-aided analysis of public comments (Schlosberg, 2007; Shulman, 2003).

Agencies have discretion in using comments for rule modification and in describing the use they might have made. In the milk-labeling case (Chapter 1) the Bureau of Food Safety and Laboratory Services of the Pennsylvania Department of Agriculture (PDA) described a modification this way:

> PDA has received a great deal of input on the standards set forth in [the new standard on milk labeling announced on

October 24, 2007]. . . . We are now in a position to inform you further as to the results of reviewing the input we received. Enclosed please find a new document titled "Revised Standards and Procedures for the Approval of Proposed Labeling of Fluid Milk" dated January 17, 2008. . . . Please review this document carefully and govern yourself accordingly.

Whereas public comment is routinely sought in federal rule making, the same is not true for state rule making. However, states must seek public comment in regulatory procedures for granting, revoking, or renewing permits for activities that affect public life as shown in Examples 3 and 4 in this chapter.

Regrettably, few citizens know about this opportunity to provide input, and few engage it. As a result, narrowly interested groups dominate the rule-making process. That is not what agencies want. Agencies want broad participation. Regulators want to get it right. Federal, state, and local agencies welcome any type of comment that can help them make and justify their decisions. The comment might be a technical analysis, a philosophical argument, an opinion based on personal experience, advocacy, or a request to hold a public meeting on the proposed action. Responsible agencies take seriously any well-prepared comment, especially any that suggests realistic and feasible alternatives.

Public comment is important because administrative public policy broadly affects present and future life. Anybody can write a useful comment. The more who do so, the better the likelihood of good government (http://www.Regulations.gov/).

How to Write a Public Comment

Goal: Knowledge of administrative procedures for implementing law, including the public's role.

Objective: To influence the administration of a law by contributing information relevant to standard setting, rule making, or permitting.

Product: Formal written comment.

Scope: Limited to the specific proposed administrative action.

Strategy: Base comments on your authority to respond, whether based on personal experience, organizational advocacy, vocational or professional background, or specialized knowledge.

Although expert commentary is always appropriate, you need not be an expert to comment. There is no template for public comments. A simple letter can have an impact. If friends or a community organization share your views, you might want to present a collective comment. You might sign for the group, all individuals involved might sign, or the organization's officers might sign.

Task 1. Find Calls for Public Comment

The U.S. government's official source for notifications of proposed rule making is the *Federal Register*, published daily. You can find the *Federal Register* either in government information depository libraries or online at http://federalregister.gov/. Look for "Proposed Rules" or "Notices." Look for announcements by agencies authorized to act on topics of concern to you.

Or, if you already know the executive branch department, and within it the relevant agency that administers laws in your area of concern, do not go initially to the *Register*. Go to the website of the relevant department (the Department of Transportation, for instance) and find the relevant agency (National Highway Traffic Safety Administration, for instance).

Or, go to the website of an advocacy group associated with your concern. Browsing there is likely to turn up the name of both the department and the agency. Sign up for the group's e-mail action alerts that make it easy to comment. For instance, here's an alert by the Pennsylvania Association for Sustainable Agriculture: ". . . It is time to submit comments on the second draft of rules issued by the Food and Drug Administration (FDA) in accordance with the Food Safety Modernization Act (FSMA). The public deadline is December 15 and it is critically important. . . . Significant progress has been made . . . FDA did listen to the thousands of voices who spoke out. . . . You can see the results by going to the FSMA Action Center (sustainableagriculture.net/fsma). . . . More changes are needed. . . . In their final form these rules will stand for two or more generations of farmers in the future. . . . Here are the links you need to comment now" (Giving Thanks and Food Safety Action Alert, 11-24-2014).

If you are concerned about a state issue, you can find calls for public comment in state notifications such as the *Pennsylvania Bulletin* or the *New York State Register*. Every state has one. Or, if you know the relevant agency for your concern, go to its website. Or go to the websites of advocacy groups for your concern.

If you want to comment on a local government matter, watch the Public Notices section of local newspapers. Local government calls for public comment are published there. Notices might be also posted in local government offices or, possibly, on their websites.

Task 2. Write the Public Comment Document

In most respects, writing a public comment is like writing any other policy document. The demands for preparation and planning are the same. The same expectations for clarity, credibility, and conciseness apply. One possible difference: some calls for public input specify the exact information needed. If the call to which you are responding does specify the contents, provide them as requested. If you have additional information, include it too, but not at the expense of requested contents.

To help ensure that your comment will be taken seriously, include the following features and qualities:

• Narrow focus;

• Evidence, analyses, and references supporting your view;

• Indication of public support of your view; and

• Positive and feasible alternatives.

Before you write, use the method (Chapter 2) to plan. After you write, check the product against the standards (Two Checklists, Chapter 2).

Four Examples

Examples here show public comments in administrative policy making. Examples 1 and 2 illustrate rule making by federal agencies, whereas Examples 3 and 4 illustrate permitting by a state agency. Comment is shown from nonprofit organizations (Examples 1 and 3), from experts (Example 2), and from community leaders (Example 4). Scenarios provide context for each example.

Example 1

Scenario

At the nonprofit National Farmer's Union headquarters in Washington, DC, a government relations specialist new on the job was assigned to write a formal public comment. His product will be the Union's submission in response to an Environmental Protection Agency (EPA) call for comments on a proposed rule to make clear "which water bodies are protected under the Clean Water Act" (D=EPQ-HQ-OW 2011-0880, http://www.regulations.gov/). He has relevant prior experience as a public affairs communicator for news clip services, blogs, and farming publications as well as legal writing experience as law student intern for the EPA.

He faced a tight deadline for submitting NFU's response to EPA's call. On advice of the NFU's board president and policy director, he first consulted the organization's current policy (http://www.nfu.org/nfu-2015-policy12066). Two policy positions stated there, opposition to extending the Clean Water Act's jurisdiction and support for environmental stewardship, become his guidelines. Next he consulted practical experts, NFU farmers in western states most likely to be affected by administrative change in the Clean Water Act, particularly South and North Dakota. As he drafted, he interacted continually with farmers, NFU state and regional chapter presidents, and NFU members who contacted him.

Through his interactions, he encountered polarized opinion, partisan politics, and misinformation about the proposed rule. This surprised him because he knew the NFU to be normally deliberative in its policy considerations (Example 3, Chapter 8). He attributed the unexpected discord to NFU's late entry into an already compromised public discourse. Well-funded industry groups, some in agriculture, had come together early to loudly convey a single negative message, stop the rule. "Ditch the Rule" advocates included the National Association of State Departments of Agriculture, American Farm Bureau Federation, National Cattlemen's Beef Association, National Pork Producers Council, National Chicken Council, U.S. Poultry and Egg Association, National Turkey Federation and the American Soybean Association (Jacqui Fatke, "Comments Finalized on EPA's Water Rule," http://www.FarmFutures.com/, November 21, 2014). Despite the EPA's issuance of an interpretation specifying 56 exemptions for conservation and farming practice in addition to traditional exemptions in the proposed rule, some farmers were made fearful by the negative public relations campaign.

Rather than simply opposing the rule, NFU's choice was to offer EPA advice on how to secure a rule that works for family agriculture. The choice was nuanced, hard to build consensus around, and hard to represent in a comment.

After three weeks of intensive drafting and revision, the writer submitted NFU's comment ahead of deadline. Subsequently, National Public Radio and local radio stations interviewed him about the Union's position. His experience shows that procedural submission to an administrative agency's formal call is not the end of the assignment. Communicators might need media skills, too.

Extracts from NFU's submitted formal comment follow.

Example 1

September 22, 2014

Water Docket
Environmental Protection Agency
Mail Code: 2822T
1200 Pennsylvania Ave. NW.
Washington, DC 20460
Docket ID No. EPA-HQ-OW-2011-0880

**ATTENTION: DOCKET ID NO. EPA-HQ-OW-2011-0880:
DEFINITION OF "WATERS OF THE UNITED STATES UNDER THE
CLEAN WATER ACT"**

Dear Administrator McCarthy and Lieutenant General Bostick:

National Farmers Union (NFU) welcomes the opportunity to submit comments to the Environmental Protection Agency (EPA) and the U.S. Army Corps of Engineers (Corps) on the proposed rule regarding the definition of "waters of the United States" under the Clean Water Act (CWA). As this rulemaking process continues, NFU may submit additional comments.

Since 1902, NFU has advocated for the economic and social well-being and quality of life of family farmers and their communities through the sustainable production of food, fiber, feed and fuel. NFU represents nearly 200,000 members nationwide, with members in all 50 states and organized divisions in 33 states. NFU is a federation of state and regional organizations.

Clean water is vital to the productivity and well-being of America's farms, ranches and rural communities. The CWA seeks to "restore and maintain the chemical, physical, and biological integrity of the Nation's waters. NFU's members understand the importance of respecting clean water as a shared resource and believe the integrity of the nation's water can be protected without unnecessarily encumbering the activities of the regulated community. NFU's policy, enacted annually by delegates to the organization's national convention, opposes broadening the definition of what waters are considered jurisdictional and supports the uniform administration of EPA policies nationwide.

The EPA and Corps' (agencies) stated goal for the proposed rule is to improve protection of public health and water resources while increasing certainty for the regulated community and reducing troublesome and costly litigation. Protecting the nation's water resources is a complicated matter, and so by necessity are the CWA and any rule implementing it. This topic requires careful consideration and measured discourse over the legitimate concerns facing the regulated community.

. . .

It is not satisfactorily clear whether the proposed rule, in its present form, would implement policies that NFU supports. However, NFU's members recognize the agencies' rulemaking process on this matter as an opportunity to achieve their policy goals because the current regulatory landscape allows for inconsistent determinations that expand the CWA's definition of jurisdictional waters. The purpose of the following comments is to provide the agencies with advice for drafting a final rule that does not increase CWA jurisdiction and promotes consistent application of EPA policies, which aligns with the agencies' stated intent. NFU will oppose a rule that does not respect these critical components of the organization's policy. These comments will help the agencies avoid language that, even when drafted in good faith, could be taken out of context and used to stretch CWA jurisdiction in the future.

. . .

Proposed Definition of "waters of the United States."
"Tributary"

The CWA establishes the agencies' permitting jurisdiction over specifically-listed waters. Paragraphs (a)(1)–(a)(5) of the proposed rule restate well-settled tenets of the agencies' jurisdiction under the CWA and do not warrant further comment. However, section (a)(5)'s inclusion of "All tributaries of waters identified in paragraphs (a)(1) through (4) of this section" warrants examination. This language has invoked significant concern in the regulated community that the proposed rule would increase the jurisdictional reach of the CWA. The agencies should address this concern and confirm this language does not increase jurisdiction by incorporating the following points in the final rule.

. . .

The preamble . . . notes that the proposed rule sets forth, for the first time, a regulatory definition of "tributary." The proposed rule defines "tributary" as "a water physically characterized by the presence of a bed and banks and ordinary high water mark . . . which contributes flow, either directly or through another water, to a water identified in paragraphs (a)(1) through (4) of this section." In order to provide more clarity to the regulated community, the agencies should note in the final rule that these features take years to form. This should mitigate concern that temporary accumulations directly related to isolated rain events will be considered jurisdictional. The agencies should add further clarifying language, including but not limited to descriptive examples of water and events that are not considered tributaries, in the final rule in order to ensure these distinctions are well-understood in the regulated community.

. . .

"Adjacent"

The proposed rule would change section (a)(6) from an articulation of the CWA's jurisdiction over wetlands adjacent to "waters of the United States" to an explanation of the CWA's jurisdiction over "All waters, including wetlands, adjacent to" waters identified in (a)(1) to (a)(5) as jurisdictional. As with the definition of "tributary" discussed above, this change is causing apprehension among the regulated community. The agencies should consider the following points in drafting the final rule to make clear that this change does not expand jurisdiction.

The proposed rule defines "adjacent" as "bordering, contiguous or neighboring" at (c)(1). It notes further that "Waters, including wetlands, separated from other waters of the United States by man-made dikes or barriers, natural river berms, beach dunes and the like are 'adjacent waters.'"

The jurisdictional reach of "adjacent waters," then, is largely dependent on the definition of "neighboring." This proposed rule defines "neighboring" for the first time. The preamble notes that the term is currently applied broadly, but the proposed rule defines "neighboring" as "waters located within the riparian area or floodplain of a water identified in (a)(1) through (5) of this section, or waters with a shallow subsurface hydrological connection or confined surface hydrologic connection to such a jurisdictional water."

. . .

The preamble also asks for specific comment "on whether the rule text should provide greater specificity with regard to how the agencies will determine if a water is located in the floodplain of a jurisdictional water." The agencies should uniformly use a 20 year flood interval zone when evaluating these waters. . . . The agencies should also provide clarity to the regulated community by stating in the final rule, "mere proximity to a jurisdictional water is not cause for a determination that a water is jurisdictional as 'neighboring' or 'adjacent,' and a scientifically-verifiable, substantial surface connection must be present for any water outside a floodplain or riparian zone to be found jurisdictional."

"Significant Nexus"

Other waters not covered by the above-discussed jurisdictional categories may fall within the CWA's jurisdiction if a case-by-case determination is made finding the water has a "significant nexus" with a water identified in sections (a)(1) through (3).

The proposed rule at section (c)(7) says "The term *significant nexus* means that a water, including wetlands, either alone or in combination with other similarly situated waters in the region (i.e., the watershed that drains to the nearest water identified in paragraphs (a)(1) through (3) of this section), significantly affects the chemical, physical, or biological integrity of a water identified in paragraphs (a)(1) through (3) of this section." The proposed rule also states "Other waters, including wetlands, are similarly situated when they perform similar functions and are located sufficiently close together or sufficiently close to a 'water of the United States' so that they can be evaluated as a single landscape unit with regard to their effect on the chemical, physical, or biological integrity of a water identified in paragraphs (a)(1) through (a)(3) of this section."
. . .

The term "similarly situated" must be examined, since it allows the agencies to consider multiple waters together in making "significant nexus" determinations. The prerequisite condition for "other waters" to be considered "similarly situated," before any assessment of geographic proximity to additional "other waters" or jurisdictional waters, is performance of similar functions. The preamble further explains that a "similarly situated" determination requires an evaluation of whether waters in a region "can reasonably be expected to function together in their effect on the chemical, physical, or biological integrity of downstream traditional navigable waters, interstate waters, or the territorial seas," and whether waters are "sufficiently close" to each other or a jurisdictional water.

The description of "similarly situated" waters above includes so many variables that it would be difficult for the regulated community to accurately anticipate the outcome of such a determination, opening the door to increased uncertainty. To give the regulated community more clarity in anticipating the results of "similarly situated" evaluations, the agencies should provide a list of functions that a group of waters must perform together in order to be considered "similarly situated." These functions include affecting the reach and flow of a jurisdictional water and allowing or barring the movement of aquatic species, nutrients, pollutants or sediments to a jurisdictional water.

. . .

This added clarity would ease concerns regarding the rule held by NFU members in the Prairie Pothole Region, in which a farm may be littered with potholes. In many cases, a pothole may be located near a jurisdictional water and have a physical surface connection to that jurisdictional water. Another pothole may be located near to the first pothole and yet have no connection to it. The agencies should assure farmers the second pothole, even though it is near to the first pothole, will not automatically be considered "similarly situated" to the first pothole strictly due to geographic proximity. At the very least, the final rule should clarify that the term "similarly situated," for purposes of determining whether "other waters" maintain a "significant nexus" with jurisdictional waters, is not a simple geographic determination. The agencies should elaborate that "similarly situated" means both waters that are near to each other and sharing an identifiable hydrogeological feature in common. A water would not be considered "similarly situated" due to geographic proximity alone.

. . .

EXCLUDED WATERS AND EXEMPTED ACTIVITIES

. . .

Exemptions for Agricultural Activities
The preamble indicates that the proposed rule does not affect existing regulatory exemptions for agricultural activities. There is nothing in the proposed rule that calls this assertion into question.

. . .

MISCELLANEOUS MATTERS

Shallow Subsurface Hydrologic Connections
. . . Until more scientific evidence is provided, groundwater connections alone should not be used to find non-navigable waters jurisdictional.

. . .

Pesticide Applications
. . . This is not the proper venue for discussing these applications.

. . .

CONCLUSION

NFU understands the agencies' stated goal of enhancing protections for our nation's water resources while providing increased certainty to the regulated community. The comments above reflect NFU's understanding of the proposed rule and explain ways the proposed rule could be improved to more effectively accomplish the agencies' stated goal in the final rule while maintaining conformity with NFU's policy. NFU stands ready to offer further assistance in this regard as the agencies may find helpful. Thank you for your consideration of these comments.

Sincerely,
Roger Johnson
President

(Content and footnotes are omitted because of space limitations. Read NFU's full comment at http://www.Regulations.gov/. Public Submission Posted: 09/24/2014 ID: EPA-HQ-OW-2011-0880-6249)

◗━◗ WHAT THIS EXAMPLE SHOWS. Administrative public policy directly affects daily life and ordinary activities. Most of us come into contact with public policy less through legislation and more through managing our affairs to comply with standards and regulations that enforce law. For water management, standards and regulations often generate controversy. The stakes are high and effects are far-reaching. Water is critical for all forms of life and many industries. Consequently, advocates for human activities, the environment, commerce, and wildlife are concerned. In all, 698,000 individuals and organizations responded to EPA's call in 2014 for comments to define terms of the Clean Water Act.

EPA issues more calls for comment than do other federal agencies except Health and Human Services (http://RegInfo.gov/, 9-23-2014). EPA's calls often entail controversy. In this example, contention focused particularly on water connectivity, or how one water body relates to another. The agency wanted to define types of connection that would qualify related water bodies for protection under the Clean Water Act. The original act protected only navigable waters such as lakes and rivers. Recent Supreme Court decisions had allowed for protecting other waters "adjacent to" or "similarly situated as" jurisdictional lakes and rivers. However, the court's decisions did not define those and other key terms. After multiple scientific and governmental assessments of the need for a new rule, EPA asked for public comment to help define the terms.

The NFU writer responded with legal argument in plain language. Legal argument is shown in the NFU comment's content organization mirroring the organization of EPA's call. By referring to EPA's proposed definitions in the order presented, by citing their exact location in the preamble or sections of the rule, then by immediately providing NFU's advice, the comment moves efficiently along, point-for-point, to meet EPA's request. The organization resembles the terms-construction phase of legal proceedings. Extraneous matter is strictly excluded.

Plain language is defined by government communicators as easy to read, understand, and use (http://www.PlainLanguage.gov/). It is reader oriented. This comment's logical organization strongly links the writer's message to the reader's use for the information. The reader is complex, representing both EPA and future followers of the codified rule. Multiaudience management is not simple; this comment manages well. Directly, it speaks to the designated recipients, EPA regulators. Indirectly, it speaks to an intended future audience, a regulated community. In effect, the writer advises EPA not only on definitions but also on ways to gain farmers' compliance with the definitions. Here's a typical construction of the complex audience: "The agencies should provide further clarity for the regulated community [farmers] . . . by stating in the final rule 'This rule does not require a permit for any plowing and planting activity that was legally conducted without a permit before this rule was issued.'"

A more obvious plain language feature is the comment's subheadings that repeat EPA's terms. The repetition makes it easier for reviewers to find the NFU comment's substantive points and to categorize them appropriately for recommendation to EPA.

Finally, declarative sentences using active voice support clarity. Most sentences in the comment are declarative and their subjects do the verb's action (Appendix A). For instance, "NFU will oppose a rule that does not respect . . . the organization's policy."

By combining these structural and stylistic features, the comment exemplifies tight writing and plain language. Its information is "actionable, sharable" (http://www.Usability.gov/). It is likely to receive the EPA's respectful attention.

Tip: Consult references such as Regulations.gov for do's and don'ts on writing effective comments. Learn plain language techniques by consulting the Plain Language Action and Information Network at http://www.plainlanguage.gov/ and http://www.Usability.gov/.

Special tip by the government relations specialist in this example: keep your eye on the *Federal Register*. You could be writing in response to a call for comment tomorrow. Keep your other eye on newspaper opinion pages and online interactive blogs in your area of concern. You could be interviewed the day after tomorrow.

Example 2

Scenario

A national transportation safety investigative board holds four days of hearings on air bag safety. The board, which reports both to the Congress and to the executive branch, is concerned about the unanticipated high rates of injury from air bag deployment. The witness list for the hearings includes representatives of auto manufacturers, insurance companies, safety institutes, auto safety advocacy groups, air bag manufacturers, and auto parts suppliers. The purpose of the hearings is to enable the board to make recommendations for improving air bag safety.

Based on the board's ensuing recommendations and its own investigations, the federal agency responsible for automotive safety regulations, the National Highway Traffic Safety Administration, announces that it intends to modify the current standard for air bags. The agency announces its proposed modification in the *Federal Register* and calls for public comment.

In response to the call for comments, two experts in automotive safety jointly write a technical comment and submit it in the rulemaking process. They point out shortcomings in the agency's proposed modification, and they propose an alternative.

COMMENT TO THE DOCKET CONCERNING AMENDMENTS TO FMVSS 208, OCCUPANT CRASH PROTECTION

Summary of Comments

Federal motor vehicle safety standards (FMVSS) must, by law, meet the need for motor vehicle safety. This proposal (Docket No. NHTSA 98–4405; Notice 1) purports to meet that need by requiring advanced air bags. In fact, it is primarily written to address the problem of inflation induced injuries and would provide little additional protection.

The worst of the inflation-induced injuries resulted in several hundred fatalities to children and out-of-position adults (including those sitting too close to the steering wheel) and from late, low-speed crash air bag deployments. NHTSA [National Highway Traffic Safety Administration] had assumed that manufacturers would conduct comprehensive air bag testing to ensure that inflation would not inflict injury under reasonable foreseeable conditions. It is arguable (although probably not practical policy) that NHTSA could address inflation-induced injuries under safety defect provisions of the National Traffic and Motor Vehicle Safety Act.

. . .

A key part of this notice proposes two options: (1) tests of air bag systems with dummies in close proximity to ensure that inflation induced injuries are unlikely, or (2) requirements for occupant sensors to ensure that air bags will not inflate if an occupant is in a position where he or she is at risk of injury from the inflating air bag.

In response to the proposed alternatives, we expect manufacturers to choose occupant sensors to prevent air bag inflation for certain occupant situations. This untested sensor technology might actually increase casualties because of inaccurate determinations of occupant risks and degraded reliability from the added complexity.

Experts in the field have suggested a number of potential air bag design and performance features that might reduce inflation induced injuries. The Canadian government and NHTSA deserve credit for their research and analysis in this field despite NHTSA's belated recognition that an official response was necessary. It is not clear which approach would be most effective, or even most cost-effective, but we think it is unlikely that NHTSA's proposed regulation will yield an optimal result.

This notice [of proposal amendments] also fails to address occupant protection challenges involving one to two orders of magnitude more casualties for which feasible technologies are available. These include raising safety belt use to near universality, protection of occupants in rollover crashes, and addressing compatibility problems between passenger cars and light trucks.

Many of these deficiencies can be overcome with a third alternative that retains the simplicity of the original automatic occupant crash protection standard; does not introduce complex, untested occupant sensors; and meets other needs for motor vehicle safety. It depends fundamentally on NHTSA's willingness to propose acceptable, effective inducements for using safety belts.

. . .

A Third Option Would Encourage Belt Use

We are proposing that a third option be added to NHTSA's notice that would ensure safety belt use with acceptable and effective belt use inducements built into the vehicle.

. . .

NHTSA must recognize that the fundamental problem with its occupant restraint policy is that a substantial minority of motorists does not use safety belts. In fact, a much larger proportion of those most likely to be involved in serious crashes drive unbelted. Nearly universal belt use is critical to any rational occupant crash protection program.

. . .

An Alternative to the Proposed Amendment

Our specific proposal is that NHTSA add a third option to its notice on advanced air bags. Under this option:

- A manufacturer must install an effective, but not onerous safety belt use inducement in a new motor vehicle of a type that would be permitted under the "interlock" amendment (15 U.S.C.1410b) to the National Traffic and Motor Vehicle Safety Act.

  . . .

- A motor vehicle must meet comparative injury criteria of FMVSS 208 and in addition [in crashworthiness tests using dummies] there can be no contact between the head of the driver or passenger dummy and any part of the vehicle (other than the air bag or belt restraint system) or any other part of the dummy, in a frontal barrier crash at a speed of up to 35 mph with belted occupants

  . . .

- Air bags may not deploy under any frontal crash speed barrier impacts below 16 mph.

  . . .

Discussion
Our alternative would provide occupant crash protection that is at least equal in all respects to that provided by the present standard and NCAP consumer information program.

. . .

This proposal would substantially increase belt use and, because of the head impact requirements, would ensure that air bags provide good head protection. Air bags that can meet this criterion would provide some frontal crash protection to the small number of unbelted occupants (who would, of course, be unbelted by their own conscious choice).

If manufacturers would choose our alternative, it would save a minimum of 7000 lives per year compared with the present FMVSS208, making it one of the most cost-effective standards ever.

(The full comment can be found at http://www.regulations.gov/. See NHTSA 1999–6407–0073. It has as Appendix 1 the commenters' additional petition on the subject.)

Later, the NHTSA summarizes all comments received in a preamble to its next published notice on air bag safety. It says how the comments influenced its plans to modify the standard. The preamble states, "In response to the public comments on our 1998 proposal and to other new information obtained since issuing the proposal, we are issuing a supplemental proposal that updates and refines the amendments under consideration." In an appendix, NHTSA states its reasons for rejecting the two experts' proposed alternative shown here.

Example 3

Scenario

A state environmental protection department's bureau of mining, which regulates mineral extraction industries in the state, announces a proposed revision in a mining company's operating permit. In accordance with "sunshine" requirements for permitting processes, the agency publishes the applicant's proposal to mine deeper than its original permit allowed. The mining company is asking the bureau to remove restrictions on the company's operation at a specific site. The primary restriction prohibits mining at levels that might adversely affect local groundwater quantity and quality. The restriction is warranted in a region where well-water supply and quality vary according to groundwater conditions and where high-quality cold-water trout fishing streams are fed by local springs near the mining site.

In response to the bureau's call for public comment on the mine operator's request for permit revision, a local environmental conservation group and a local civic organization write letters of comment (Examples 3 and 4, this chapter). Other interested parties write letters, too, including a national sport fishing group, local businesses dependent on tourism, and individual citizens. At the request of the civic organization, the agency holds a public meeting. The conservation group hires a professional stenographer (who is also a notary public) to transcribe the meeting. In addition, the group invites local news reporters. The meeting is well attended. The bureau officials, the mine operator, and the residents of the region affected by the mine vigorously discuss the request to lift restrictions on the mine. After the meeting, the conservation group provides the transcript to the bureau as a written record of public comment. If administrative litigation regarding this permit ensues, the transcript will provide evidence.

Following the public meeting, an attorney member of the local environmental conservation group, in collaboration with members who are expert in hydrogeology and water quality engineering, writes a technical and legal analysis of the mining company's application for permit modifications. The chair of the group's relevant committee signs and submits the comment. Selections are given here.

TECHNICAL ANALYSIS

July 29, 2001

Michael W. Smith
District Mining Manager
Pennsylvania Department of Environmental Protection
P.O. Box 209 Hawk Run, PA 16840–0209
VIA Hand Delivery

Re: Con-Stone, Inc's, June 7, 2001, application to revise permit #14920301

Dear Mr. Smith:

The Penns Valley Conservation Association (PVCA) has reviewed Con-Stone, Inc.'s, June 7, 2001, application to revise permit #14920301 to allow removal of the Valentine Limestone below the 1080' elevation. PVCA wishes to work cooperatively with Con-Stone and the Pennsylvania Department of Environmental Protection (DEP) to ensure that mining operations protect the watershed surrounding the Aaronsburg Operation, including Elk and Pine Creeks [state-designated Exceptional Value (EV) stream] and Penns Creek [state-designated High-Quality (HQ) stream]. In that spirit of cooperation, and for protection of those streams, PVCA requests denial of Con-Stone's current application for the following reasons.

1. PVCA recommends retaining special conditions 1, 2, and 4 in Part B, Noncoal Surface Mining Permit No 14920301, Revised July 13, 1999, Special Conditions or Requirements. As District Mining Manager Michael W. Smith said in an August 27, 1999, letter to Con-Stone, "The mining limit of 1080 feet was originally established to keep mining activity out of the average seasonal low water table to minimize the potential for impacts to groundwater and to Spring S-26. We are not convinced that mining below 1080 feet can be accomplished without added risk of water impact."

   . . .

2. To manage the risks of mining below the water table, the proposed amendment calls for phased mining with a progressively deeper penetration of the water table. However, there is a total lack of detail in the permit amendment regarding the specific steps to be taken in the phased mining process. There should be clear language in the permit that stipulates consecutive mining and reclamation and attaches some time schedule and methodology for data analysis and reporting prior to advancing to the next phase of mining.

3. In PVCA's original discussions with DEP, Mike Smith indicated that Con-Stone would have to develop a new infiltration basin system to dispose of the groundwater pumped from the quarry. The permit amendment is contrary to this position as it utilizes the infiltration galleries currently designated for storm water disposal. PVCA requests that separate infiltration systems covered by separate NPDES permits be developed for the storm water and groundwater pumped from the pit.

4. The materials contained in the permit amendment do not adequately describe the hydrogeologic conditions. An appropriately scaled map showing the current pit location, the water table configuration, the location of all boreholes, the sedimentation basin, and infiltration galleries should be prepared. Without water table

contour mapping, it is impossible to address issues such as recirculation of the water pumped from the mine.

5. The May 7–10, 2001, pit pumping test performed by the mine operator provides little useful information regarding the extent of [potential loss of water supply] due to mining operations. . . . If DEP is going to grant the requested amendment, PVCA requests a special condition that Con-Stone is responsible for replacing the water supply for any water losses that result from mining operations. . . .

6. . . . In the context of the EV protection of the watershed, a much more comprehensive modeling effort is warranted. "Ideal aquifer" calculations such as those used to calculate inflow to the pit are not applicable in this setting.

7. Monitoring should be expanded, again at Con-Stone's cost, to be more complete by including all biological and chemical monitoring required by DEP's water quality anti-degradation regulations and implementation guidelines.

   . . .

10. The permit amendment submission does not appear to be signed and sealed by a licensed professional geologist.

11. PVCA believes Con-Stone must apply for a new or revised NPDES [National Pollution Discharge] permit for the proposed quarry dewatering activities.

    . . .

12. PVCA does not believe that Con-Stone has complied with all necessary pre-permit requirements under DEP's water quality antidegradation regulations and implementation guidelines. . . . Further, the application has not sought review by local and county governments to ensure compatibility with applicable regulations, ordinances, and comprehensive plans and to allow government to identify local and regional environmental and economic issues that should be considered.

Sincerely,

J. Thomas Doman Chair,

Watershed Committee Member,

Board of Directors, PVCA

cc: Jeff Confer, Con-Stone, Inc.
Hon. Jake Corman, Pennsylvania Senate
Hon. Kerry Benninghoff, Pennsylvania
House of Representatives
Pennsylvania Trout Unlimited

In announcing its decision later, the agency says, "The many public comments the Department received regarding this application formed the basis for modifications to the permit revision and resulted in changes in [the mining company's] proposed mining plan." The bureau's decision is to allow deeper mining, but to require new modifications intended to protect groundwater conditions.

Example 4

This is a letter by a citizens group requesting the public meeting described in the scenario given earlier.

LETTER

July 16, 2001

Re: Application for amendment for Con-Stone mining permit #14920301, Aaronsburg Operation

District Mining Manager
Department of Environmental Protection
Bureau of Mining
Hawk Run District Office
PO Box 209 Hawk Run, PA 16840–0209

On behalf of the Aaronsburg Civic Club I am requesting a public conference on the proposed amendment to the above permit. Again this year, we are offering our facility, the Aaronsburg Civic Club Community Building, for that purpose. As you are aware last year's public meeting was well attended and provided an opportunity for residents to state their concerns and for Con-Stone and DEP to address them. This is as it should be in a free and democratic society.

I strongly urge you to hold a public meeting on the latest proposed permit revisions. Two concerns that have been brought to my attention are (1) the potential degradation of underground and surface water, and (2) mining on land previously designated for storage.

Please contact me to reserve our facility.

Sincerely yours,
Earl Weaver, President
Aaronsburg Civic Club

►━• **WHAT THESE EXAMPLES SHOW.** All the examples exhibit qualities of effective public policy communication (Two Checklists, Chapter 2). They illustrate useful public comments made from a variety of legitimate perspectives. They suggest a range of policy actors who exercise the right to comment on proposed government action. Taken together, the examples suggest the robust potential of the genre, formal public comment, for getting concerns on the public agenda and in the public record.

Summary and Preview

It is surprising that few of us comment on action that government intends to take when the responsible agencies directly ask us to do so. This chapter aims to encourage and enable the practice of publicly commenting. Democratic self-governance depends on our willingness to intervene in the process.

References

Bullock, D. (2014, March 12). Research Triangle Institute. Interview.

Federal plain language guidelines 2011. (2014, September 27). http://www .Language.gov/.

Public comments make a difference. (2014, September 27). http://www .Regulations.gov/.

Schlosberg, D., Zavestoski, S., & Shulman, S. W. (2007). Democracy and e-rulemaking: Web-based technologies, participation, and the potential for deliberation. *Journal of Information Technology & Politics,* 4(1), 37–55.

Shulman, S. W., Schlosberg, D., Zavestoski, S., & Courard-Hauri, D. (2003). E-rulemaking: A social science agenda. *Social Science Computer Review,* 21(2), 162–178.

Tips for submitting effective comments. (2014, September 27). http://www .Regulations.gov/.

What Writing Public Policy Means

In this guide, writing public policy means communicating by writing or speaking in political democracy to influence action, usually government action, to address public problems. Communicators are policy actors. Policy making depends on communication. As the congressional intern quoted in this guide's preface said, in policy work if you can't write it or say it, you can't do it.

That's the bad news–good news truth. The bad news is that communicating is hard. Complex thinking goes into writing or speaking to communicate. You make many conscious as well as unconscious choices about audience, purpose, subject or topic, form or genre, structure, tone, and expression. You need both know-how and skills for executing your choices. If your communication is to be useful to recipients, you must account for context and situation, not just content. You must be aware of pluralism or your own and others' values. Finally, your ideas must be feasible. Actuality should be kept in mind while you construct abstractions.

The good news is that you can learn to do it. Chapters and appendices here show diverse policy communicators at work. They illustrate typical policy communication demands and they demonstrate adaptive uses of language resources. Be guided by their examples, methods, standards, and tips derived from experience.

About Clarity

"Don't go for convincing. Go for clear."
A director of legislative research, investigative, and legal services once gave that advice to novice communicators. He was speaking as an experienced public administrator who, every day, must make sense of ambiguity often mixed with uncertainty. He firmly believed that communication can make a difference only if it is understandable.

   In agreement, this guide advocates clarity, with the caveat that clear does not mean simply transparent. The important dimensions of clarity in policy communication are accuracy, reliability, and functionality. Clear policy communication is realistic, accountable, and meaningful or relevant for recipients. A lot goes into creating communications with those attributes (see General Method and Two Checklists, Chapter 2).

Preview

Two appendices follow this conclusion to illustrate basic principles that apply widely in policy communication. They address requests for help made by users of this guide. Appendix A shows you how to write clear sentences. Appendix B shows you how to find meaning in research results and tell readers what you find.

Writing Clearly

To show its relevance to policy work, clear sentence construction is here linked to the task of writing a policy memo. Tips by an experienced practitioner and teacher of policy memo writing are generalized to demonstrate a key principle of clarity, identifying the action and the actor. Links to tools for assessing plain language are provided at the end.

Tips on Writing a Policy Memo

By Peter J Wilcoxen
Center for Environmental Policy and Administration
The Maxwell School, Syracuse University
Used by permission of the author.

There's no single formula for writing an effective policy memo because every policy is different. However, here are a few guidelines that may help:

Be Concise

Remember that being concise does not just mean the memo should be short; it means that it should be no longer *than necessary*. Being concise does not mean leaving important things out; rather, it means don't write a paragraph when a sentence or two will do.

> *Bad*: "Some people will react to the increase in the gas tax by taking taxis, buses or other public transportation since those forms

of transportation are now somewhat less expensive than using a private automobile. However, some people may not be willing or able to make such a change: they might live far from public transportation or might have medical conditions that made it necessary for them to drive. These people will continue driving but they would generally be likely to take fewer trips than before the tax."
Problem: Far too many words for the basic points being made!
Better: "A higher gas tax would reduce the amount of driving by people who can easily use other forms of transportation. People who can't switch would continue to drive, although they would probably drive fewer miles than before."

Focus on Results Rather Than Methods

You should focus on *what* you calculated rather than on *how* you calculated it. The details can be put in a separate report to be circulated to people interested in the technical issues.

Bad: "To calculate the effect of the proposed $5 tax on each new tire sold, it is first necessary to convert the tax to an equivalent percentage change in the price. The average price of a tire is $100 so the tax would raise the price by 5%. Next, the percentage change in the price is multiplied by the price elasticity of demand for the good. The elasticity shows the percentage change in the quantity demanded for a percentage change in the good's price. Multiplying it by the price change thus shows the percentage change in the amount of the good that will be demanded. The demand elasticity for tires has been estimated to be in the range of −0.2 to −0.4. Thus, the 5% increase in tire prices would reduce tire sales by 1% to 2%."
Problem: The reader does not want to be taught how to do the calculation, she just wants to know the answer.
Better: "The tax would raise tire prices by 5%. Historically, tire sales fall by 2–4% for a 10% increase in price, so in this case it is likely that tire sales would fall by 1% to 2%."

The only time you'd need to put in much detail about the underlying calculations would be when there are multiple competing methods that give conflicting results. For example, suppose you needed to report the average number of cigarettes consumed by women between the ages of 19 and 25. It would be important for the reader to know whether the data was obtained by surveying women about their smoking habits or by observing the sales of cigarettes. People tend to underreport their consumption of cigarettes so survey data would be biased downward.

Identify the Winners and Losers

It's very important to figure out who would be helped and who would be hurt by a proposal. After all, the point of public policy is to solve public problems and thereby make people (at least some people) better off. No policy analysis is really complete until the winners and losers have been identified.

In addition, knowing who gains and loses can be very helpful in anticipating how the political process will play out. It will indicate which groups could be expected to support the policy and which groups would be likely to oppose it. Moreover, calculating compensating variations or changes in consumer and producer surplus will show how much it would cost to compensate the losers. To the extent that compensation can be built into the policy, political obstacles will be reduced.

> *Bad*: "Eliminating rent control will benefit an average tenant by $75."
> *Problem*: Too little detail; it sounds like everyone gains when really some tenants lose.
> *Better*: "Eliminating rent control will cause rents to rise by $600 for 500 tenants currently in rent controlled apartments. However, it will also bring 300 new apartments on the market. The average value of each new apartment to its tenant will be $1,200 above the amount the tenant pays in rent."

Anticipate Questions

Look over your preliminary results and try to anticipate what questions a reader would be most likely to ask, or what additional calculations he might want to do to understand your results fully.

> *Bad*: "The policy reduces the average wages for entry level clerical workers from $6.00 per hour to $5.50 per hour."
> *Problem*: Virtually every reader will mentally convert this to a percentage to gauge how important it is.

Better: "The policy reduces the average wages for entry level clerical workers from $6.00 to $5.50, a decline of 8.3%."

Don't Use Unnecessary Jargon

Avoiding jargon will make it easier for your results to be understood by a wide range of readers.

Bad: "The income elasticity of medical care is 1.5 so a 20% increase in average household income would increase the consumption of medical care by 30%."
Problem: Incomprehensible to anyone not thoroughly trained in economics.
Better: "Statistical evidence shows that a 1% increase in household income leads to a 1.5% increase in expenditure on medical care. Since the proposed policy would raise household income by 20%, it should raise the demand for medical care by 30%.

Use Tables

A table can often be worth a thousand words. It's a much faster way to present a set of numbers than to include them in the text and it can be a lot easier for a reader to understand. That's especially true when you need to show results for different demographic groups.

Make sure the rows and columns of the table are labeled clearly and avoid including unimportant data.

Bad: "The benefit of the food stamp program to eligible households having two children would be $5,000. These households have an average income of $15,000 so the benefit would be equivalent to a 33% increase in their income. Eligible households with three children would receive $6,000 in benefits and have an average income of $17,000 (benefits are 35% of income). Households with four or more children have an average income of $18,000 and would receive $6,500 (36% of income). Households with one child would receive $4,000 and households with no children would receive $3,000. The average incomes of these two groups is $14,000 and $18,000 respectively."
Problem: Lots of information but it's tedious to read and it's hard for the reader to compare across groups.

Table A.1 Benefits received by households with different numbers of children.

Number of Children	Average Income	Food Stamp Benefit	Relative Gain
0	$18,000	$3,000	17%
1	$14,000	$4,000	29%
2	$15,000	$5,000	33%
3	$17,000	$6,000	35%
4	$18,000	$6,500	36%

Better: "Table 1 shows the food stamp benefits and average income for eligible households with different numbers of children. Also shown is the benefit as a percent of the household's income."

Write for an Intelligent Nonspecialist

You'll usually know more about the policy problem and the analytical methods you use than the reader of the memo. That makes it easy to inadvertently write the memo as though the reader were ignorant or stupid. The problem is subtle because it usually happens as a result of the best of intentions on your part: in trying to be as clear as possible you end up explaining things that the reader already knows or can easily figure out for herself.

Bad: "The policy will lower the price faced by consumers. When a good's price declines, consumers generally buy more of the good. Therefore, we would expect more units of the good to be sold."
Problem: It's both basic economics and common sense.
Better: "The policy will lower the price faced by consumers and thus increase total sales of the good."

Focus on Your Results, Not Your Opinions

Wherever possible, the memo should include all the facts a policy maker would need to reach her own conclusions and should not emphasize your personal opinion.

Bad: "US car manufacturers would gain by $1 billion per year if fuel economy standards were relaxed while US consumers would not be hurt significantly."

Problem: The reader doesn't know what you consider significant.
Better: "US car manufacturers would save $1 billion per year in costs if federal fuel economy standards were relaxed. The net effect on consumers is much smaller: the reduction in vehicle prices would save a typical household $200 but the drop in fuel economy would increase gas expenditure by $220."

Please note: these figures were made up as an illustration and are not based on real facts about US automobile industry.

Evaluate Means, Not Ends

Finally, focus on whether the policy is a good means for achieving its stated or implicit purpose, not whether the purpose itself is good or bad. For example, suppose Policy A intended to help Group X is grossly inefficient. The memo could argue that Policy A is a bad way to help Group X (i.e., that there are other policies that could achieve the same goal with less waste). However, it should avoid arguing that helping Group X is good or bad per se. That is, take it as given that Group X is to be helped and evaluate whether or not the policy is a good way of doing so.

Bad: Policy A is worthwhile because it helps Group X.
Problem: Helping Group X is the purpose of the policy so this is a statement about the goals of the policy, not about its means. It's not addressing whether or not Policy A is the best way to help Group X.
Better: Policy A helps Group X but is much more expensive than delivering the same benefits via Policy B.

WHAT THESE TIPS SHOW. A key principle of clarity applies in each of these suggestions. The principle: identify the action and the actor. To tell readers clearly what you mean, build each sentence to answer the question "who's doing what?" (Lanham, 2000). Make the main actors subjects of verbs and make important actions verbs (Williams & Colomb, 2012). Show who (subject) is doing (verb) what.

Writing sentences (or rewriting them) in accordance with the action–actor principle would eliminate most of the problems exhibited by the examples shown here. Those problems are created, variously, by failure to focus on the main action and actor. To illustrate, look again at the bad sentence in the first tip, *Be Concise*, with the principle of clarity in mind. In the bad sentence, the subject (*italicized*) is not the main actor. The verbs (underlined) show too many actions by that not-main actor. Which action matters most? The reader must guess.

> *Bad*: "*Some people* will react to the increase in the gas tax by taking taxis, buses or other public transportation since those forms of transportation are now somewhat less expensive than using a private automobile. However, *some people* may not be willing or able to make such a change: they might live far from public transportation or might have medical conditions that made it necessary for them to drive. *These people* will continue driving but they would generally be likely to take fewer trips than before the tax."

Now look at the better sentence with the principle of clarity in mind. The subjects (*italicized*) are the main actors. The verbs (underlined) show only the most important actions by each actor.

> *Better*: "A higher *gas tax* would reduce the amount of driving by people who can easily use other forms of transportation. *People* who can't switch would continue to drive, although they would probably drive fewer miles than before."

Crafting clear sentences takes practice. Probably the best way to learn is by rewriting. "Most experienced writers get something down as fast as they can. Then as they rewrite that first draft into something clearer, they understand their ideas better. And when they understand their ideas better, they express them more clearly" (Williams & Colomb, 2012, p. 5).

References

Lanham, R. A. (2000). *Revising business prose*. Boston, MA: Pearson Allyn & Bacon.

Williams, J. M., & Colomb, G. G. (2012). *Style: The basics of clarity and grace*. (4th ed.). Boston, MA: Pearson Longman.

Further Reading

Federal plain language guidelines. http://PlainLanguage.gov/.

Interpreting Data to Support Policy Argument

Instructor: "What is hardest about stating a policy position to advise policy makers?"

Students: "Saying what the data mean. Putting words to tables."

That exchange occurred in a public policy studies seminar. It points to the difficulty of interpretation. Policy analysts and issue advocates regularly face the difficulty. Students face it when writing policy arguments or extensive research papers. This appendix is intended to help by describing ways of inferring meaning from data and communicating meaning to readers.

The description draws on old ideas about how communication works (Day, 2001, p. 38) and new hypotheses about how the human brain works (Wolchover, 2014) as well as current practices of information retrieval (*Exploratory Search*, 2015). The description is in accordance with the argumentative approach to policy analysis that emphasizes the importance of language and meaning (Stone, 2012; Wagenaar, 2011).

Interpretation is the focus. For other research tasks such as collecting data or reviewing scholarly literature, you must rely on instruction given elsewhere or on your experienced know-how. Here, you learn about making inferences to reach an understanding of data that is usable as evidence in argument. Additionally, as teachers who use this guide have requested, you will be referred to previous chapters for reminders on constructing a policy argument (Chapter 6) and communicating it to intended audiences (Chapter 2).

How to Interpret Data for Policy Argument

> *Goal*: An intentional argument for the meaning that you find in data.
>
> *Objective*: To infer meaning by successively reducing data to pattern that supports generalization about the data.
>
> *Overview of the process*: Data have layers of potential significance. Within layers, data can be clustered according to simple criteria to reach a next-level generalization or characterization. Similarly, clusters can be grouped to show pattern. Then, patterns can be grouped and regrouped. By iteratively clustering, grouping, and regrouping, you reduce the detail in data to achieve generalization. Generalizations yield to other generalizations as your understanding evolves. You are inferring the data's meaning for your purpose.

The following composite account of analytical experience illustrates. Its analysis is rudimentary, but it demonstrates the progression from data to insight.

Illustration

You work as a U.S. Department of Agriculture Cooperative Research and Extension Services program administrator. Your division has received appropriation for public education in conservation. Objectives for spending are given, but implementations are unspecified. You have authority and opportunity to develop new initiatives. You are professionally trained in forestry with concentration in ecology, so you are interested in developing ecological approaches to conservation. Personally, you own and live on an old 68-acre farm in Pennsylvania that you have taken out of agriculture production. It has woods, wetlands, and grasslands, and you now manage it for conservation. You have relied on advice and benefitted from cost sharing by several conservation agencies. Nonetheless, you are aware that there are gaps in your practice, particularly of woodland conservation. You wonder whether other landowners might have similar needs for practical knowledge, particularly if their land has varied environments including woods.

Prompted by your values as a conservation-minded landowner and by the workplace opportunity to develop new educational initiatives, you are interested in learning whether conservation programs aimed at owners of 10 to 100 acres of land having varied environments would find an audience. You are aware of other, more specialized programming. You know about landscaping with native trees and shrubs to enhance wildlife habitat around private homes on 1 to 10 acres. Similarly, you know about sustainable timber harvesting to conserve commercial forests on 1,000 to 10,000 acres. These programs do not fit the scope and scale that interests you, land with varied environments that is larger than a home lot but smaller than a timber farm. However, they suggest that you might productively focus on woodland conservation as you explore ideas for new education initiatives.

As background, you know that reforestation is occurring at different rates in the United States. In Pennsylvania where your farm is located, forests have recovered from earlier overharvesting to remain relatively stable. However, their composition has altered. Climate change, planting practices, and dynamics of land use are creating new forest types. The increasing private ownership of wooded land is also influential. Private ownership results in forests becoming broken into smaller and smaller parcels, partly because of the effects of inheritance taxation and estate planning that divides land holdings among heirs. As a conservationist, you recognize that parcelization threatens the sustainability of many social, ecological, and economic values associated with woodlands.

You want to account for these changing conditions in conservation education for landowners, especially owners of noncommercial woodlands. To move forward, you must know more about that potential audience. Not having the resources to commission a custom survey, you look for existing data that might be helpful. One promising source is a recent survey of forest landowners in Pennsylvania. It documents the increasing trend for the Pennsylvania forest to be divided into smaller parcels held by more numerous owners (Metcalf, Finley, Luloff, & Muth, 2012; Gruver, Metcalf, Finley, Luloff, & Muth, 2012). You are interested in knowing whether such owners could benefit from ecological education. You analyze the survey results with that interest in mind.

Table B.1 Area and Number of Family Forest Owners by Size of Forest Landholdings, Pennsylvania, 2006. (McCaskill et al., 2013, p. 12)

Size of landowners' forest (acres)	Total acres (1,000s)	Sampling error (%)	Number of owners (1,000s)	Sampling error (%)
1–9	885	21.4	301	11.3
10–19	822	22.5	66	9.5
20–49	2,018	10.4	72	6.2
50–99	2,274	10.0	36	6.1
100–199	1,902	12.1	15	7.4
200–499	1,402	15.8	5	9.3
500–999	611	32.8	1	16.2
1,000–4,999	824	26.7	1	24.9
5,000–9,999	168	99.3	<1	82.1
10,000+	832	24.1	<1	38.6
Total	11,738	1.7	497	6.8

The researchers conducting the survey began with data taken from a joint U.S. Department of Agriculture and U.S. Forest Service publication, *Pennsylvania's Forests 2009* (McCaskill et al., 2013). Table B.1 shows the original data.

In the original data, two columns are devoted to sampling error, a statistical measure of reliability of the sample data surveyed versus the data for the entire population of interest. Although it is important for other purposes, sampling error is not critical for your interest in seeing broad patterns.

To find patterns, you first transform the data by computing percentages of the whole for numbers of landowners and sizes of parcels. Table B.2 shows that result.

Table B.2 Total Acres and Number of Landowners Converted to Percentages

Size of landowners' forest (acres)	Total acres (1,000s)	Percent of total	Number of owners (1,000s)	Percent of total
1–9	885	7.5	301	60.6
10–19	822	7.0	66	13.3
20–49	2,018	17.2	72	14.5
50–99	2,274	19.4	36	7.2
100–199	1,902	16.2	15	3.0
200–499	1,402	11.9	5	1.0
500–999	611	5.2	1	0.2
1,000–4,999	824	7.0	1	0.2
5,000–9,999	168	1.4	<1	<0.1
10,000+	832	7.1	<1	<0.1
Total	11,738	100.0	497	100.0

This simple change from absolute numbers to percentages of the whole shows a significant bulge in the middle of the data for parcel size and, as parcel size increases, a general decrease in the percentage of landowners. However, the breakdown in parcel size is more fine-grained than you need. Consequently, your second transformation is to consolidate parcel sizes into three orders-of-magnitude sets.

For each set, you compute the percentages of the whole represented by both total number of landowners and total acreage. Table B.3 shows the result.

Table B.3 Size of Landowner Forests Consolidated into Order-of-Magnitude Groups

Size of landowners' forest (acres)	Total acres (1,000s)	Percent of total	Number of owners (1,000s)	Percent of total
1–9	885	7.5	301	60.6
10–99	5,114	43.6	174	35.0
100–10,000+	5,739	48.9	22	4.4
Total	11,738	100.00	497	100.00

The interesting pattern in the data becomes clearer with this change. That pattern is the relationship between landowner numbers and parcel size. This pattern speaks most strongly when presented in graphical form. Chart B.1 shows a strong inverse relation between percentage of landowners and percentage of total acres.

Chart B.1 Numerical Data Converted to Visual Form

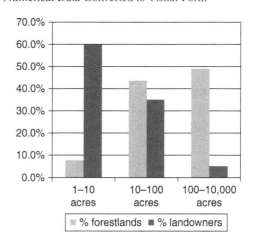

The inverse relationship is significant for your purpose of determining which landowners might be the best audience for new educational initiatives. Based on that significant relationship, you infer the following:

Takeaways

1–10 acres	Small scale, potentially high receptivity, large numbers needed to make marginally significant impact with regard to acres.
10–100 acres	Moderate scale, moderate numbers could make significant impact, ecological enhancement plausible first or second priority goal; sweet spot!
100–10,000 acres	Large scale, relatively few owners have great potential impact, but ecological goals beyond harvest enhancement and sustainability likely to be secondary.

These takeaways or inferences put words to the tables. Now you can say what the data mean for your purpose. You can confidently advocate programming targeted to landowners of parcels ranging from 10 to 100 acres. Further, you can argue that these landowners have holdings large enough to make a significant contribution to the overall ecology of their area.

———

•⇒• **WHAT THIS ILLUSTRATION SHOWS.** By transforming the data—from absolute numbers to proportional percentages and then to aggregated groupings—the analyst inferred a pattern meaningful for a purpose. It was done intuitively. With intuition prepared by background knowledge and professional know-how, the analyst iteratively made several passes through the data. Letting the results of each pass successively direct the next, the analyst reached an interpretation of the data that supported an idea. With different data or for a different idea, a different approach might be necessary.

A principle of policy argumentation is illustrated here. That principle says that data alone mean little. Data must be purposefully, thoughtfully interpreted if they are to become persuasive evidence for a position.

The following guidance to the inferential process is prescriptive. Because your data are likely to be complex enough, interpretive thinking is rendered here simply as sequential steps with a variety of techniques. For familiarity, the steps refer to previous chapters in this guide where you might have encountered or used a technique before.

Process:

- You have a body of data (regardless of methodology used).
- You have intention (purpose and audience) and freedom to decide relevance according to your viewpoint and intention.
- Your audience has intention (purpose), a viewpoint, and freedom to attend to you and to others.

Step 1: Understand the data.
Used alone or in combination, the following strategies for discovery can help you to make sense of your data and to purposefully distinguish what is important from what is not. If you already have other favorite strategies, use them, too.

- Given your data, ask what is happening. What can happen? What can't happen? (Imagine possibilities and impossibilities.)
- Ask What if? (write scenarios to show possibilities) (Task 1, Chapter 3).
- Ask What's the story here? (write narratives from the viewpoint of several policy actors; write causal stories, some with simple cause–effect and others with reversed effect–cause to show complex causality) (Tasks 1, 2, and 3, Chapter 3; Example 2, Chapter 4; Example 2, Chapter 9).
- Ask What is missing? (transform the data to reveal more potentiality) (Illustration, this appendix).
- Recognize metaphor in your thinking (note likeness or unlikeness that you perceive between the data and something else; name the likeness or unlikeness) (Example 3, Chapter 7; Example 3, Chapter 8).
- Ask What might be gained/What might be lost? (assess the politics).

- Ask Who might benefit?/Who might be harmed? (empathize) (Task 4, Chapter 3).
- Portray actual conditions or people implicated by the data (ground-truth them) (Example 2, Chapter 9).
- Draw a picture or design a chart or make a table based on the data (visualize relationship) (Illustration, this appendix; Tips, Appendix A).

Step 2: Construct your argument (reminder: refer to Chapter 6).
Good policy arguments are logical. You must categorize information to order it logically. Common devices of categorizing are question lists, outlines, diagrams, and charts. Use the following questions (or others if you prefer) alone or in combination to identify salience for policy in your understanding of the data.

- Given your understanding of the data (Step 1, this appendix), what problematic conditions are revealed?
- What policy problem(s) do the conditions present?
- What are the issues?
- What is your concern? What is your intended reader's concern?
- Who else is concerned?
- What are the main agreements/disagreements? (Task 4, Chapter 3)
- Characterize the policy problem according to size or scale, scope, incidence, effects, perceptions of it, and influences on it (Task 4, Chapter 4).
- Finally, outline the logic of a policy argument by stating a problem; an issue in that problem; a question about the issue that has at least two answers; your answer or claim; support for your claim categorized as justification (reasons and assumptions), elaboration (grounds, evidence), and anticipated reactions (Task 1, Chapter 6).
- If visualization helps you, draw your intended argument in an organization diagram with conclusion at top and support arrayed below.

Step 3: Represent and communicate your argument (reminder: refer to Chapter 2).

Persuasive argument enables minds to meet. The meeting ground, so to speak, is symbolic representation of ideas in words, numbers, and perhaps images (Viewpoint 3, Chapter 2). Symbolic representation requires many acts of thinking, not all of them conscious. Nonetheless, conscious control comes from using a deliberate method of thinking about the intended audience's need and use for information. The following methodical devices used alone or in combination can help you to communicate the argument you outlined in Step 2 above:

- Ask and answer the questions in the General Method (Viewpoint 4, Chapter 2).
- Prepare a complete working draft in accordance with your answers to the general questions.
- Test the draft's effectiveness and quality in accordance with standards for public policy communication (Two Checklists, Chapter 2).
- Revise as needed.
- Test the revised draft's clarity. Use the following short question list (contributed by experienced policy communicators) to review and revise as needed to make your communication usefully clear. Does your argument:
  - Focus on results rather than methods?
  - Focus on results rather than opinions or perceptions?
  - Evaluate means, not ends?
  - Anticipate questions a reader will likely ask or additional calculations the reader might make to understand your results fully?
  - Address the intelligent nonspecialist (regardless of the intended audience's specialty)?
  - Acknowledge your analytic approach, its value, and its limits?
  - Anticipate other arguments on the issue to look for potential conflict and common ground?
  - Justify its recommendations by comparison with alternatives?
  - (Wilcoxen, 2014; Helfert, 2014)

References

Day, R. E. (2001). *The modern invention of information: Discourse, history, and power.* Carbondale, IL. Southern Illinois University Press.

Exploratory search. (2015, January 6). http://wikipedia.org/wiki/Exploratory_search/.

Gruver, J., Metcalf, A. L., Finley, J. C., Luloff, A. E., & Muth, A. B. (2012). *The future of Penn's Woods: A mixed-methods study of parcelization and Pennsylvania's private forests.* Final Report to PA Department of Conservation and Natural Resources, Bureau of Forestry.

Helfert, D. (2014). *Policy position papers*; *Memoranda writing.* Instructional guides available from the author (dhelfert@verizon.net).

McCaskill, G. L., McWilliams, W. H., Alerich, C. A., Butler, B. J., Crocker, S. J., Domke, G M., . . . Westfall, J. A. (2013). *Pennsylvania's forests, 2009.* Resource Bulletin NRS-82. Newtown Square, PA: U.S. Department of Agriculture.

Metcalf, A. L., Finley, J. C., Luloff, A. E., & Muth, A. B. 2012. *Pennsylvania's private forests: 2010 Private forest landowner survey summary.* Final report to PA Department of Conservation and Natural Resources, Bureau of Forestry.

Stone, D. (2012). *Policy paradox: The art of political decision making* (3rd ed.). New York, NY: Norton.

Wagenaar, H. (2011). *Meaning in action: Interpretation and dialogue in policy analysis.* Armonk, NY: Sharpe.

Wilcoxen, P. (2014). *Tips for writing a policy memo.* Appendix A, this guide.

Wolchover, N. (2014, December 3). A common logic to seeing cats and cosmos. *Quanta Magazine.*

Suggestion for Further Reading

Coplin, W. D., with Sandefer, E. (2007). *The Maxwell manual for good citizenship: Public policy skills in action.* Lanham, MD: Rowman & Littlefield.

Index